Editor:
Gail L. Green

Cover Design and Page Layout:
James W. Donnelly

Technical Information:
Will Perry, Sports Information Director,
The University of Michigan, and Bill
Cusumano, Assistant Sports Information
Director, The University of Michigan

Price $6.95

Man in Motion
by JOE FALLS

THE VICTORS

Hail! to The Victors valiant
Hail! to the conquering heroes
Hail! Hail! to Michigan, the leaders and best—
Hail! to The Victors valiant
Hail! to the conquering heroes
Hail! Hail! to Michigan, the Champions of the West.

This fight song, reflecting the great glory and tradition of The University of Michigan, was written by a senior music student named Louis Elbel in 1898.

He became so inspired when a substitute halfback, Charles Widman, dashed 98 yards for a touchdown that he immediately went back to his room and wrote "The Victors".

Glenn E. (Bo) Schembechler is carrying on this great tradition—except that when he goes 98 yards, it is in 18 plays with his fullback carrying the ball 14 times.

Today's Victor is his own man. Believe me.

—Joe Falls

Published By
School-Tech Press
745 State Circle
Ann Arbor, Michigan 48104 U.S.A.

DEDICATION

Joe Falls: *The only time I have ever deferred to Bo Schembechler is in the dedication of "our" book, so here it is:*

I will pass along my Ghost's deference to my wife, Millie, to whom I dedicate this book.

—Glenn E. "Bo" Schembechler

First Printing September 1, 1973

Library of Congress Catalog Number: 73-85215

Printed in the United States of America

TABLE OF CONTENTS

Bo's Record Third Best in Nation

Glenn E. (Bo) Schembechler, Michigan's 13th head football coach, is in his fifth season in charge of the Wolverines and during that time his teams have won 86 per cent of their games.

Going into the 1973 season Bo ranks third among all active coaches in winning percentage with a mark of .764 built over 10 years as head football coach at Miami of Ohio and Michigan.

Meanwhile, Bo has been voted national Coach of the Year (1969) and the Big Ten's Coach of the Year (1972) as he compiled the best winning percentage of any Michigan football coach since 1900 (.864).

He conducts a football clinic each spring for high school coaches, is a guest lecturer at several of the top national clinics, coaches in all-star football games, maintains a busy and exacting recruiting schedule and still reserves two or three weeks vacation time with his family.

Schembechler (pronounced SCHEM-beck-lur), brought a solid football background to Michigan. In his six seasons as head football coach of Miami of Ohio his teams posted a 40-17-3 overall record, and a 27-8-1 record in the Mid-American Conference. His teams won two MAC co-championships, finished second twice and tied for third once. He has never coached a losing team.

Schembechler was the fourth straight head coach at Miami to take over a Big Ten team. Woody Hayes (Ohio State), Ara Parseghian (Northwestern), and John Pont (Indiana) had coached Miami teams since 1949. He replaced Bump Elliot, now Iowa's Athletic Director, as head coach at Michigan and is only the fourth head coach of the Wolverines since Fritz Crisler was appointed in 1938.

Voted MAC Coach of the Year in 1965 and Ohio Coach of the Year in 1966, Bo engineered upsets of Northwestern in 1964 (28-27) and Indiana in 1966 (20-10).

Schembechler, who graduated from Miami in 1951 and received a master's degree in education from Ohio State in 1952 has an extensive background in coaching. He started as a graduate assistant under Hayes at Ohio State in 1951, then served two years in the Army.

He was line coach at Presbyterian College in 1954, a line coach at Bowling Green in 1955, and joined Parseghian's staff at Northwestern in 1956. Schembechler rejoined Hayes at Ohio State in 1958 and served five seasons as line coach before taking over the head job at Miami in 1963.

The former Barberton, Ohio prep all-stater was an offensive tackle at Miami for three years, playing under George Blackburn and Hayes. He also was an outstanding left-handed pitcher for Miami. He was a teammate and roommate of Indiana's John Pont on the 1950 Miami football team.

Bo and his wife, Millie, have four children: Chip, 17, Geoffrey, 15, Matthew 14, and Glenn E. III, almost 4.

SCHEMBECHLER'S RECORD

	Year	W	L	T	Pct.	Pts.	Opp.
AT MIAMI	1963 ------	5	3	2	.625	208	178
	1964 ------	6	3	1	.667	209	142
	*1965 ------	7	3	0	.700	247	137
	*1966 ------	9	1	0	.900	229	76
	1967 ------	6	4	0	.600	181	114
	1968 ------	7	3	0	.700	240	99
	Total ------	40	17	3	.702	1314	746
AT MICHIGAN	*1969 ------	8	3	0	.727	352	148
	1970 ------	9	1	0	.900	288	90
	†1971 ------	11	1	0	.917	421	83
	*1972 ------	10	1	0	.909	264	57
	Total	38	6	0	.864	1325	378
	Career Totals	78	23	3	.772	2639	1124

*—Co-Championship Season   †—Outright Championship

Chapter *1*

Heart Attack: "The Coke Stuck in My Throat. I Couldn't Swallow the Damn Thing."

I'm lucky to be doing this book. I'm lucky to be alive. I mean, how do you handle a heart attack when it hits you? How can you prepare yourself for it? You can't. Bang—it just hits you and there you are, wondering what happened?

What do I remember about it? I'm in intensive care and they've got wires coming out of all parts of me. I look up at the ceiling and they've got dials up there and there's all kinds of equipment all over the room. I remember there was a window where the nurse could stand and look in at us. There I am, flat on my back. . .scared stiff because I didn't know what the heck is going on.

I remember George Allen. He was one of my first visitors at St. Luke's Hospital in Pasadena after I left the intensive care unit. George was the Los Angeles Rams coach, and he can be pretty dramatic. He started to come into my room, and he suddenly stopped in his tracks and looked at me.

"Bo, he says, "Bo. . .tell me. . .what can I do to prevent this from happening to me?"

I want to die laughing whenever I think about it.

I look back now on my heart attack and I see where it had to be building up in me for a long time. In a lot of ways it was my own fault for letting myself get out of shape.

When I was at Miami of Ohio, I really took care of myself. I'd play handball every noon. Chuck Stobart and I used to have some hellish battles. When I came here I was fired up, I mean really fired up. All I thought about was football. I junked everything but my job—the handball, my eating habits, my sleeping habits. . .the whole works. All I thought about was coaching the University of Michigan football team.

I felt I was well known in Ohio but it wasn't that way in the state of Michigan. I had to cover a lot of ground in Michigan if the people here were going to get to know me. If someone wanted me for a banquet on the other side of the state, I would go. I said "yes" to everyone. I'd get home at two o'clock in the morning and I'd be up early, with almost no sleep, and in my office working before anyone else showed up.

I took the job in 1968, just around Christmas time. That meant we were behind in recruiting. I had to hustle to get our program started and especially to start competing with Michigan State. Take some of those kids State got. I went to see Brad Ven Pelt and Joe DeLamielleure. My name wasn't exactly magic to them but Duffy Daugherty's was and there was no way I could have recruited them. I lost key players like this and what I was up against is that everyone was saying to these kids, "Why go to Michigan and play with all those Ohio players?" But that was my salvation. Duffy could beat me in Michigan but he couldn't beat me in Ohio. All I had to do was go down there and get good enough talent from Woody Hayes to offset the fact I was not winning in the State of Michigan. That isn't true any more. We've put together a winning program at The University of Michigan. Now I have something to sell in Michigan.

Anyway, I drove myself pretty hard in those early days. I'm not really what you'd call a drinker or a smoker. I'll take an occasional drink, a beer or two at times, and I've smoked some cigars but I've never smoked cigarettes. But eating is what was doing it to me. I'd come back from a recruiting trip or a banquet and I'd find some old greasy restaurant in a gas station and there I'd be eating a bowl of chili at two o'clock in the morning, just wolfing it down. There was just no sense to it but I was nervous and I kept driving myself.

When spring practice came around we were still going at it very hard. I figured right off, following Bump Elliott, that my style was going to be different from what they knew and they

"If you had one more eye, you'd be a Cyclops!"

Defensive Coach Jim Young (Left) and Bo Discuss a Decision with an Official During Michigan's 31-20 Victory over Purdue in 1969.

Joe Falls
Sports Editor

U-M's Bo Scores His First Points

Dec. 28, 1968   ANN ARBOR

THE COLOR OF HIS TIE wasn't exactly Maize and Blue. But, for being new around here, it was close enough. It was yellow and blue, with a touch of red in it—probably for his dear old Redskins from Miami of Ohio.

At least he didn't come in wearing green and white and this was an impressive beginning.

They came from near and far to meet the new coach of the Michigan football team Friday morning. They came in on the ice-coated toboggan runs from Detroit and Kalamazoo and Toledo (where was Lansing?), at the ungodly hour of 9:30 in the morning, but as soon as they got inside the plush lounge of the University Events Building, they knew immediately that things are different at this old indifferent institute.

Don Canham, the Madison Avenue man, had hot coffee and buns waiting for the boys, and if I were Biggie Munn, I'd start doing a little thinking.

Canham is even thinking about providing hot coffee for the boys AFTER the games next fall as they try to write their stories and maybe even put heat into the front row of the pressbox, which would be an all-time Michigan record.

He is talking about building a special carpeted room next to the dressing room where the boys can talk to the coach and you can only wonder if Bunny girl hostesses can be far behind.

Next thing you know they'll be challenging those hot beef and turkey dinners they serve up in East Lansing before the games and the fight of the filets will be on.

The trip out here in all that snow and sleet was well worth it because the new man—Bo Schembechler—seems like a bright, witty, articulate, no-nonsense individual who is dedicated to one thing in life, and that is winning football games.

Lives Game 12 Months a Year

BUT REALLY NOW, what other kind of man do you think Canham would have hired to head up the football program around here? Donald is no dummy. He knows what gets the bills paid, what builds up the old image, what makes Don a successful athletic director.

If you are impressed with Canham—and what else can you be when he is so open and honest about his aims and ambitions?—then you have to be impressed by his hand-picked choice to run the Michigan football team.

Sight unseen, you had the notion Schembechler was an impressive individual—and he was indeed that as he handled the members of all the media. He answered their questions easily, almost effortlessly, and nobody got the idea he was saying things he really didn't mean.

As for his dedication to football . . . well, th came burning through like a slap of white-hot stee He tells you he lives this game 12 months a year an he tells you in a way that makes you believe it.

You suspect he will be able to talk more than a fe high school hot shots into doing their playing at Mich igan, and isn't this one reason—maybe the main reaso — why the change was made in the first place?

Schembechler, in trying to explain what type o person he is, said: "Well, I don't smoke, so I hav a weight problem. I eat a lot, especially when I'r nervous, and it's always the same after a game. I' eat a lot and then go to bed. I'll sleep to maybe 1 o'clock on Sunday morning and then I'll get up."

He was asked: "Why 10 o'clock?"

"That's when the movies of the game are ready, he said with a smile.

Determination, desire and dedication—it seems lik Schembechler is bringing it all into his new assignmen Also, a sense of humor, and this could be his mos important product—especially when he goes out t face Duffy and Woody, which is also why he is bein brought in to coach this team.

Pronounce His Name? Well, Uh . .

HE COACHED FOR WOODY HAYES not once, bu twice, and that should be worth some points. Wha impressed him the most about W.W. God?

"It is his enormous capacity for work and his tre mendous enthusiasm," said Schembechler. "I've neve met a man like him. He goes on and on and on. H can take a routine play, a play you've seen for 10 years and go to the blackboard and make it seem like revelation to you."

Standing there before the kleig lights, with th battery of cameras grinding away, Schembechler knev he had finally scaled the heights of his profession

He had come a long way from those early year at Presbyterian College, where he was the line coac "and got thirty-four hundred bucks a year and cafeteri rights and I thought I had the best job in the world Why not? I was even allowed to eat with the basketba team."

Schembechler, it appears, brought everything wit him from Miami of Ohio except a pronunciation guid on how to pronounce his name.

"It's, ah . . . leeme see, 'SHEM-beck-lur' . . . no er I think it's 'shem-BECK-lur' . . . oh, heck, what's th difference. Call me anything you want."

Personally, we're going to call him "Sir."

You see, Bo Schembechler says that sports writer are "great, wonderful people—kind, considerate an thoughtful."

Anybody got a "coach-of-the-year" ballot?

4

may as well find out about it right away. We had some "occasions" that were really something. I can remember going after the players, pulling Jim Mandich off a guy one day and yelling at him and throwing him off the field. We had a rugged spring. Our scrimmages would get intense and I remember the time when old Barry Pierson was really putting some licks on Mandich. Everytime he'd go down there on a pass pattern, Pierson would put it to him. Mandich went after him and they had the wildest fight I ever saw. I damn near killed Mandich. But let me tell you something about him. He was my kind of player. He was tough. I had great respect for him but the tangles we had set the tone for the camp.

I wasn't feeling good. Physically, I mean. I was getting awfully tired and working myself to the state of exhaustion. I would go to sleep and it seemed like I was getting up only minutes later. Everything seemed to be going so fast. I'd get up and look at myself in the mirror and say, "You dummy, what's the matter with you?" I'd get on the scales and I'd feel like the dumbest guy I ever knew. But I just kept going and going, figuring everything would be okay. I was fooling myself but I didn't know it then.

The only time I ever relaxed was when Bennie Oosterbaan talked me into going up to Lake Lelanau for a couple of weeks during the summer. I got up there but stayed only five days. I had a football clinic over in Milwaukee and Millie and the kids stayed alone while I flew to Milwaukee. I came back a couple of days later and picked her up and we returned to Ann Arbor. That was the only time I took off.

Now we started getting ready for the season. We won our first two games and got blown out by Missouri. We came back to upset Purdue but went to Michigan State and blew that one. I was so wrapped up in everything, going around the clock, that I just never gave any thought to myself.

We went up to Minnesota and that's when the season turned around for us. We went up there without two of our best players, John Gabler and Glenn Doughty, but we played a tremendous second half and won the game. We started to move after that. Billy Taylor got into the lineup and Doughty came back and we started to become a good team.

We blew out Iowa, which was a decent team, and after that game I knew. . .I just knew. . .we could beat those son of a guns from Ohio State. I could feel it right there, in the locker room at Iowa. I looked around at the players and I knew we could do it.

That's when they were calling Ohio State such a super team. We came back to Ann Arbor and I knew I was fat and sloppy and I said to myself that as soon as the season is over I'm going to get my weight down and start working out again. I'm going to feel good and stop killing myself.

But now there it was: Ohio State and Woody Hayes. My first shot at them. I kept eating. I never stopped eating.

On Tuesday of Ohio State week we had this sleety rain that froze on the practice field and we had no place to practice. We had all the guys out with shovels. We must have had 60 of them shoveling off the field. I'm out there with them, shoveling away like a mad fool. I'm standing there shoveling and I'm saying to myself, "You dummy, you're going to get into shape as soon as this season is over." It was freezing out and I was getting tired. I was starting to puff, but no way was I going to stop shoveling.

We beat Ohio State that Saturday but there was no time to rest. I'd never gone to a major bowl game in my life and now I was faced with a trip to the Rose Bowl. I tried to be casual about it but when you do something for the first time, you just don't know what you're getting into. So now I've got to get the team ready for the game in Pasadena and I've got to get into our first real recruiting program. If we don't recruit right, I know we're going to get buried. So we jump right into that—on the road for a couple of weeks—and then we come back to Ann Arbor and start getting ready for the Rose Bowl.

When we got to Pasadena, I try to act very casual about the whole thing. But my insides are churning. I can feel it. I get on the scales one day and I weigh 220 pounds! I couldn't believe it. I said, "You big slob, that's ridiculous." My second day in Pasadena, where it's so sunny and nice, and I weigh 220 pounds! You must remember I weighed only 195 when I came to Michigan. In less than a year's time, I've gained 25 pounds. That's absurd.

The whole scene around the Huntington Hotel in Pasadena

was upsetting. I wasn't used to having that many people around my ball players. They were very friendly, but I felt it was hurting our players. It just didn't seem like we were getting ready for a game as big as the Rose Bowl.

So now it's two days before the game and we're practicing pretty well and so I'm feeling pretty good. We had these press conferences every day, late in the afternoon, and so when I get back to the hotel I'm feeling pretty good when I go up to my room. We've got a little refrigerator up there where we keep Cokes and stuff and I pulled out a Coke and started to drink it. You know, the whole thing stuck right in my throat. I couldn't swallow the damned thing. It was a funny feeling. Did you ever try to swallow something that you can't swallow?

It just stuck there and I couldn't figure what the hell it was. Then I started to get a pain in the top of my chest. I went in on the bed and Millie came in—Millie is a nurse by trade—and I said I drank a Coke and couldn't swallow the thing.

She said, "Where does it hurt?"

I said, "In my chest. It's getting worse."

She said she was going to call the two team doctors, Dr. Gerald (Jerry) O'Connor and Dr. Robert (Bob) Anderson. They came into the room and they asked me where it hurt.

I said, "Right here. My chest hurts! I can't even lay still."

Now my arms are starting to burn, too. It's one of those things where they say to just lay there still but I can't. I want to get up but it hurts. They gave me some pills, tranquilizers or something, and I said I have to go to that press conference. They said I'd better have somebody else handle it. So I called Jim Young, our defensive coach, and told him I wasn't feeling well and would he handle the press conference.

The doctors gave me some stuff to settle my stomach but the moment I took it I got up and vomited. I laid back down and then the pain started to subside. So right now I'm thinking of indigestion, right? That's what it had to be. Dr. Anderson said it could have been something to give me a spasm which gives you the same effect as having heart pains. But he said we should go to the hospital and take an EKG anyway, just to be sure. Dr. O'Connor said he had a friend at the clinic in Pasadena and so after a brief nap we went down there—Millie and me and the two doctors.

I'm not scared at this point because I'm feeling pretty good. I'm kind of limp but I figure that's to be expected. We took the EKG but they didn't have anything to compare it with and they thought it looked okay.

So what do I do? I'm starved. I haven't eaten since noon and so I go back to the room and order up the two biggest hamburgers you ever saw. There I am, eating again.

Both Millie and the doctors are pretty smart. They're worried. Even though things looked okay, they were watching me very close. The next day, everybody is asking me, "What's the matter, Bo?" I just shrug. "Nothing," I tell them. "I just didn't feel well last night."

The team has gone up to the monastery by now, but Millie and I stay at the hotel. Now it's the day before the game and we are practicing in the park across from the Rose Bowl—Brookside Park. It's only a 45-minute practice and I don't hardly have anything for breakfast. They had this kick-off luncheon but I didn't touch a thing. I felt kind of drab. I got up and talked but I just didn't feel sharp. The thing that was sticking in my mind more than anything else was that for the first time I have ever coached I couldn't get up for the game.

I kept saying to myself, "You dumb so and so, this is the biggest game you are ever going to play in. . .and you can't get up for it." I couldn't believe it. Here we're getting ready for the Rose Bowl and I'm not feeling a thing.

At practice that day we were timing up a few plays, the way we do the day before a game, and I purposely grabbed a football and started running around with it. I went from hash mark to hash mark, just like they do in the newsreels. The doctors are looking at me and I can only wonder what they're thinking. But I've got to get myself up. I've just got to. The truth is, I felt completely wrung out.

You know, you're never able to look at yourself properly. Here I am a 40 year old guy and I'm out of shape but no way am I ever going to admit I'm going to have a heart attack. You just don't think like that, and I didn't. After the EKG, I dropped the whole thing from my mind.

Now we're up at the monastery. It's the night before the game. The priests, they're good old guys and they like to make things nice for the coaches. So they have this little cocktail party, hors d'oeuvres and everything, and we spend some time with them before dinner. While we're going over there, my stomach is starting to hurt. It's bad. One of the priests says, "Why don't you have a 7 Up?" I drank a can of 7 Up, hoping it would make me burp and get the indigestion out. I get a call from Don Canham that he's up in the guest house with Robben Fleming, the president of our school, and they're with the players and Fleming wants to say a few words to the players. They want me there, and I go out the door and start up the road to the guest house.

Now this is only about a hundred yards away. I've got to go up a circular road and I get about two-thirds of the way—I could see Fleming's car and I can see the driver—and I'm walking up there when this pain hits me across the chest and through my arm. It's the same thing I had the night before, only worse. I couldn't walk and I couldn't breath and it feels so bad I can't believe it.

I stop and I try to catch my breath. I'm looking at the car and I know they're waiting for me, so I wait a few moments and then I start walking up the hill again.

I got up before the squad and I guess I'm sweaty and shaking but I introduce the president to them and then I sit down. Canham leans over to me and says it's impolite to sit down after introducing the president but what am I going to say to him, that I just had a heart attack out on that hill?

Fleming spoke to the players and then we went down to eat. I'm not sure if I ate anything. Maybe very little. I didn't want to say anything to anybody. I said to myself I was going in for a checkup as soon as the game was over.

We have a movie the night before our games. I usually sit through it with our kids. But now I keep walking back to my room and laying down. I'd lay down for a while and try to get everything out of my mind. Usually, on the night before a game, I'm going over everything—every possible situation that might come up. But now I'm not thinking about anything and I'm getting mad about it. I can't understand it. Here's the biggest game of my life and I couldn't care less about it.

I said to myself, "Maybe if I get a good night's sleep. . ."

After the movie is over, I call the kids together and say a few words to them. I'll never forget one of our kids. I said to him, "You don't look as if you're having a good time." He kind of looked down at the floor. He said, "I'm not, coach." I can't tell you his name because he had a girl in trouble and this is the first time he is telling me about it. It's right before the game and you know I'm really interested when a kid is in a bind like that. I want to talk to him. I want to calm him down. You know, when you don't give a kid your time at a time like that it is the worst thing you can do. They know your time is valuable, and when you give it to them, they appreciate it. It makes them feel important.

But I just couldn't talk to him. I am trying to talk to ALL of the kids but I want to get to bed so bad it isn't funny. After I checked them all in, I went to my room and took my clothes off and laid down on the bed. It's a tradition that the other coaches stop around and sort of talk over last-minute things.

They came in and we started talking but after a while I said, "Why don't we knock it off tonight, guys, okay?"

I told them I wanted to get some sleep. But these guys know me. They looked at me and asked me if everything was all right. I said I was okay. I said, "I just walked up that stupid road and I got the worst pain in my chest, it just about killed me." This was the first time I talked about it. They said, sure, okay, and left the room.

Jim Young slept in the next room and he said I snored real loud that night. When I got up in the morning, I had a headache. I felt just terrible.

The doctors came into my room. The coaches had called them. They told the doctors that I didn't want to talk to them the previous night, that I wanted to go to sleep, and they thought something was wrong and they'd better come around and take a look at me.

The doctors asked me how I felt. I said, "Kind of blah, but I'll be okay." They said we'd better take another EKG, just to be sure. They said we could do it during the pre-game meal—that one of the priests would run us down to St. Luke's

Hospital.

"You know," the doctors said, "you will feel better and we will feel better if we have one more checkup."

I said, "Okay, cripes, let's get it over with. We've got a ball game to play."

We go to the hospital and they hook me up again and here we go with our second EKG. I've got my plays with me and I'm studying them. I think I really have to make up time because I just haven't done a good job of getting ready for the game.

I'm sitting there looking at the plays when Dr. Anderson and Dr. O'Connor walk back into the room with another doctor—Dr. Weinstein, head of cardiology at St. Luke's. He is really a sharp guy and I was lucky to have him at the time. He comes in and says, "Coach, I hate to tell you this but you are out of the game."

I look at him. "What do you mean?"

He tells me I have just had a heart attack and I must be placed in intensive care. I start to cry. No way can I believe it. A heart attack? No game? No Rose Bowl?

He said, "I'm sorry but it's true."

It's funny, I'm not even thinking of the heart attack. All I'm thinking of is the game—missing it. I knew something was wrong. I knew it for two days. But I didn't want to admit it. Now, to finally know it—it was just too much.

I asked them could I talk to my coaches. They said that would be all right. By this time, they've put some shots into me to calm me down. They've got some tubes stuck into me and I'm feeling pretty groggy. Jim Young came in with Jerry Hanlon and Chuck Stobart. I tell Jim to take the team. Stobart and Hanlon would run the offense and Young would handle the defense.

I remember them saying to me, "Don't worry, everything is going to be all right." But things were getting pretty hazy. They wheel me into this room with these three or four other guys and I'm saying to myself, "Son of a gun, what am I doing in here?" I conk out and fall asleep.

I remember waking up when some nurse would come in and I'd ask her what the score of the game was. She wasn't a football fan and didn't know what score I was talking about. "The Rose Bowl! The Rose Bowl!" I said. She'd kind of back away and say she'd try to find out.

She came back and said it was 3 - 0. Then 3 - 3. Finally, when I woke up the last time. . .it seemed like I was sleeping a long time. . .there was a little red-headed gal there—Millie remembers her name but I don't—and I said I had to know the score and she said: "It was 10 - 3. Your team lost."

I felt just awful. If we had won, it wouldn't have been so bad. But we lost and I'm there in bed and I'm not even sure where I am or what's happening. The only thing that saved it for me is that they kept knocking me out and I slept a lot. If they hadn't done that, I don't know if I would have made it.

Dr. Gerald O'Connor:

Bo is a tough individual and it is hard for him to under-stand that he can be prone to the human frailties. When he had his first attack in Pasadena, he wouldn't even admit the next day that he had any of the symptoms.

In retrospect, I think he probably had a significant attack at about three o'clock in the morning on New Year's Day. Even then he wouldn't admit it. I saw him the next morning and he didn't look well.

He was standing up shaving and I asked him, "How are you feeling?"

He said, "Fine. . .I feel just fine."

I repeated, "Are you sure you're all right?"

He looked at me and said, "Yes, I said I was fine."

I went to Jim Young's room and told him that Bo didn't look well. I felt it was our responsibility to get him to the hospital for another EKG, no matter what he was saying to me.

Even on the way to the hospital, he wouldn't admit any-thing. In fact, he was humoring us, trying to convince us he was all right. He kept going over his game plan in the car.

It was evident the moment we looked at the EKG that there was a definite change in his condition.

Only when we told him at the hospital that the evidence was pretty strong that he'd had a heart attack would he admit that he wasn't feeling well.

A lot of people have coronaries and don't know it. I think it was fortunate we were there that morning with him. If we'd have met him out at the game, I don't think he would have ever admitted he wasn't feeling right.

I was in the hospital for 18 days. I started getting books on the heart and I read every one of them. I wanted to know how such a thing could happen to me. I read about overweight and smoking and eating too much and I knew I could do something about all of those things. But when they talked about tension, that's something I wasn't sure about. It wouldn't make any difference if I never smoked another cigar or never had another beer, but if we're playing a game of marbles—I'm going to try to beat you. I'm going to get fired up and I'm going to try to beat you.

I'd lay there in bed and look down at my chest. It looked normal but I'd wonder—would it ever happen again? What would I feel?

I'd been named coach of the year that year and this was really something because it was picked by the other coaches. That's when I got my first test. They asked me if I could go to Washington, D.C. for the dinner, which of course I couldn't, and so that night Jim Young went in my place. They set up a conference call where they could talk to me on the telephone and my voice could be heard all around the banquet room. I was very excited about it because I had beaten out Darrell Royal and he had one of his great Texas teams that year and why kid about it, when the other coaches vote for you—that's really something.

If this had been one of those sentimental things—I mean because of my heart attack—I wouldn't want it. But the nice thing is that they voted before the bowl games.

So now I haven't done anything for 10 days or so and here comes the big night and when I get the call I'm trying to keep myself down but I start breathing heavy and I can actually feel my heart beat. I can actually feel it! But everything goes okay and I feel real good when it's over. It is my first step back.

You can't imagine how much mail I got. I couldn't believe it. I'd spend all day just opening mail. I mean, it came from all over the country. Little kids would scrawl things—their mothers would write letters and I brought boxes and boxes of the stuff back home with me. I got a tremendous letter from Woody Hayes. I had Millie dig it out and I think we should let the readers see it:

Dear Bo:

If you were going to have a sick spell why didn't you have it at our game, for your team didn't look the same without you. On television it appeared that they stuck in there real well, but they lacked the coordination that they had against us. Anne is always accusing me of practicing medicine without a license, but even at that hazard I'm going to offer a little free advice. A few years back I headed up the Central Ohio Heart Fund Drive two years. During that time I talked with scores of good heart doctors and with hundreds of "happy cardiacs" who were the best and most enthusiastic fund raisers we had. In their cases their complete recovery was truly amazing. At one luncheon a man thirty-two years old told me he had suffered an attack a year and one-half before while playing tennis. That morning his doctor had told him that he could start playing tennis again. I'm not suggesting that you go back to handball for you never were very good at it.

Ten years ago Monk Strine had an attack, at 40, and he swears that his sex life is better now than ever. Dr. Bob Murphy scared Monk into doing exactly what Dr. Bob wanted.

All I'm trying to say is: If you won't get stubborn and heroic you can be in better health than ever.

I'll see you next November 21st.

Your old coach and long-time friend,

Woody

Millie would sit there all day and read the letters to me. You'll never know what a lift they gave me. But already I was getting a little edgy. I kept asking the doctor when I could go home. He'd look at me and smile. "You just lay there and act like a dishrag," he'd say. Can you imagine me just laying there acting like a dishrag? I guess that's why they kept me doped up so much.

As the days passed, I began to do some serious thinking. I was only thinking of myself, but now I realized that I had a wife and four children depending on me. I HAD to get better—for them if nothing else. Still, I couldn't believe I had a heart attack. I was only 40 years old!

I did the obvious thing. I asked Dr. Weinstein, "How bad was it?" You know how doctors are—they think everything is serious and they treat everyone the same way. But I wanted to know. He said to me, "Let's just say that you took a pretty good jolt." That's all he ever told me about it.

We flew back to Ann Arbor on January 18th. They had a bed set up for me in the front room of my house. I wasn't even allowed to walk up and down the stairs. I was lucky that Rudy Reichart was my doctor. He's some kind of a guy—in his middle 40's and he still plays oldtimer's hockey.

When I got home, I made up my mind I wouldn't do anything to jeopardize my chances of coaching again. If he told me to lay on my back for two or three months. I was going to lay there. If he told me not to eat certain foods, I just wasn't going to eat them. I decided—for once in my life—to listen to somebody else.

Don Canham was just great all through the whole ordeal. He'd come to see me and I'd look into his eyes for any signs of doubt but I could never find any.

I said to him, "You know, I'm not going to be able to make spring practice."

He said, "Forget spring practice. Jim Young and the guys can handle it. You just get well. You're going to be all right."

You know me. I went to practice every day. They got me a golf cart to sit on and I'd just sit around and watch. I guess I got a little too close at times. Some of the guys were running into the cart.

I've thought about the possibility of another heart attack. I guess every guy thinks that. I can only say this: I feel great and my EKG has been back to normal and as long as I take care of myself, I don't see why I should have any more problems. I don't feel there was a lot of severe damage in there. If there was, it'd be another question. But I've gone through several football seasons now and never felt better. It is probably corny but I think all the discipline I learned in football has helped me. You have to believe this if you're going to coach and if you see it work, then you begin to believe it yourself. I remember I was scared the first time I started running out on our track. I didn't know if I'd collapse or what. But I was able to work into it because of the discipline I'd learned.

One of the tough things. . .and this is going to sound silly. . .is when they told me I couldn't have any more hamburgers. If there is one thing I like to eat, it's hamburgers. But for months and months, all I could do was think about them.

During my diet, I went from 220 pounds to 175. I took off 45 pounds from New Year's Day until the first day of practice on August 20. They wouldn't let me have any fatty foods—none at all. No whole milk, fatty meats, cheese, bread, butter or bacon. Breakfast was a bowl of cereal with skimmed milk. In fact, it still is. I never put sugar on anything. For lunch I stuck pretty much to chicken. I didn't even eat the dark meat. White meat chicken, salads and fruit. Dinner I would eat a piece of meat and vegetables. You must understand I also had no ice cream or candy. But the hamburgs. . .do you know what it's like to dream of hamburgers covered with fried onions?

I began running in May, four months after my heart attack. It was right out there at Ferry Field, behind the athletic office. Now you understand I'm not taking any outside engagements, but I did all the recruiting. I had every kid come to my house with his parents and they all wanted to know the same thing: Is Bo Schembechler going to coach again? The coaches would bring them over every night, every weekend. I had to sell myself as well as my program. I never told them I was definitely going to coach again, just that I knew what I have to do and I was going to do it. I'd be lying around in my pajamas all day and I'd put on a suit and a tie when they came in at night. I would sit there and look them in the eye and tell them exactly how I felt about everything. I never tried to kid them. . .and we had some real class kids come in there—Ed Shuttlesworth and Bob Thornbladh and Clint Haslerig and Dave Gallagher. It was a great class.

I think some of the other coaches used my heart attack against me—in fact, I know they did. The kids would tell me about it. I don't think the coaches did it maliciously but they would raise the questions about whether I could come back or not.

One complication came up after I got back to Ann Arbor. Usually after I would eat, I would start getting a pain in my chest. Well, you know what I thought that was. I mentioned this to Dr. Reichart and he sent me in to the University Hospital for another examination. It turned out that I had a hiatal hernia and that kind of hernia lets out gas and gives you the same feeling as a heart attack. I don't even like to hear the words and here I am still suffering the symptoms of it.

I got the hernia when I let my weight get out of hand. As I lost weight, it slowly disappeared. But it gave me some anxious moments.

So now I'm starting in on my exercise program. I'm just walking around the track—four times around, one mile. Every week I'm going back to the doctor and I'm feeling good.

I tell him I'm going to start jogging a bit, but I start feeling some pain again because the hernia isn't fully gone, and I'm getting a little nervous again. But I keep at it and soon I'm running on the straightaways and walking around the curves. Pretty soon I've got it up to three miles a day. It's always by myself, too. I never wanted to run with other people, and still don't. I like to set my own pace and do things my way. Guys would come by and say, "Hi, Bo. . .how are things going?" They were all very thoughtful. When the weather got nice, you'd find a hundred guys out there jogging. Personally, I hated jogging. Jogging—I would rather run than jog and pretty soon I'm turning it on until I'm doing that three miles in under 27 minutes. The doc sees me doing this and says, "Throw the watch away." I told him I had to compete against something. I told him I liked ripping off those three miles in under 27 minutes. I thought he was going to faint. He made me put the watch away.

I guess there are two ways you can look at a heart attack. You can either accept the challenge that you have had a problem and do something about changing your life or you can continue to kid yourself and lapse back into doing things the way you used to do them. I took the challenge and that was my motivation—to conquer something else in my life. This was the toughest challenge of all because it was me I had to beat.

So I just sat there and did everything—absolutely everything—the doctors told me. I had to be one of the greatest patients in the history of modern medicine. I didn't cheat once with my food. If they told me to nap for 30 minutes, I napped for 30 minutes. I went all the way with them.

I suppose you could say the heart attack was a costly one to me. Here I am, coach of the year, my first year at Michigan, and I can't make a dime out of it. Not one dime. The school was great to me, though. It took care of all the doctor bills and I didn't have to come up with a dime. So I guess it came out even.

You always wonder what it'll be like when you go back to work. I knew I'd have it licked when I could go into that stadium and perform with all the enthusiasm of before. I mean, when I had the guts to do it.

Because of that hiatal hernia—it always worried me—I began to get a nervous stomach. So I'd be drinking skimmed milk all the time. The first game back was the opener against Arizona in 1970. I'm feeling pretty confident about things. It doesn't really matter if you have a heart attack or not. The big thing, the thing you think about on Friday nights, is 'Are you giving them the right stuff to work the next day?' In this case, I didn't. We had a bad game plan because we didn't have our people in the right positions. We lost Garvie Craw and we made a mistake by playing Billy Taylor at fullback and Glenn Doughty at tailback. I would have been 10 times better off if I would have gone with Fritzie Seyferth at fullback, Taylor at tailback and Doughty at wingback.

So we come out for the game and I admit it, I'm looking for signs of trouble. I run on the field with the rest of the players, and later, I run off with them. I'm watching the doctors because I know they're watching me. At halftime some of the guys would stick their head into my office and say, "Everything okay?" I'd look back and smile and say, "Everything's okay."

The players took it all in stride. We'd gone through two-a-day practices and they knew I was in good shape. We could have done better that day but we won, 20 - 9. I was back on the sidelines and that was the big thing. I was back where I wanted to be. I was back where I had to be.

Millie Schembechler:

I was terrified when I learned of Bo's illness. We were at a luncheon, a few hours before the Rose Bowl game, when we got word he'd been stricken and placed in the intensive care ward at St. Luke's Hospital.

It was awful because that's all we knew. We couldn't get any more information until we got to the hospital.

A million thoughts ran through my mind.

Here I was, the mother of three children whose first father had died—and I am thinking, "Will these poor boys have to go through this again?"

And then there was "Shemy," who was just three months old. I kept thinking, "Wouldn't it be terrible if I had to raise him without a father."

It all hit me at once. I was so much in love, you see. We had been married only a year and a half and our marriage was still very much in the stage of excitement.

Following Bo's heart attack, I found myself watching him more than I was watching the games. That first game was a terribly anxious moment.

You know, of course, that Bo doesn't stay at home the night before the games. He is with his team. . .and I was terribly anxious about this first game because I was trying to get him to talk to his doctor to see if he could get some sort of mild tranquilizer to calm him down. I kept trying to get him to take one but you know how Bo is. "Yeah, yeah," he would say. I kept trying to reassure him that it wouldn't be any hazard to his thinking processes. I don't know if he believed me. In fact, I don't even know if he ever took a pill.

I knew he looked great and he said he felt great. But I hadn't seen him under any pressure and this worried me a great deal. We almost always have someone from out of town—family or friends—and they go to the games with me and the children.

I remember sitting there thinking, "Oh dear. . .let's just get through this first one." I can't even remember the game. I was watching only him.

I could see a change in him. He just wasn't. . .well, he wasn't uptight the way he'd been in all of the other games. I didn't see him arguing or yelling. I felt he had great control of himself and his emotions and that was a great relief to me.

I think this is the best thing that has come out of all this. He has learned patience and tolerance and not to get uptight about things he knows he can't do anything about.

He still gets upset at times and when he comes home after losing a game. . .or even when he loses a boy in the recruiting season. . .that's when we try to have things run a little smoother in the house and try to have fewer arguments and few disagreements among the boys.

You see, I love him because he is such a good father and a good husband. Others must love him, too.

Telegram

All Ohio is praying for your fast recovery.

James A. Rhoades
Governor of Ohio

Telegram

We are pleased that you are making great progress. Looking forward to seeing you in Michigan real soon. Congratulations on a great year.

Cordially,
Duffy Daugherty

Telegram

A speedy recovery. A little fire water in the Redskin should get you going again. Will call you when your body guards permit it.

Ara Parseghian and staff
University of Notre Dame

Dr. Gerald O'Connor speaking. . .

When he came back to coach, Dr. Anderson and myself kept a very close eye on him. In that first game, he had some discomfort in the top section of his stomach.

I said to him, "What did you eat this morning?"

He said, "Nothing."

So we got him a little milk to drink.

It was a burning discomfort he had and when he drank the milk, it disappeared. He had that hernia—he was correct about that—but he also developed some gastritis on an empty stomach and that caused him the pain. You can imagine what he was thinking.

People tell me he has calmed down a lot, and I suppose he has. But you watch him in practice and he can still get pretty excited. In fact, he can get bombastic at times.

I'll tell you this, though. He has recovered so well that I've had people come to me and say, "I don't believe Bo ever had a heart attack."

Most times I don't even bother to comment to these people but if it's another physician, I'll tell him it is a well-documented fact that he had an attack.

"Doc, are you sure I'm supposed to give up hamburgers?"

Bo and Team Physician Dr. Gerald O'Connor

Joe Falls
Sports Editor

Not Enough Time
For U-M's Bo

Sept 19, 1969

ANN ARBOR

WHEN THE MICHIGAN FOOTBALL team lines up for the kickoff against Vanderbilt in the season's opener at 1:30 p.m. (EST) on Saturday, the new head coach of the Wolverines, Glenn Edward (Bo) Schembechler, will have been on the job for a total of 269 days.

That's 6,454 hours . . . or 387,270 minutes . . . or 21,636,200 seconds.

And it hasn't been enough.

"We haven't worked enough," our boy Bo was saying at the end of Thursday's practice session in the big stadium. "We've still got a lot to do."

That shows you just how intense this man is . . . because to those who have seen Schembechler operate since becoming the head coach last Dec. 26, he has worked at his job 24 hours a day, seven days a week . . . or a total of 6,454 hours . . . or 387,270 minutes . . . or 21,636,200 seconds.

If the Michigan team isn't ready, it won't be for a lack of effort on the coach's part.

Some people are born to be bankers. Others are born to be truck drivers. A few of the more unfortunate are born to be sports writers.

Bo Schembechler was born to be a football coach.

If he'd devoted as much time in the past nine months to studying the stock market or the racing form or even to digging ditches out on I-94, he'd be a rich man today.

Instead he is a man who is apprehensive about this biggest moment in his career.

Bo is THE Boss

"I THINK WE'VE GOT A GOOD football team but you really can't tell," he was saying as he looked wistfully into the darkening skies. "Remember, we've only played ourselves so far—we've only scrimmaged against ourselves. You never know how your players will react until they start bumping into other players."

This is a highly emotional moment for Schembechler because he has made it that way. He has given almost his entire being to getting the Michigan football team ready for the 1969 season. He has gone at it body and soul from the very moment he was given the job . . . and you need only to watch him for a few moments on the practice field to know that it is all business with him.

You also know who is the boss.

Some head coaches step back and let their assistants do most of the work. Not Schembechler. He puts his nose right into it and he screams louder than anyone else.

His assistants scream, too, and pretty soon the cool evening air is filled with some rather colorful words, some Maize, some blue.

He is almost another Woody Hayes. All that is missing is the pot belly and the baseball cap. And maybe the fullback drive off tackle. That we'll see.

His players call him "Sir" . . . "Yes, sir" . . . "No, sir."

But there is also humor out on the field because it is a part of football.

Reason to Be Nervous

"SURE, I'M GOING TO BE nervous for this game but no more nervous than I am for any other game," Schembechler said. "Remember, I've spent the last 15 years getting ready for this moment. I may blow some plays but it won't be because I'm tight."

Schembechler has been on a dawn-to-midnight schedule and maybe that's not so unusual among modern-day football coaches, except that he's been under some added strain. His wife is expecting their fourth child any day now and has had such difficulty that she's been hospitalized several times.

The due date, in fact, is Sept. 27, the day Washington comes to town.

Schembechler sends out for hamburgs at lunch so he can stay on the job. He does make one concession, however. When lunch is done, he tells his secretary: "No calls, no visitors for 20 minutes."

He sits back in his chair and sleeps.

Our boy Bo tries to think of everything, including "Wolverine-Ade" for his players to drink on the sidelines. That's his substitute for the popular "Gatorade."

"But I can't do anything about the weather," smiled, "and if it comes up hot on Saturday we'll be in trouble. We haven't worked in the heat."

Bo also might keep his eye on Lindsy McLean, the new trainer of the Wolverines. Word is around that he's a graduate of Vanderbilt and if the "Wolverine-Ade" comes up looking green . . .

"If you can change the score I'd feel even better."

Tournament of Roses Committee Presents Bo with Get Well Wishes at St. Luke Hospital, Pasadena, California on January 16, 1970–(Left to Right, Top)–Bill Nicholas, Bo Schembechler, Lathrop K. Leishmen–(Left to Right, Bottom)–Stan Hahn, Raymond A. Dorn

1969 Michigan Team at 1970 Rose Bowl

Chapter 2

The Ghost Speaks

Joe Falls
Sports Editor

Has Success Come Too Fast for Bo?

Dec. 31, 1969   PASADENA

BO SCHEMBECHLER. AS WE NOW KNOW, is an intense individual. All you have to do is look into his face to see the deep determination, the deadly dedication—the total committment—that this man has for his job.

Bo Schembechler is almost scary.

You can see his intensity, and you can also feel it. You can feel it burning inside of him like a white-hot flame and you ask yourself: "Is this what it takes to be a great football coach anymore?"

Vince Lombardi has this sort of intensity, and so does Woody Hayes. Ara Parseghian has it, Bear Bryant has

it and, while he likes to tell funny stories to keep the members of the press happy, John McKay, the Southern California coach, has it.

I guess it's part of the job. The competition is so keen, the talent so even, that it takes this sort of personality to be a success in the coaching business.

I've a l w a y s had the feeling that every minute Bo Schembechler gives me to answer my questions, it is one less minute he can be looking at his precious

Bo's grudging . . .

movies. He gives his time, but gives it grudgingly.

He is a man of great organization. His idea of a perfect day, I suspect, would be eight hours of meetings, eight hours of movies and eight hours of practice.

Bo Schembechler doesn't have dinner at eight; he schedules dinner for eight. You trot, never walk, to the nearest exit.

He is a very intense individual—and very complex.

But he is also a bad actor. He is a give-away guy who doesn't know how to mask his true feelings. Those eyes of his give him away every time.

Meaning Something Else?

WHEN YOU SEE Bo's eyes start darting around and looking down toward the floor, you know he may be elling you one thing but meaning something else.

Every evening here they bring him into the press room at the Huntington Sheraton Hotel and he sits there while the writers from around the country shoot questions at him.

And Bo has been very good—surprisingly good. Even better than the quick-witted McKay. He answers all of the questions and he answers them fully and honestly,

even mixing in some humor of his own.

But he sits there and squirms in his chair and you know he'd rather be some place else. He stays as long as the writers want him to stay because he is smart enough to know that this is a part of his job.

They ask him about all the distractions of trying to get a football team ready to play a game in this fantasyland of California. Bo says, yes, there are many distractions but that he has enjoyed himself, the visits to Disneyland and Marineland and the tours through the studios on the Universal lots.

"I even went on some of the rides in Disneyland," he said, smiling.

He looks around and quickly adds: "Don't get the idea I'm not enjoying myself. I am. It's a great experience."

But then you look at those eyes. They're moving around quickly and he is looking down at the floor as he is speaking, and then — suddenly — the whole thing hits you: "This man is in a terrific spot. He's got tremendous pressure on him."

And you admire him even more that he can even give up these few moments to satisfy the members of the press.

Beating Bucks Created Monster

YOU SEE, THE MICHIGAN football coach has created something of a monster. He did it by whipping Ohio State. Nobody expected that, no one believed it could happen.

But Schembechler not only brought down the mighty Buckeyes, he brought them down with a crash, and

now, instead of being a guy with a difficult name to spell and even pronounce, he is a national figure — one of the ranking coaches in his profession.

Now they expect great things from him. They expect him to beat Southern Cal on New Year's Day, and if he doesn't, it'll be a blight—not just a loss—on his record.

All of this has come swiftly for Schembechler, really much too swiftly. He has barely been on the job

. . . And Intense

for a year and already he has been acclaimed "coach of the year." He has taken his place with the leaders in his field.

When I think about it, I'm amazed that Bo is handling it all as well as he is. He is about as up-tight as a coach can get and yet he'll sit there with us and swap funny lines and try to help us in our jobs . . . while all the while you know he is dying a little bit.

Duffy Daugherty does it, but Duffy enjoys it. Duffy is part actor.

Schembechler's only break is that Notre Dame is in the Cotton Bowl and, from a national standpoint, that game rates the top priority on New Year's Day. But once that one is over, they'll flip their dials and start sitting in judgment of this man with the long funny name.

I hope he does well.

Joe Falls:

Who were they trying to kid? The guy came on the P.A. system about 90 minutes before game time and said: "Attention, press. Here is an announcement from the University of Michigan. Head coach Bo Schembechler has not accompanied his team to the Rose Bowl game today. He is suffering from a case of the virus.

"Repeating: Head coach Bo Schembechler of the University of Michigan. . ."

I turned and looked at Curt Sylvester, our football writer at the Free Press. The two of us were sitting in the press box at Pasadena watching the Notre Dame-Texas game on TV.

Virus?

"Something's wrong, Curt," I said. "They'd have to cut that man's legs off at the knees to keep him away from this game."

And there began one of the longest and most exhausting days of my life.

We had to find out what was going on—what was wrong. Where do you begin?

"I'll go look for Don Canham. You look for Bump Elliott. We gotta find out what's happening."

Curt and I took off in different directions.

The press box at Pasadena is on different levels. Writers on one level. Broadcasters on another. Photographers on the third.

We scoured the place. We looked around from one end to another.

"You see Bump around?"

"Where's Canham?"

Nothing. No one was around.

Our problem was acute. We're a morning newspaper, which means we print at night. Our first-edition deadline is normally about seven o'clock. That's our copy close. Anything after that doesn't get in our first edition. But now it was a holiday, New Year's Day, which meant the editions were changed and the deadlines moved up by as much as two hours. And, with the three-hour time difference between

California and Detroit, it was already past three o'clock back home.

I felt clammy.

"What are we going to do?" I asked Curt.

"I don't know," he said. "We've got to talk to somebody but nobody is around."

I left my seat and made another search of the press box.

While I was gone, little Robin Wright came into the press box and started talking to Curt. She was whispering to him. Robin worked for the Michigan Daily and she was whispering because she didn't want me—the ogre—to hear what she had to say.

For the want of a better way to put it, Robin thought I was a very nasty man. That's because of the things I had written about the Michigan football team. She told Curt: "I was just down on the field. The players told me Bo has had a heart attack."

I returned and Robin smiled at me. I smiled back at her. When she left, Curt said, "Robin says she talked to the players and they told her Bo has had a heart attack."

I should have been surprised. Even stunned. But I wasn't.

I couldn't quite bring myself to believe it but it did make some sense.

I thought back to that press conference at the Huntington Hotel a few days earlier and what I had written about Bo.

Curt had flown out to California with the team when it left before Christmas. I came in about three days before the game.

Every day they have a press conference at the Huntington. They bring in the visiting coach so that all the writers can get some fresh material from him.

I walked in just as Bo's conference was starting and the moment I looked at him, I knew something was wrong. He looked ashen. His face was white. He looked nervous. He looked worried. I knew he didn't like all the hoopla that goes on with the Rose Bowl. Hell, I knew he didn't like having us writers around all the time.

But this was different. He looked—well, he didn't look right.

As he was talking to the guys, I watched him. His eyes were

darting around the room. He was tapping his foot on the floor, bouncing his knee up and down.

I didn't want to ask any questions, since I had just arrived and figured the other guys might take it the wrong way.

But I couldn't help myself. I blurted out: "Are you having a good time, Bo?"

His eyes shot straight at me. They were hard. He was glaring at me.

"Sure, I'm having a good time," he said.

He told me he enjoyed going to Disneyland and to Marineland and to all the places that the Big Ten teams go in Los Angeles. He said this was all part of the Rose Bowl game.

I nodded at his answer.

Bo went back talking football with the other writers. The conference lasted about 40 minutes or so. He laughed a few times but it sounded very forced.

I had no more questions.

I just sat there and listened.

When it was all over, Bo got up to leave. He looked back at me and said: "Now, Joe, I'm having a good time here. Do you understand that? I'm having a fine time."

I told him: "Okay, Bo. I'm glad."

I went to my room and wrote a column saying how awful it must be to be a big time football coach and be under all the pressure that a man like Bo Schembechler is under at a big game like the Rose Bowl. I also wrote that something seemed to be bothering the man—I didn't know what—but hoped he would do well for himself on New Year's Day.

This is what I thought about as Curt told me what Robin Wright had said. But we couldn't go on hearsay. We couldn't write any stories from what a student newspaper gal told us. It was too risky.

Somehow, I thought Robin had it right but we had to get it officially before we could put it in our newspaper.

Still, nobody was around. . .and now the game was about to start.

"You watch the game," I told Curt. "I'll keep looking for the Michigan people."

I went around to the coaching booth, which is centered in

the middle of the press box on the writer's level. There were three Michigan coaches in there. I only knew one of them. George Mans.

He was crying.

George was sitting there with earphones on his head and tears was streaming down his cheeks.

That clinched it for me. Something definitely was wrong— something drastic.

But still it wasn't enough to write.

All we could do was call our office, tell them what was going on, and put a little piece on the wire saying that Bo wasn't at the game—that the school had announced he was suffering from a virus.

Our hands were tied until the game was over, until we could talk to the team doctors in the dressing room.

I tried to watch the game. Impossible. To this day I can't recall one play in the game. Not one. I kept thinking of Bo and what was going on.

We were really up against it now. . .because the game ended about five o'clock, California time, which meant it was eight o'clock in Detroit. Our presses were running non-stop, so that every minute that passed meant so many papers were going out without Bo's story in it.

It seemed like the game lasted forever. We couldn't get down to the dressing room quickly enough. By now, the word was around that something bad had happened to Bo and there were dozens of reporters waiting outside of the Michigan dressing room.

They let us in right away and Jim Young did the best he could to try to explain what was happening. Jim was on a terrible spot. He didn't know what to say because, at this point, they didn't know what type or how severe a heart attack Bo had had. The doctors tried to talk to us, too. They were on the spot, too. Of all people, they didn't want to commit-themselves.

So they began talking in medical terms and because the writers didn't understand what they were saying, we let them ramble on.

Finally, Pete Waldmeir of the Detroit News had enough

courage to ask the question.

"Did Bo have a heart attack?" asked Pete.

It was out. Those dreaded words—"heart attack."

Again the doctors hemmed and hawed. Well, yes and no, they said. They couldn't be quite sure yet.

Time was running out, so I went in to see the players. I knew only a few of them—Jim Mandich and Garvie Craw. I asked them straight. To their credit, they gave it to me straight. Yes, they were told Bo had had a heart attack. Yes, the team was shaken by it. Yes, some of the players broke down and cried.

I headed back to the press box and Curt and I began writing as fast as we could— a page one piece, a sub on my column, a new lead for Curt's story, a sidebar story.

We went as strong as we could. We called it a "possible heart attack." We could have gone stronger. It WAS a heart attack.

I remember feeling exhilerated because we had done such a good job of writing the story but also drained because it was such an emotional experience.

It may sound crass that we relate so much to how it appears in print but this is our job. As we walked out of the press box in darkness, I felt satisfied we had done our best. . .and frustrated that we couldn't make more papers than we did.

Curt and I had a quiet supper and talked about Bo. We began recalling all the little incidents of the previous days— how uptight he was becoming. Curt remembered one of the assistant coaches telling him: "There's a big story happening here but nobody knows it."

The next day, I was horrified at how the Los Angeles papers handled the story. They not only almost overlooked it, but one columnist poked fun at the whole affair.

"This," he wrote, "is what happens to Big Ten coaches when they come out to the West Coast to play our teams. Remind me to send Bo some flowers."

I was appalled. I couldn't believe what I had read. How could anyone possibly make light of what was a very serious situation.

I didn't know much about heart attacks, and still don't but

M's Grid Future Hangs in Balance

Jan. 2, 1970   PASADENA

IT IS ODD that a university such as Michigan could ⸋t so much hope—so many of its dreams—into the ⸋nds of one man.

But that's what they did when Don Canham went out ⸋d hired Bo Schembechler to be the coach of the Mich-⸋an football team.

And so now not only an entire university, but a mas-⸋ve alumni and every Michigan man in the country-**⸋ll anxiously await the next doctor's report from St.** ⸋ke's Hospital in Pasadena.**

It is a cruel blow that has been struck here — a ⸋cious blow.

Because all of those hopes and all of those dreams ⸋uld come c r a s h i n g down if they decide that Bo ⸋hembechler has to go easy.

This is a man who doesn't know how to go easy.

He lives for but one thing — football.

It is his entire life.

He has a wife and a family but his wife must be the ⸋ost understanding woman in the world.

She knows of her husband's love for his job, and she ⸋es right down the line with him—waking him up in **⸋ose dark early hours of the morning and waiting up** ⸋r him when he returns home late at night.**

Bo Schembechler IS football at Michigan and what ⸋e Wolverines accomplished this season, they accom-⸋ished b e c a u s e of his great drive, ability and ⸋nagination.

Mostly his drive.

Bo Did it All

LET'S NOT KID ABOUT THIS. Canham hired ⸋hembechler for the sole purpose of restoring the old ⸋lories to the ancient school out in Ann Arbor.

Too long had Michigan State dominated the football ⸋cture in our state.

Too long once-mighty Michigan had to take a back ⸋at to the live, bold, imaginative Spartans of Michigan ⸋tate.

So Canham, an ambitious man himself, went out ⸋nd hired a man who was totally dedicated to this business of winning f o o t b a l l game . . . and I will never forget that day in Canham's office early last autumn when he sat there shaking his head and saying, "I don't know whether I've got a genius on my hands or what."

Michigan had opened up with a pair of resounding victories over Vanderbilt and Washington, and all of a sudden there was a stirring in the land.

Perhaps Michigan was on the way back.

Schembechler   "I r e a l l y don't know what I've ⸋ot," said Canham. "Frankly, I'm a little scared by it ⸋ll."

Genius or not, only history will tell.

But Bo did it all in his first year. He woke up a few of the old echoes and restored much of the pride and prestige to ⸋his school.

He lost to Michiang State but pulled it together and reeled off five straight at the end of the year, topped by that smashing victory over Ohio State.

They were afraid, out here, that the Big Ten would be sending its second best team to the Rose Bowl.

Team Missed the Leader

BUT BO SHOWED THEM.

He won the co-championship of the Big Ten the Wolverines flew west with its head high.

And then Bo ran into a very unsettling thing.

He ran into the Hollywood atmosphere of this bowl game.

It bothered him. It bothered him greatly. He tried to keep it but if he is not working at his profession around the clock, he is a restless man.

His idea of a perfect day would be eight hours of movies, eight hours of meetings and eight hours of practice.

He was on the spot here. They wanted to see if the Ohio State game was a fluke, one of those once-in-a-lifetime upsets.

But Bo never got a chance to show them . . . and if

you saw it on TV, you saw how flat this Michigan team performed against Southern Cal.

Nobody will ever know if it would have been dif-ferent had Bo been here for the game, and anything you say in this respect will have the ring of an alibi.

But he was the leader of this team—the unquestioned leader—and when they looked around for him, he wasn't there.

And they seemed like lost children.

This loss will hurt. It will hurt in the important days ahead, the recruiting days. This may sound calloused, but it is true.

You don't build champions unless you have the play-ers, and you don't get the players unless you work at it.

Bo Schembechler was prepared to launch the great-est recruiting campaign ever known to the University of Michigan.

But now everybody will have to wait for that next report out of St. Luke's.

"Here I am Mickey-Mousin' around when I have a game to play."

A Distracted Schembechler at Disneyland, 1970 Rose Bowl

Michigan's "Missing Man" Formation

1970 Michigan Rose Bowl Team on Sidelines, without Schembechler

33

The Ghost Says: *"Here was a man who was putting a football empire together. He had brought the old greatness, the old traditions back to Michigan."*

when you are hit by one, they can't be minor.

The morning paper barely made mention of Schembech-ler's absence. The story was buried back on the bottom of page seven of the sports section. The man writing the main story of the game gave it a quick mention in his third para-graph and never alluded to it again.

You'd have thought the whole thing was a hoax—that somebody made it all up. Here was the coach of the Michigan football team— the coach of the year—suffering a heart attack just before the start of the Rose Bowl game, the biggest of all the bowl games, and one paper is sneering at it and the other is all but ignoring it.

After all, Southern Cal had won the game, 10-3, and the game is still the thing. Right, men!

I was ashamed of my profession that day.

But something came out of all this. . .because it was then, in this time of trial, that I began taking a closer look at this man who was coaching the Michigan football team.

Maybe you have read some of the things I have written about him over the years—particularly in the 1972 season, when I said he was a very stubborn man and that his brand of football was very dull and boring to watch. I did not do that for effect—to sell newspapers, as it were. I did it because I believed it.

I also did it because I care for the man and I would have been less than honest with him if I did not let him know how I felt about him.

Let me tell you another story about Bo.

This is the 1970 game against Ohio State. Bo's second sea-son. He was back now from his heart attack, as good as ever, and I couldn't help but be impressed the way he disciplined himself and lost all that weight. I've had a weight problem my entire life. I'm going on a diet—tomorrow.

When I saw what Bo had done, I acquired a great admira-tion for him.

So now we are down in Columbus to play the hated Woody Hayes and the hated Ohio State Buckeyes. I know I am not the most popular writer among the University of Michigan football fans, especially those who live in Ann Arbor.

But the truth is, I have always rooted for Michigan—sometimes actively, sometimes passively. But I've always wanted to see the Blue win. I really don't know why, except that it was the first college team I ever covered and I liked them from the start. I liked the whole scene at Michigan—the drive out to Ann Arbor, the big stadium, the big crowds. We never had anything like it in New York.

Some people won't believe this but I wanted Michigan to beat Ohio State so bad on this day in 1970 that my stomach was growling at game time. Curt Sylvester can tell you. We sit together at these games and root. (The trick is not to let it color your judgment or your work. You still have to be impartial. But I gave up long ago trying to play the role of a neutral. That's the bunk. It's not honest. When Michigan plays Ohio State, I hope Michigan kills them).

Since this was such a special game, I knew we had to have special preparations. So I bought a Playboy Magazine in the lobby of our hotel and pasted the centerfold to the window in front of our seats.

"That," I told young Mr. Sylvester, "ought to inspire you."

Ohio State kicked off. Lance Scheffler caught the ball. Lance Scheffler fumbled the ball. Ohio State recovered the ball. Soon, all was in disarray, including our Bunny Girl. We took her down in the middle of the third quarter and dropped her into a waste basket.

It was an embarrassing afternoon. A humiliating afternoon. Ohio State did a job on Michigan.

But now we had to do our work. We had to talk to the Michigan players—to see how they felt, to get their reactions. . .to paint the familiar losing locker room scene.

Again there were dozens of writers outside of the Michigan dressing room. We stood there and waited. And waited. And waited.

Five o'clock.
Five oh five.
Five ten.
"Come on, Bo. . .open the door."
"Hey, how about letting us in?"
Five fifteen.

'We Made Mistakes All Over the Place,' Bo Admits Grimly

November 22, 1970

BY JOE FALLS, Free Press Sports Editor

COLUMBUS—It was a bad moment for Bo Schembechler. . .possibly the worst in his career. . .and the anguish showed in his eyes and in his voice.

"We made a great effort, but we didn't play well," the grim Michigan football coach told a corps of reporters after his Wolverines lost the big one to Ohio State Saturday.

This was more than 30 minutes after the game. That's how long Bo kept the members of the media waiting outside his dressing room.

And then, when he permitted them inside, he wouldn't let anyone talk to his players.

"Just me. . .leave the players alone," he said, "I'll talk to you, but I don't want any one talking to my players."

SCHEMBECHLER, of course, was trying to ease as much of the hurt as possible for the young men who had played so brilliantly for him all season.

But they will carry the memory of this painful defeat for the rest of their lives—and it was painful.

Schembechler put it the best when he said "We made mistakes all over the place. . .dropped passes, fumbles, penalties. . .and you just can't do those things against a team like Ohio State."

Schembechler twice lost his temper when a reporter in the rear asked him if he could speak up.

He glowered at the reporter and fumed: "That's as loud as I can talk."

IT WAS a very difficult moment for the man who tried to make it two straight over his former tutor, Wayne Woodrow Hayes.

Bo spoke in short, clipped tones and the interview lasted only five minutes.

"We didn't move on the ground," he said, "That was the ball game. I don't know why we couldn't move. . . We didn't seem to block very much.

"Our trouble was that we had to play too much defense today. But give Ohio State credit. They jammed our running game.

"But we were dropping passes and fumbling the ball and you just can't do those things."

Bo wanted to take some shots at the officials but held himself back.

He was particularly disturbed about the face mask call which deprived the Wolverines of a 71-yard punt by Paul Staroba in the second period.

Staroba was asked to punt a second time, and Michigan lost 39 yards in field position. That put the Buckeyes in a spot to score their first touchdown and take a 10-3 lead at the half.

"I was told that we were guilty of face-masking while the ball was in the air," he said, putting a strong accent on the word "while".

"I never heard of such a thing in my life, but that's what I was told."

He would not identify the player charged with the penalty.

He was also incensed at the officials' confusion near the end of the first half.

This was when Ohio State tried to get on the scoreboard again with time running out. The Bucks called a fifth time out—an illegal move since they already had their prescribed four timeouts and tried to get into position for a field-goal try.

They never got the play off, and after the gun sounded, Schembechler went to the officials and began complaining.

"No way could they do what they did," he told the reporters. "Ohio sent a player into the huddle, then pulled him out and you can't do anything like that. That's what I was complaining about, not the extra timeout."

THE BRIEF question-and-answer session, strained from the very first moment, got a little awkward when some of the questions came out sounding like second guesses.

A reporter, for instance, asked Schembechler why he persisted on running on first down on almost every play when the maneuver wasn't producing much result.

Bo replied tersely: 'I believe you've got to run. Their defense had to crack if we were going to win. But it just didn't.'

Another writer asked if his players were nervous at the outset.

"Nervous?" Schembechler looked up. "We were high, not nervous."

HE WAS asked why Glenn Doughty carried only one time, gaining just one yard.

"It just wasn't in our plans for him to carry very much," siad Bo.

Then he offered a comment of his own.

"We started off by dropping the opening kickoff and that's just the way it went."

It was Lance Scheffler who bobbled the ball and Schembechler grimaced and said: "And he was through for the day. A thigh. He never got back in there."

FINALLY, they asked him how he saw the play when Ohio State's Tim Anderson blocked Michigan's extra point try in the third quarter.

"I'll have to look at the films on that one." said Schmebechler, laughing briefly for the first time. It was a half-hearted laugh. "It looked as if he came in from the outside. I don't know if we missed a block or we kicked slowly. I'll have to look at it."

Then Bo looked around and asked: "Is that it?"

Nobody said a word.

"So that's it, then," he said with a wave and walked away.

His players dressed in silence and filed out quietly. None of them uttered a word. They didn't have to. The expressions on their faces asid it all.

(This Column Reproduced)

Ohio State's Harry Howard Closes in as Michigan's Lance Scheffler (45) Fumbles the Opening Kickoff in the 1970 Game which Ohio Won, 20-9.

I knew what was happening. Bo was letting his players dress and leave without giving us the chance to talk to them. Now I was embarrassed. I was standing there among my colleagues, the other writers from around the midwest and some from New York and cities like that, and our coach was keeping his dressing room door closed.

The players started coming out now. They pushed past us. They wouldn't talk. Anyway, few of us knew who they were since they were in street clothes.

Now I was getting angry. I'd missed my first edition and didn't think that was fair. It wasn't fair to the Michigan fans back home. I felt, win or lose, they deserved to read about their team.

But Bo had shut us out, shut us off.

He finally let us in but he'd have done better to keep the door barred. He was curt. He was rude. He threw up his hands after only a few minutes and said: "That's it! That's all! I have nothing else to say!" And he stomped off.

I wrote some of this that night. You never like to do this because it seems like you are crying to your readers about your own problems and it should be no concern of theirs. But, in this case, we got such little information out of the Michigan room that I felt the readers should know why.

When I got home, I sat down and wrote Bo a very long letter. I thought it out at great length.

I told him, first of all, that I was on his side—that, if he was going to believe any of the things I had to say, he had to first believe that.

Then I gave him all the reasons why I thought he was wrong in how he handled the press in Columbus.

I told him his players deserved better. He was, by keeping us away from them, saying they couldn't handle adversity. I told him if I were one of his players, I'd take this as an insult.

Secondly, I told him we had gone in to talk to his players for nine straight Saturdays—all winning days—and I didn't think it was fair to us to keep us out just because the team finally lost a game.

"We were there when you won and we deserved the chance to be there when you lost," I wrote.

I also told him that I thought he hurt his own image with the other writers—that, perhaps, they didn't understand the great importance of this game, or how he felt, and all they would remember was his rebuff at the dressing room.

Oh, I was beautiful in my letter.

I wondered how Bo would answer me. I wondered what he would say the next time he saw me.

Well, to this day Bo Schembechler has never mentioned my letter to him. . .and the curious thing is that this didn't turn me off. It made me more fascinated by him. I wondered what kind of man could receive such a missive and ignore it. I figured he must be one helluva tough individual and I must get to know more about him.

I got the idea for this book near the end of the 1972 season. It happened right in the press box in Ann Arbor. I don't remember the game, but I do remember sitting there pretty bored by what I was seeing. Michigan was pounding somebody into the turf but when I looked around the press box, the rest of the guys were sitting there staring straight ahead. Nobody was making any noise. Nobody was moving. Nobody was doing anything.

I thought to myself: "What's going on here? Here the team is doing what it is supposed to do—it is winning and winning big—but nobody is very excited about it."

Okay, that was the press box. Most of us don't demonstrate. We're pretty quiet people when we work—and sometimes pretty cynical. I could understand the mood in the box.

But then I looked out to the stands. They were almost filled. They must have had 70,000, 80,000 or whatever. I studied those people, particulary the students below us. They didn't seem bored at all. In fact, they seemed to be having a helluva time for themselves.

That made me think some more.

Maybe it was us. Maybe it was me. Why weren't we excited by what was happening, when seventy or eighty thousand people were?

I thought about the man who was responsible for this great double mood—Glenn E. Schembechler, my boy Bo. I thought, right then, I've got to find out more about this man.

"Nobody really knows him," I thought. That was true. Who really knows Bo Schembechler? His wife? His kids? His players? Don Canham? That was about it.

Yet, here, before our very eyes was a man who was putting a football empire together; in four years he had brought the old greatness, the old traditions, back to Michigan.

And he was spoiling us all by winning so much.

We'd go out to Ann Arbor expecting Michigan to win, knowing Michigan would win. So, show us something different, Bo. Show us a different way to win.

Not our Bo.

He'd hammered away at the middle of the line, until that line caved in. 7-0. 14-0. 21-0. Click, Click. Click. Not very exciting. Not very imaginative.

But effective as hell.

We would see Bo for maybe 10 minutes after the game. Then again at his noon press conference on Monday—maybe an hour and 10 minutes a week. What was that? How can you learn anything about a man—what he does and why he does it—in an hour and 10 minutes a week?

I walked to the back of the press box and sat down with Don Canham.

"I've got an idea."

Canham looked at me. Idea. That's a word he likes. "How about a book on Bo Schembechler?"

Don turned around in his seat and looked at me. He gave himself away in that instant. A book on Bo! Click. Click. Whirrrrr. Whirrrrr. He, too, knew what it could mean. . .a way to tell the world about this man. Especially the people who buy tickets to Michigan football games. And—most especially—those who don't.

So that's how this book was born. The fun part was trying to sell Bo on the idea.

It happened in Canham's office one morning after the season was over. Canham picked up his phone. "Bo, Don," he said. "I need 10 minutes." That was all—Bo, Don, I need 10 minutes. I wondered if Canham saw the smile on my face.

Bo came into the office. He took one look at me and said: "What the hell are you doing here?"

I was still smiling.

"Joe's got an idea," said Canham. "Sit down and let's talk about it."

Now I knew I had to make a sound presentation to him. I knew it had to make sense to him, so I had a prepared speech for Bo.

"I want to write a book about you," I began, and his eyes got THIS BIG. "Now, wait, let me explain. . ."

I explained:

1. Nobody knew him.

2. He was successful.

3. He had made Michigan a winner.

4. He had instilled discipline in young men at a time when young men don't want discipline.

(Bo stirred in his seat. This is when I knew I had him.)

5. And he had overcome a heart attack—a truly great accomplishment.

He launched into the obvious: "A book? Me? Me write a book? You're crazy. Who cares what I've got to say? Who cares what I do?"

I let him talk.

Then I said: "I care. . .and I think some other people do."

"Hey," I said, "I'm coming to you—your great critic asking to work with you. If I think you've got some things to say, other people might, too."

Now he was rubbing his chin and looking at the floor. I had him. I had him, cold. But I kept a straight face. I didn't want to blow it now. (I loved this moment—me, talking Bo Schembechler into something. Not too many people had ever done that, I thought. I meant all I said, though, and I could see he believed me. That was the key to it all—belief.)

Well, with Canham's help—and I would like this man to be my financial adviser someday if I ever have any finances—we sold him.

Through the winter months, I had to keep selling Bo.

He would weaken. We'd be sitting in his office or in his home and he'd say: "I don't know. . .I don't like this. I don't like talking about myself. You write it. Leave me out of it."

He didn't even like reading what I wrote and, at this

moment, which is the end of April, 1973, Bo still hadn't read his own manuscript.

But he talked. Oh, my, how he talked. We'd turn the tape recorder on and the Bo Schembechler mind would start and swoooooooooosh!

Actually, I could write a book about writing a book about Bo Schembechler.

The toughest part was getting him to sit down, even for 10 minutes. Twenty minutes was a bonus. A half hour was unbelievable. You talk about a man going at his job 24 hours a day; believe me, in this case it is true.

Here it is December, January, February, March and April of the year. An important time, certainly, for football coaches since this is the recruiting season. But sitting in Bo's office, trying to get him to talk into the tape recorder, was like sitting in the office of the president of U.S. Steel.

The phone never stopped ringing. His secretary was in and out of the office with one message after another. The coaches were forever coming by with questions. The players were always there.

Bo never stopped. He was talking all the time to me, to the tape recorder, into the telephone, to whoever came into the office.

In all the time I was with him—and it wasn't nearly what I wanted—his mind never turned off. Let me show you one page of a transcript—the man's flow of consciousness. Then maybe you'll understand his intensity, his dedication, his consuming passion for his profession. . .why he is how he is:

Jerry Hanlon and I are driving down to Cleveland to go in and see a family—we had a great prospect and the mother of the boy had remarried and had a different name than the boy and her husband was living in another city quite a distance away (the boy's father) so we went in there and Jerry and I are driving in there and we are talking about morality—morality in people today and all this you know—I said you know Jerry, you and I are a couple of stiffs and he said well why do you say that and I said you know we don't do anything—I mean all we do is coach football and go home to the family and you know we don't do anything. You see all the other guys are having a good time chasing around and you know he said you know I really don't want to do it and so we go into the house and we are sitting down and the kid isn't home yet and there is a program on television about a guy who was in the hospital with a heart attack (it was Dr. Kildare) and it was funny because the guy had a gal who came in to see him and one of his daughter's caught him you know and at the end of the program they had it all worked out where the guy was going to go back home with the family and the nurse said to the doctors that there is no way it will work because the guy is a weak willed guy and—all men are alike they can be had you know—he is weak willed and he will go back to the girl and the boy's mother turns over to us and said that is absolutely right—every man is weak willed. Jerry and I looked at her and said you mean every man and she said every man every one of you is alike and so we assumed right there that the old man had moved out on her you see and Jerry and I had just been telling each other how good we were you know and she said every man is the same way and I looked at Jerry and Jerry looked at me—tell me that isn't funny—we were driving down there and telling each other how nice we were and she said every one of you.

Everybody has had their say about Bo, their reasons why they like or respect him. I have mine.

I believe he is eminently honest.

Maybe he cheats a little, as all coaches do, as all coaches must, but I didn't uncover any of this in my days with him.

I am taken mostly by his complete dedication to what he does. He believes in football. He believes in coaching football. He does all in his power to be a success at what he does. . .and I can't get mad at any man who is so dedicated to excellence.

You know what Bo would do to me? We'd start talking about him, his career and such, and pretty soon he'd be interviewing me. He'd ask me about Billy Martin, what kind of guy was he? What about Johnny Wilson of the Red Wings? Joe Schmidt? He wanted to know everything about everything.

I worked with Bo through his recruiting season. He went out to Jackson one night to visit the parents of a player he called "the best quarterback in the whole damned state of Michigan."

Bo wanted this young man and wanted him badly.

As he was speaking to the boy's father, the father's face turned into a frown and he said: "You know, Mr. Schembechler, there's something which has been bothering me. I mean, the way this Joe Falls has been writing about you and your program at Michigan."

"What about it?" said Bo.

"Well, it seems that he is very bitter about you. . .and I just don't understand it."

"He's not bitter," said Bo.

"Well, it seems that way," said the man.

"What if I told you Joe and I are working on a book," said Bo.

The man's eyes brightened. "A book?"

"Yeah, what if I told you Joe came into my office one day and said, 'I want to write a book about you?' "

"Did that happen?" the man wondered.

"Sure, it happened," said Bo. "We're writing it right now."

"Well, I'll be. . ."

How's that for turning things around? Bo Schembechler now has Joe Falls recruiting players for The University of Michigan!

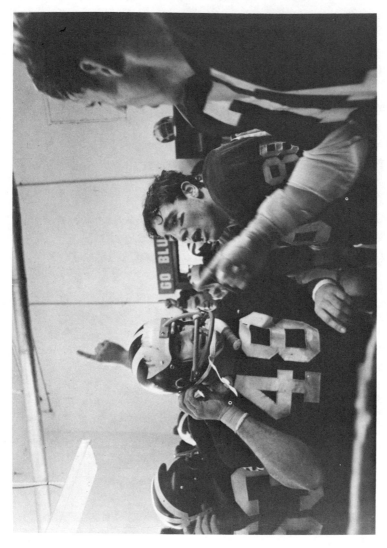

"We knew we could do it all the time, didn't we Garvie?"

Captain Jim Mandich (88) with Garvie Craw (48) and Jack Harpring (71) following the Wolverines 24-12 upset win over Ohio State in 1969

Chapter 3

Ohio State: "No Way Are They Going to Blow Us Out of There!"

If anything means anything in this business of football, it is the way a team. . .a collection of men. . .can perform the way we did against Ohio State in 1969.

It doesn't happen very often. Sometimes it never happens. Not in a whole lifetime. Everything has to be right. The time. The place. The conditions. The setting. And the men.

We had it all—just once maybe—but we had it. It was the highlight of my whole career. I want it again. But, if it doesn't happen again, it happened once. I'm a pretty lucky guy.

To understand what we did you have to understand our season. The team is new to me. I'm new to them. Nobody knows what's going to happen. Everyone is wondering.

We open with two wins, then get blown out by Missouri. They kill us. We come back with a big one against Purdue but we go up to East Lansing and lose to Michigan State. Now we're 3-2 and everybody is really won.ering, even me.

But it all turned around in the sixth week when we go up to play Minnesota in Minneapolis. We were crippled up but we won the game with a great second-half flurry. That got us going. It got us straightened out. We beat Wisconsin, then blew out Illinois, 57-0.

Now we're in Iowa and I'll never forget the Friday before the game. We're practicing in the snow and it's a miserable day—snowing and gray. I call them all together, right there in the middle of the field, and I say, "Men, you're playing in the snow today but we're going to be playing in the sun on New Year's Day." They look at me. I tell them, "You're going to win tomorrow and you're going to win next week and you're going

47

to the Rose Bowl."

They were hustling and they were playing good football and we went out and bombed Iowa. I mean, Iowa was decent and we bombed them, 51 to 6.

When we came into the locker room. . .and you can ask Canham. . .or you can ask anybody that was allowed in the locker room. . .there was no way you could silence those guys. There were tears in their eyes. We beat Iowa. We bombed Iowa. We were ready. We were confident. We knew we could play over our injuries. We knew we could do anything.

I told them: "All right, now! I said we can beat Ohio State and we can beat them!"

You should have heard them. Like kids. Grown up kids. They're screaming and yelling. I wanted to play the game right then and there.

We're talking about a super team now. Ohio State. I mean, this is supposed to be one of the great teams in history. But I'm so enthused, I can't believe it. I'm so pleased the way this team has come along. . .well, imagine me standing there in the middle of the room telling them we're going to beat Ohio State. I'm glad you writers weren't in there then. You'd have thought I was crazy.

You just don't get this feeling very often. It's special. I think you've got to be a coach to understand it. All of a sudden I feel I have control of a team that is good. Damned good. They're hard to beat. They're eager. They're hungry. We had everything.

Ohio State had just come back from the Rose Bowl. They had been walking through their opponents. Everything was easy for them. It wasn't for us. We had to struggle to get where we were, but now we were there.

The minute we get home Saturday night, we go down to the office and start in on the Iowa film. The guy has it ready for us in two hours. Nobody's thinking of dinner or going home. Iowa. Then, Ohio State. You could just feel the crackle in the air.

Our staff met again at one o'clock Sunday afternoon. We went over the Iowa film real quickly, then we started to put the Ohio State film on. We met the squad at four o'clock and showed them the Iowa film. It was a complete blowout. We knocked them out of there and everything was good. We looked good.

We closed the film and I got up and said, "Okay, that's it. It's over with. Now everything is Ohio State from now on."

I tell them that we're in an ideal position to win. I tell them there is no way anybody figures we are going to win. But we are going to win. I swear to them we are going to win.

Sunday night we grab a bite to eat and go back to the office and go over our Ohio State films and decide on our game plan. The game plan was to run at them. We felt we could run on them. We would run off tackle and we would run the draw and we would fake the draw and pass.

We felt if we could get ahead of them—put them into a position they weren't accustomed to—we could break them.

Monday morning we're still working on the game plan. It's finished by noon. We know exactly what we're going to do.

When you set up a game plan, you have to decide on every adjustment you have to make. You have to take every play you are going to run, every defense they can put in there, every possible adjustment you can think of. What will they do? What if they move him over here? What if they bring in that guy two steps? What if the fire game is on? How do you handle this? How do you handle that? We have to block everything they're going to do.

It's like saying you are going to run a certain play—you have to go back over 10 games and know everything they have done defensively. Would that stop this play—yeah, it would. . .unless we block it this way. So this means a change in technique. We will make sure we will be able to adjust. I mean, we have to get it down cold. No guesswork. No experimenting. Cold.

Since we knew we were going to run at them, we weren't going to take the easy way. We were going to attack their sideline.

The other thing is that we weren't going to back off Jack Tatum, their great linebacker. We were going to take it right to him. We knew he was a great player. No question about that. But I didn't want to go into the game with a negative attitude, saying Tatum is going to line up on the wide side of the field so I

Bo's Dedication
Awesome to Behold

November, 1969

ANN ARBOR

Who's afraid of big, bad Bo?

Well, would you believe the sports writers and sportscasters from around the state of Michigan?

'Tis true.

Sad, but true.

Here it is the weekly Monday luncheon at Weber's Inn with the head coach of the Michigan football team, Glenn Schembechler, and he is sitting at the head table. (Where else do you expect head coaches to sit?)

He is talking about something he dislikes almost as much as he dislikes losing to Ohio State.

He is talking about food.

They've asked him about his diet, how he's keeping the weight off, and he picks up the basket of bread, crackers and garlic toast in front of him and says how this stuff is murder on you. He points to a platter of butter and says "this is the stuff that'll really kill you."

He calls it "cholesterol jazz" and says who needs it . . . and so we sit there, the toughest, hardest-hitting crew of newsmen that can be collected at one sitting—right, guys?—and not a one of us touches so much as even one pat of butter!

Now that's what you call intimidation. It is also a new field-house record for restraint.

In the old days, when Bump Elliott was the boss, the weekly luncheons were quiet, intimate affairs, like the weekly meeting of the PTA. Les Etter, the PR man, would be there and maybe a couple of writers and, if the weather was nice enough to drive out, possibly one whole radio man.

Now our boy Bo was playing to almost a full house—11 writers and two flesh-and-blood broadcasters. Even Don Canham and Dave Strack showed up for a while. And there were—count em—three PR men in the audience, two from Michigan, one from Ohio State, and can you imagine anyone from Ohio State passing up lunch with Woody to break bread with Bo.

Except, of course, nobody dared to touch any bread either.

Nothing Else Seems to Exist

This shows you the hold that Schembechler has taken on everyone even remotely connected with Michigan football. When he is around, nothing else matters. Nothing else even seems to exist. It is as if the entire world spins on the axis of Bo's Big Blue Machine . . . and you can understand, after just one of these luncheon sessions, how he can push his players to a 10-0 record, the Big Ten title and another trip to the Rose Bowl.

You get the idea if they didn't do it, he'd play all 11 positions by himself.

His dedication is an awesome thing to behold.

They asked him what he thought about the way the Chicago Bears beat the Washington Redskins Sunday—on that pass to Dick Butkus in the end zone.

"I don't know," said Schembechler, "I don't follow pro football that much."

He had just finished reeling off data on a string of Ohio State players—almost everyone who plays defense for the Buckeyes, first and last names and a little bit of information about each player, but he hadn't heard a thing about what was probably the wildest play of the entire football season, pro or college.

He is so wrapped up in his occupation that you get the idea he never fully says what is on his mind, for fear he might say the wrong thing, or perhaps be misquoted or misunderstood, and hurt his team.

Other coaches do the same thing. They guard their every word, cover their every thought. But Bo seems to go a little further with it than most. He carries it to the extreme.

For instance, he has built a magnificent football team b how many people around the country really know very muc about it? Who knows just how great Tom Darden is at his safe spot? Or the mighty Mike Taylor at linebacker? Or Regg McKenzie and Jim Coode in the offensive line?

Bo just doesn't talk about them that much.

It is not fair to compare coaches but if Duffy Daugherty ha these players he would be singing their praises every week ar they would get nationwide recognition.

It is sad, in a way, that a coach has to promote his player for them to get attention. It is sad that the ability of the player can't carry it alone. This may say something about press cove age, too.

But that's the way it is. Fair or unfair, the coach has to bea the drums, especially for his linemen. If he doesn't, who will?

No Punch, Power to Comments

It is simply not Bo's way to get carried away in praise of h players. He was asked at the luncheon if he ever saw thre backs quite like Billy Taylor, Glenn Doughty and Ed Shuttle worth in the same backfield.

The opening was there to really boost his players — to polit a little for them. But all Bo would say was that they were ver good, but Ohio State also had some good backfields in recer years.

He was also asked about Billy Taylor, as an individual. H said he was the best back who had ever played for him. B his comments had no punch to them, no power — if you excuse it, no pizazz.

Bo gets torn between not wanting to say anything — and the not being able to help himself and talking about what he didn want to talk about.

The Rose Bowl, for example. He said he wasn't even thinkin of the Rose Bowl this week — not with the Scarlet Scourg coming to town. But then, moments later, he said that thing were going to be different in Pasadena this time, he was goin to do a much better job of getting his team ready to play o New Year's Day.

Bo seems to cover every contingency about his job, includin putting his foot in his mouth.

But you sure can't argue with his results. He has brough Michigan back to the old heights and that's why they hired hin He has done everything, and more, that anyone could expec from him.

You just know he would like to put it to Woody, and put to him good, on Saturday. He remembers only too well wha happened in Columbus last year.

But it's been an odd thing — nobody has really made much the revenge motive for this year's game. You suspect Bo like that fine, just fine.

You also suspect he has been mentioning last year's debacl to his players as this season has worn on, so that by Saturday they won't need any more motives to tear into the Buckeyes.

It's not likely Bo will run up the score, even if he gets th chance, because he knows he is going to have to play Ohio Stat again. Our man thinks of everything.

But I've also got some bad news for him. He may think h has us under his thumb, too, but it must be reported in th interest of accuracy, that when he left the room to return t work on Monday, five guys ordered stawberry cheese cake an one had rum pie.

can't go to the wide side of the field. To hell with that. There are certain plays Tatum can't cover. So we went at him with the tailback draw. You'll recall we got him on a key pass, coming off a fake draw. We hit Jim Mandich in behind Tatum. We broke contain on him when he was involved in the fire game. When he was coming across trying to smash us in the backfield we went around him.

We spent almost two full days on our game plan and it was ready for the team at Monday's practice.

I spoke to our alumni at a noon luncheon. I told them flat-out we were going to beat Ohio State. You should have heard them. They cheered. Some of them thought this is what I should be saying, being new on the job and all. But I meant it. Every word of it.

I was cuter with the writers. I "hinted" that we had a chance. I talked about Ohio State. Remember? I told you how good they were. But I knew we were going to win.

We went into Monday's practice and put in the adjustments we had to make. We worked about 40 minutes, a lot of running mostly, and then went back inside. We gave them the Ohio State film and then I gave them the scouting report.

I went over all of their basic personnel. You judge them and evaluate them and then you say to your guys: "Okay, we go man on man with them. Moorhead against Kern—who plays the best game? Henry Hill against Jim Stillwagon." That's the way we match them up. We do it man for man. I do this in front of all the players and I say. "Are you going to let him out-play you?"

It all boils down to if we're going to beat them, we have to outplay them, man for man.

"Dierdorf against Shad Williams. . .Tom Darden against the great Tatum. . .Mandich against Jan White."

I'm psyching them right down the line. When we got to their backs, I was hoping they wouldn't use John Brockington. We could handle Jim Otis, but Otis and Brockington—no way! Luckily, they kept Brockington out of there. Our strategy was to stop Kern and contain Otis. Otis got a lot of yardage, but we held Kern real well.

You could feel the charge in that room. You could see it in

their faces. All you had to do was pick up Sports Illustrated, pick up the newspapers—it was all there: Ohio State, the super team; Ohio State, the unbeatable team; Ohio State, Ohio State, Ohio State. . .

Remember Doyt Perry, my old boss at Bowling Green? Elliot Uzelac, who is on my staff now, tells a great story about Doyt. He was working for him at Bowling Green and Doyt comes in Monday morning and says to the guys, "Well, how do you think the game will come out?" Everyone says Ohio State is super. Doyt says, "I'll tell you what I think. I think Woody can name his own score. Yes, sir. I think they are going to blow them clear out of the stadium."

That night there's a radio show and they're interviewing me and asking me about the big game. They pick up the show in Bowling Green and coaches are listening to it.

The radio man asks me what coaches have helped me the most in my career. I say, "Doyt Perry down at Bowling Green has been a great influence on me. I owe an awful lot to Doyt."

It turns out that Doyt also was listening in and don't you think he comes in the next day and sits down with the guys and says, "You know, I been thinking about it—I'm not so damned sure Bo isn't going to beat him on Saturday."

Now it's Tuesday morning and the coaches meet from eight until ten. We break up because we have to have individual meetings with the players. Everything is done for the convenience of the players. We work around their schedules. If they have an off period between ten and eleven, my coaches have to be free to talk to them. When they're not talking to the kids, they're inside watching Ohio State films.

We have one policy—no night meetings with the players. That's why we stay up so late at night, so we can have the stuff ready for them in the morning.

I am primarily concerned with the quarterbacks. I am dealing with Don Moorhead. Moorhead has to play great football in order for us to win. Moorehead comes in an hour every day, just like all the quarterbacks do, and we talk about adjustments. We talk about keys and how he has to read them and react to them. He has to be letter perfect, no mistakes. We talk about how we're going to run into the sidelines. We tell him we're not going to back off from Tatum. We look for places we can run and pass. Moorhead is smart. He knows what's going on. It's easy to work with him.

We look at the films together. Every game. We know their blitzes. We know everything they're going to do. We know their strengths and weaknesses, both from a personnel and tactical standpoint. Moorhead picks it all up.

He's a confident guy. . .but we also had Mandich and Dierdorf and Huff and Hill, guys like that—guys who just aren't overawed by Ohio State. I mean, it isn't going to shake them up to play them. You look at your films and say, "Hey, wait a minute! We have a great tight end here." Or, "We have a great quarterback and a great tailback. We have some pretty good blocking up front. We have Henry Hill—how much better is their middle guard than ours? Maybe he isn't better at all." You look at these films and you can just feel the confidence surging up in you.

So it's Tuesday. . .and Tuesday and Wednesday are the tough practice days. That's when you get it done. We go out to practice on Tuesday and you'll never believe this. We walk out on the practice field and the ground crew has failed to cover the field. It has snowed overnight and the field is covered with snow and ice. I can't believe it. We're ready to do our big work and the field is iced over. We call out the freshmen—50 or 60 of them. We give them shovels and get them going. I'm out there shoveling away. My coaches are shoveling away. Even Dave Strack, Assistant Athletic Director, is out there shoveling away.

I'm madder than hell. I'm standing there looking at this scene and saying to myself: "Tuesday, and we can't even get on the field!"

We keep the varsity in the locker room while the freshmen and all the coaches are out there trying to scrape off the field. We finally get out late, and practice is bad. Everyone is eager to get going but the field is in bad condition and the weather is miserable and nothing happens right.

Wednesday morning we're back in the office at eight o'clock and all we're doing is groaning and griping about the way things are going. I'm still mad because the field still isn't ready to play on yet. I know I'm not easy to live with but I can't help myself; I let the ground crew know exactly how I feel. Let's face it, our big game and they blew it.

On Thursday, we shorten up the practice because you just can't go hard on Thursday. Even though we haven't had good practices, the spirit is up. You can just feel it. I walk around talking to the players.

"How do you feel?" I say to each one.

"Great," one kid tells me. "All I'm thinking about is the game."

"Good," I tell him. "That's exactly what I want to hear."

It's that way with everyone. This is one week when the old school books come second.

You could also feel the electricity in the staff. When they came in Friday morning, it seemed like everyone was talking at once. We knew they weren't going to blow us out. They might beat us but it was going to be close. It wasn't going to be any runaway. We wouldn't quit. We'd hit them right to the end. I mean, that's fundamental. There is no way they were going to blow us out because the only way you blow a team out is when they quit and there was no way we were going to quit.

We take the team into the stadium on Friday afternoon. We have a spirited workout. You could just feel the excitement growing.

Now it's Friday night and we take them into the motel. It's the old Sheraton. We have a whole set of rooms and a hall set aside just for us. Do you remember how cold it was that night? It's the Friday night before the game and the snow is piled up all around the motel.

It's freezing outside and all of a sudden I hear someone say that the furnace in the motel blows. Now I'm running around at midnight trying to find out what's going on.

It's getting colder and colder and I say to the manager. "How cold is it going to get in here?" He says, "By three o'clock in the morning, it's going to be freezing in those rooms."

Now I'm in a panic. The night before the Ohio State game and my players are going to freeze to death.

I say, "Where are the guys who can fix the furnace?" He says they sent to Detroit to get a couple of engineers.

The engineers finally show up and I'm trying to hustle them

54

around into getting the furnace fixed. I talk to my coaches, but they're in bed already. I finally say: "Do the kids know what's going on?" They say no. I say, "Okay, the heck with it. Let's all go to bed and forget about it."

I climb under the covers and do you know something? It doesn't bother me a bit. I guess a few of the players got up and thought it was a little cold in their rooms but nobody was complaining about it. It wasn't the disaster I thought it would be. There was just no way anything was going to upset them on this night. That's beautiful—when you've got only one thing on your mind and you want to do it and now you've got the opportunity and nothing is going to keep you from doing it. That's the way I felt and that's the way the players felt. There was just no way we were going to be distracted even if we had to sleep out in the snow. Here we'd had a poor week of practice. . .one thing after another seemed to go wrong. . .and now we're all sleeping in these ice-cold rooms and it didn't matter. It didn't matter one bit.

Psychologically, we were ready.

I guess they got the furnace fixed at about 5 a.m., so the rooms were warming up when we got up Saturday morning. We had our usual meeting. It was a very tense meeting. Everyone was alert. Everyone was sitting there just eager to get going. You could just look at them and see the anxiety written all over their faces. This is a great feeling for a coach.

I got up and said only one thing: "It's here. Don't foul it up."

You can give them the right stuff but you never know if it's going to work. Coaches tell you that practice is everything—that if you haven't done the job during the week you can't do it on Saturday. The old business about the hay being in the barn.

I don't buy that. That isn't what coaching is about. It's only part of it. When you get into the game, that counts, too. Do I do the right things? Do I make the right calls? Do I have in the right defenses? This business that you don't coach on the sidelines is a lot of hogwash. If you can't coach on the sidelines, you're not going to win.

As we started over to the stadium, the same thought kept going through my head: "No way are they going to blow us out of there."

We get dressed and I send my team out for the pre-game warmup. They go down the tunnel and suddenly come to a stop. I wonder what's holding them up.

I'm behind them and I go to the front and say. "What's going on here?"

Jim Mandich says, "Hey, Bo, look where Woody has his team."

Wouldn't you know it. . .the old man has his team warming up on our side of the field. He's been up here a dozen times and everybody knows Michigan warms up on the north side of the field.

I look at Mandich and say, "So, the old guy is going to test me, eh?"

I go right out there and say, "Hey, Woody, you're warming up on the wrong side of the field." I don't say hello or anything else. He turns around and says, "Oh, hi, Bo," and he waves his players down to the other end.

I go back to the tunnel and say, "Okay, dammit. Let's go!" And out they go like a rocket. No kidding, they took that field like a rocket.

Everyone was so fired up that when I got them back in the locker room I don't even remember what I said to them. The game was on national TV and I can only imagine what the viewers must have thought when we came out for the start of the game. It wasn't one of those things where they jump on each other in piles—I mean they were really taking off and landing in the middle of everyone. I never saw anything like it in my life.

They took the football and drove right down to our 10, fourth down and a yard to go. They gave the ball to Otis and Henry Hill stopped him with a great play. We couldn't move and had to punt. Now Larry Zelina, I believe it was, brought it back to our 20 and they went in to score.

Now they kick to us and we jam it right down their throats. We score to tie it up. After an exchange they hit a pass to Jan White, a new pass play that we weren't ready for, and he runs in for a touchdown. They're on top again.

Back it up. We're ahead 7-6 when they score. Now it's 12-7 in their favor and they line up for the extra point but we're offsides on the play. Woody nixes the point and decides to go for two. He sends Rex Kern out on a counter rollout pass and Mike Keller and Cecil Pryor nail him back on the 20. They fail to get their two points and that really gives us a lift.

The guys come off the field and everyone is fired up. We take the ball and knock it in there and when we kick the point, it's 14 to 12 in our favor.

Then little Barry Pierson. . .isn't he a lovely boy?. . .made his great punt return. He took it near midfield and ran it in close, so we knock another one home and we're up. 21 to 12

What did I tell them? Get on top and make them come from behind and we'll beat them. Now we've got them where we want. We get the ball again and hit Mandich on a pass coming across the middle and it looks like it's going to be 28-12. But they call it back because we were supposed to have illegal procedure on our split man. It had nothing to do with the play but they called it back.

Then we kick a field goal and go ahead, 24 to 12, and that's the way it is at the half.

Now if you know my defensive coach, Jim Young, you know he is not a demonstrative guy. They'd moved the ball on us. They'd broken off some plays on us. They even fooled us a couple of times.

But Young went up to the blackboard, hit it with his hand and said, "That's it! No more!" He chalked out some adjustments for them—just a few—and we were ready to go out and play again.

We knew they had to come to us. Some way or another we were going to crack their game plan. What we had to do was go out there and control the ball. I kept telling them, "We will not gamble. We will not gamble." We were up by 12 and that meant they had to score twice to beat us.

I kept repeating over and over. "We must control the ball. We must eat the clock. We must not gamble."

All of a sudden, it happened. It was late in the third quarter or early in the fourth and Woody decided to go to the pass. I wanted to jump off the ground I was so glad. We had broken their game plan.

Kern threw one up and Pierson intercepted it. Before the day was over, we picked off six of their passes. Pierson got three of them. The St. Louis Cardinals picked him fairly high in the draft and I always felt they did it on the basis of his great play in this one game.

They could throw on us all day if they wanted. No way was our defense going to crack. You've got to remember they were saying this was one of the great teams in football history. The newspapers were saying that the only team which could challenge them was the Minnesota Vikings. They'd beaten a good Purdue the week before and there seemed no stopping them. Now we had them backed up to where they were putting the ball up into the air.

What a moment. We came from a 3-2 record and won the rest of our games. None of them was even close. We buried everybody. Then we took on a team that couldn't possibly be beaten. . .and before a national TV audience and a record crowd, we beat them.

They scored first and we came back and scored. They scored again and we could have quit right there. We came back again and took it to them. There is no way you can add it up and say we didn't win it. I mean, we won the game. No luck. No flukes. No crazy bounces. We went after them and beat them.

It's like this: a guy comes in and takes over a team and accomplishes something that is the epitome of his profession. Here's a team with a new coach and a new system—veteran players who were set in their ways. Good players, too. For some reason or another, they had the character to believe that maybe what the new man was trying to do was right. . .and it all came together in the second half of the Minnesota game.

Maybe this will never happen again. Maybe you can't ever have the same set of circumstances. We're taking on the No. 1 team in the nation and everybody is feeling sorry for us. They're saying no way we can win. People down in Texas are saying no way can they win the national title. No way can Michigan beat Ohio State.

The only people who really knew what was going on was my staff and my team. I really believe that. Yet, there were 103,588 people who came in that day because they weren't sure either. I mean, they weren't absolutely sure. If we had gotten blown out, they would have said, "Well, that's what I expected." But we didn't get blown out, did we?

Fritz Crisler (speaking to the U-M Alumni Club on the following Monday):

It was grand to see this Michigan team do what it did in its final game against Ohio, to go out as co-champions and earn the invitation to the Rose Bowl. This will be the fifth Michigan team that has gone to the Rose Bowl.

I think this team was well endowed with ability. I think they were as well coached as any team of Michigan that has gone out to the Rose Bowl. I think Bo did an amazing, just amazing job this year.

I have seen teams go into games with tremendous odds against them but I have never seen a team that has gone into a game where they were the underdogs and were as well prepared mentally, physically and technically as Bo had this team in its final conference game. I thought it was a masterpiece.

It is a victory that will live long in history and it will be one of the great achievements that has contributed so much to Michigan's proud tradition.

Bill Cusumano, U-M Assistant Sports Information Director, when he was a student:

You should have seen the campus that night. Everyone was in love with everyone else. It was like a national holiday. No, it was like a religious holiday. We were fulfilled. Our time had been sanctified. We beat Ohio State!

We roamed through the quad, drunk and singing, when a law student yelled out the window he was trying to study. We ran up to his room, dragged him out and told him, "Hey, man, this is no time to study. Don't you know we beat Woody?"

Jim Mandich, U-M player:

All I know is if we got one more touchdown we were going for two points—we didn't care what Bo would have wanted.

Former Michigan Athletic Director and Head Coach H. O. "Fritz" Crisler (Left), who Masterminded Michigan's Legendary 1949 Rose Bowl Victory, Says of Bo's 1969 Ohio State Win: *"A Masterpiece."* He is Shown Here With Don Canham, Michigan's Athletic Director, in 1972.

The Ghost Speaks:

This was one of the most nervous days of my life. I mean, for getting involved in something I was covering.

For years I'd try to kid myself. I'd tell myself, and those around me, that I was The One Great Neutral—that I could cover all of these sports events and take a very detached view of the whole thing.

Who was I kidding?

Deep down I was always rooting for somebody to beat somebody else. I just didn't want to show it. I thought it would make me look bad. . .since a newspaperman is supposed to be unbiased, impartial and very fair.

Well, sorry. I can't make it. I root and root very hard. All I try to do is turn the Neutral Switch when I sit down to write. It would be unfair to use my typewriter for personal reasons—though that's hard to combat, too.

Anyway, I wanted Michigan to beat Ohio State so bad in this 1969 game, I couldn't believe it. I was nervous all week long writing my column leading into the game. I tried to act very professional about it but my stomach was churning all week long. I know old Bo is going to find this hard to believe. But it's true.

Whenever you cover a big event, you usually get out there early. Very early. I don't know why. You just do. It's not to beat the crowd and it's certainly not to get a good parking place or a good seat in the press box. These things are assigned to you in advance. Whenever I cover an event of this magnitude, I have to get out there early to work off some of my anxieties. The way I do it is to talk to the other writers and see how they feel about things.

I got to the Michigan press box this day three hours before the game. I was the first writer in there.

I waited until the concession counter opened and got a cup of coffee. Then I got a cup of soup. Then a Coke. Then another Coke. Then a hot dog. Then a cup of Vernor's ginger ale.

Who was nervous?

Three of us covered the game that day—Curt Sylvester, Jack Berry and I. Curt would write the lead. Jack would write the Ohio State dressing room story. I would do Michigan's.

Anyway, we were clearly divided as to who we wanted to win.

Curt and I were on one side—Michigan's. Jack, a grad of Michigan State, certainly wasn't going to root for The Blue. . .and not only did he show up with that leer on his face but he brought along his "lucky Buckeye."

Now get that—Jack Berry, who works at the Detroit News now, showing up for a Michigan-Ohio State game with a "lucky Buckeye" in his pocket.

That's pure hatred.

Anyway, Jack was pretty smug about things. He'd seen what Ohio State had done to Michigan in recent years, and he knew the sort of team the Buckeyes had this time. How sweet it would be to sit there, among those 100,000 fanatics, and relish in Woody putting it to the Wolverines once again.

When Ohio State scored first, and scored rather easily, Jack sat there with a sneer on his face. When it was our turn to score, I played it cool. I didn't say much. Frankly, I thought they were going to do a job on Michigan, too.

When Ohio State went ahead again, Jack was really yukking it up. He was laughing and singing the Ohio State fight song. Sports writers can be very cruel people. Even to other sports writers.

When Michigan took the lead, I again played it cool. But I could sense something. I thought: "Hell, if they can score twice on Ohio State in such a short time, maybe it's going to be a wide open game and anything can happen."

I watched closely now.

The Michigan team really surprised me.

They were playing with great aggressiveness. They didn't seem the least bit awed by Ohio State.

They were holding their own and even starting to put it to the Bucks. They were running that power sweep and running it to the short side of the field. That really amazed me—that they'd go to where they had the least room to run and were making yardage at it.

Bang, bang, bang, bang. . .

I couldn't believe what I was seeing. The whole team was

moving as a unit, as one; they'd snap out of the huddle, line up crisply and, on the quarterback's count, take off in the same instant.

Four yards. . .

Seven yards. . .

Five yards. . .

They were putting it to the Buckeyes and Ohio State couldn't do anything about it.

When Barry Pierson took that punt near midfield and ran it in close—oh, my! The stadium was in an uproar. The press box was in an uproar. I was in an uproar. I was pounding my table top. This was something I hadn't done since that day in Yankee Stadium in 1959 when Steve Myra kicked that field goal for the Baltimore Colts to force the NFL title game against the N.Y. Giants into overtime. I didn't care. I could feel Michigan had them and it was the sweetest feeling in the world.

Jack Berry sat there and to his credit, he was smiling, too. I think Jack felt what was going to happen.

He said: "Guess I'd better put this away." He slipped the Buckeye into his pocket.

I can only say this: For pure execution. . .for running the plays with the greatest precision and perfect timing. . .I have never seen any football team do it better than Michigan did to Ohio State in the first half of this game.

I had a lot of fun that day.

Don Canham Said: *"This is what it's all about."*

The Michigan Bench Celebrates Following 1969 Victory Over Ohio State.

Bo Tells World

'We're Going as Champs'

November 23, 1969

BY JOE FALLS, Free Press Sports Editor

ANN ARBOR—"Unbelievable. . .fantastic. . .the greatest victory in the history of the world."

Garvie Craw, the hard-working football player, stood in the middle of the Michigan dressing room after Saturday's stunning 24-12 victory over the Ohio State Buckeyes and he said it all.

". . .in the history of the world!" he bellowed.

Craw, like all his teammates, couldn't hide his elation.

"I think," the young man said with a smile, "Bo has Woody's number. They didn't do a thing our coach hadn't told us they would do. Bo's got to be Coach of the Year, and if they don't give him a million awards, It'll be a sin.

It was a mad, mad scene in the Michigan room. The players thundered up the tunnel shouting and screaming and belting each other on the back.

"We're No. 1. We're No. 1" They kept yelling.

THE WALLS of their room shook and the tremor probably could be felt all the way to Columbus, O.

"Bring on the Vikings!" someone shouted. "Yeah!" answered a group of players. "Bring on the Vikings."

The Boss, Bo Schembechler, had that wild look of victory on his face.

"We're going to the Rose Bowl as the co-champions and don't forget that." he said almost defiantly. "You know what they were saying out on the West Coast—that they didn't even want us.

"I wouldn't even have wanted to go if we didn't win today, but now we're going and we're going as champs."

Quarterback Don Moorhead, who outplayed the celebrated Rex Kern all the way, spoke easily, confidently about the stirring triumph.

"We felt we could do it all along." he said. "All that business about them being supermen was such a bunch of bull. We knew thay could be had.

"We didn't do anything differently," Moorhead went on. "We just went ont there and punched it to them." We thought they'd be weak off the tackles, and so that's the way we went."

MOOREHEAD HAD it all over Kern, who was eventually removed from the game in the final quarter.

"Yeah, I feel good about getting the best of him," said Moorhead. "That's what our coach told us at the start of the week—that we all had to beat the man across the way from us.

"Kern happened to be the guy I had to play against."

Moorhead couldn't keep the smile off his boyish face.

"It made us sick all that stuff we were reading about Ohio State," he said. "You know, that petition they got up out on the West Coast about them wanting them in the Rose Bowl.

"It just made us want it all the more."

MICHIGAN'S PLAN was simple, according to Bo Schembechler.

"We just decided to run at them." he said. "We watch all of their movies and we saw that whenever anyone ma a mistake against Ohio State, they got behind and co never catch up.

"We just determined not to make those mistakes. knew (Jim) Otis would get his yardage, but we knew had to stop Kern."

Henry Hill, Michigan's middle guard and a key man the defensive alignment, said the plan was to keep ke hemmed in.

"The picture showed us that every big play he made, made to the outside," said Hill. "We just tried to ke him from going wide."

BARRY PIERSON, the defensive back who played superbly picking off three of Kerns' passes and setting a touchdown with a magnificent punt return, spoke as he knew the Wolverines were going to win all the time.

"Yeah"! he said, "We know it—we knew it last Monda In fact we knew if all season. You could feel it in the guy

"You could tell right after the first series of dow The guys up front could feel it. and Ohio felt it. Th moved on us, but we adjusted and stopped them."

Michigan captain Jim Mandich sat quietly in front his locker accepting the congratulations of well-wishe He said, "When they put those first six points up there had visions of last year.

"But our confidence came right back. I think when came back and scored so quickly. It demoralized them little."

Mandich said that the Wolverines put in no new pla for the game.

"Oh!" he corrected himself. 'We had one new one b never used it."

CRAW, WHO scored the first two touchdowns—the on which put Michigan ahead each time, kept shaking his hea in astonishment.

"That's just got to be the best victory this school h ever had," he said.

"It's unbelievable, that's all. I still can't believe it. can't wait until I read the newspapers, Then maybe I believe it."

Craw broke into a laugh.

"You know," he said, "I got those four touchdow at Illinois, but I gained only 18 yards all day and I felt little guilty. But, man, I don't feel guilty today."

AS SCHEMBECHLER walked off the field, he was me by Woody Hayes.

Woody offered him one word: "Congratulations."

What did Bo say to his old boss.

"I didn't say anything." he said. "I just shook his hand.

One game statistic stunned Schembechler, an Ohio Sta assistant for six seasons.

"You mean we intercepted six passes against Ohi State? I can't believe it." he said.

(This Column Reproduced)

Chapter 4

Woody Who?

W. W. Hayes. Wayne Woodrow Hayes. Where do you begin to talk about this man? Where do you end? Sometimes I think Woody Hayes will coach at Ohio State forever. He is one of the great institutions of our land.

I have been called his pupil, his protege, and even some names I don't like, such as "Little Woody"—most with good reason. You are talking eight years that I spent with this man. Eight years! Two as a player, one as a graduate assistant and five as a coach. You might say he had somewhat of an influence on me.

You also might say I'd rather beat him than anyone else in the country. Woody Hayes is special, all right. I haven't let many people throw chairs at me. Woody did. I threw them right back at him. We had what you'd call a mutual understanding of each other.

The first time I met him was in the lounge of Ogden Hall at Miami of Ohio. I had been recruited by Sid Gillman and played my sophomore year under George Blackburn. But now this new man—Woody Hayes—was the coach and we all lined up and he came right down the line and shook hands with everybody. He had something to say to everybody. No loss of words for this man. Right away I knew he was very special.

I guess you'd have to say Woody stepped into a tough spot at Miami. I mean, following Sid Gillman. Everybody there was Sid Gillman-conscious. He was a brilliant mind—a great winner. Everybody who played at Miami felt we were better coached and knew more football than anyone else—that we were a full ten years ahead of everyone—and it was all because of Sid.

Gillman created a special atmosphere at Miami and then all of a sudden he was gone to coach at West Point under Red

Blaik. He went there when Vince Lombardi was also an assistant, so you know that they had some kind of coaching staff. Sid went to West Point for one year and then came back to Cincinnati as the head coach.

Blackburn took his place at Miami but he lasted only one season. I played for him but I'm no superstar, you understand—I'm a guy struggling to play offensive tackle. I'm 190 pounds and I'm just fighting to get into the lineup.

Gillman had done a fantastic job of recruiting. We had a whale of a freshman team. We beat everybody. We had great intra-squad games—we had everything. I'd been a regular tackle on the freshman team under Gillman and so when he left, I was sick. I played a little for Blackburn in my sophomore year, but not very much. It was a tough year for me. I didn't make some of the trips and that was really hard to take. I was ticked off and I wouldn't leave my room for the whole weekend. The team would go away and I'd just stay in my room. I didn't want anybody to see my face because no way should I have been in that room.

Halfway through the season, Ernie Plank, who was the captain of the team, went to Blackburn and told him he thought Schembechler was getting a bad deal. Joe Madro, who was our line coach, said, "Okay, let's get him out to practice early. We'll see what he can do."

Madro asks Plank if he'll come out early, too, so that can put me to the test. Ernie is a big defensive tackle and what Madro has in mind is to put us head to head and see what kind of stuff I have. I think what he wants is to show me up and shut me up.

Ernie is a good guy and comes to me and says, "Now listen you, I want to see you blowing off that line!"

I said to him, "Don't you worry, I'll blow you right off the line!"

So we go out there and Madro is coaching and it's one on one—Ernie is playing defense and I'm playing offense. The first time I take off I jam my head gear right up in front of Ernie's nose and I tear up his nose. I'm really fired up, but he's standing there bleeding and I think that Madro wants to kill me. I guess they thought I was eager and so they moved me up to the second team so that I was playing some. They had real

"There he is, biting the hand that fed him."

Sid Gillman, Bo's Coach Until the End of His Freshman Year as Miami Player.

good tackles and I shouldn't have been a first stringer, but I was good enough to make the traveling squad. I went to Dayton once. Big deal. When they went to Virginia, they left me home.

Anyway, now it's the following spring—just before I'm going to become a junior—and Woody has the team in spring practice and he is something else. This guy is unbelievable. He is grabbing the players and turning them around and shouting at them. I find it all very interesting. That's because I'm playing baseball. I'd get these reports second hand—the guys are coming in complaining and saying "that so and so," and "you can't believe this man." I'm looking at them and laughing and saying nobody can be that tough.

What happened was that we had a very intricate system under Gillman and Blackburn and now we had to adjust to Woody's ways. He put in his own system. There was really nothing wrong with his system. It was just that the players were unwilling to change. Woody is out there yelling and screaming and everybody is upset. We had only a 5-4 season and that was the worst they'd had in a long time. Gillman never had one like that, and that's what everyone thought about.

I played with a bad knee in my junior year and it was a bad deal all around. The players were calling Woody names behind his back and the more we lost, the harder he drove us. If you think he gets uptight now, you should have seen him then.

To complicate matters, when Gillman went to Cincinnati at the end of my sophomore year, he came to Miami and raided our team. He took six or eight of our top players and had them transfer to Cincinnati. This meant they wouldn't play as juniors—they'd be "redshirted" for a year—but it showed everyone on the campus just what regard the players had for Gillman. He took Jim Driscoll, one of the best tackles. He took Danny McKeever, who was our best back, and he took our No. 1 quarterback, Gino Rossi.

There was great resentment between Gillman and Hayes. They'd never been friends—only mortal enemies. They were at each other's throats. The whole thing got pretty bad.

Here we were going through our third coach in three years and he comes in and starts raising a storm with everything. The guys at Miami were a pretty cocky group because they felt they were always superbly coached. So a guy comes in from Denison, which nobody cares about, and he puts in a new system and Gillman is gone and the whole thing is a mess.

So now my senior year comes up. I played baseball again—how Woody let me do it, I'll never know. We opened the 1950 season with Bowling Green and we beat them by a big score. Forty or fifty to nothing.

Woody had done a great job of recruiting. He got our first black player out of Hamilton, Ohio; a guy by the name of Jim "Boxcar" Bailey. He was just super. We had a great back in John Pont, and the quarterback was Norbert "Nobby" Wirkowski. He was a little guy but he had a great throwing arm and he was a good leader. We had a pretty good defense and a real good offense. So we blew out Bowling Green, but then we went up against Xavier. Our backs got hurt and Woody went to the shotgun formation. He put Wirkowski back there and we didn't run our basic stuff and we got beaten, 7-0. Doc Urich was on that team and so was Carmen Cozza. The talent was there all right. Boy, were the guys ticked off. They wanted to stay with our basic stuff but Woody felt we would have to pass to win. I do not think he has ever felt that way since.

We got squared around the next week, using our basic stuff, and then we started beating everyone in sight. Then we got down to the final game against Cincinnati. You can imagine what that was like. The game was played on the same day Michigan and Ohio State played the "Snow Bowl" game in Columbus. So you can imagine what the weather was like, too.

We had a chance to go to the Salad Bowl in Phoenix, but we had to beat Cincinnati. Cincinnati already agreed to go to the Sun Bowl. They had a great team with Gino Rossi at quarterback, Danny McKeever at halfback and Jim Driscoll at tackle. It was Miami against Miami. Hatred against hatred.

So here we go—Sid against Woody. . .and it's snowing so hard you can't even see. I can't believe what's happening. I mean, there's Rossi, the quarterback on our freshman team, warming up with the other guys. McKeever was my roommate when I was a sophomore, and now I've got to play across the line from Driscoll.

The game starts and for one half we kick the daylights out of them. We score five times but have one called back. We lead 28-0 at halftime. We had a 60-yard draw play called back. I got off one hell of a block but I was offside. So I cost us a TD but Cincinnati couldn't move a lick and we've got 'em. You couldn't believe the second half. You can't see. You can't stand. You can't do anything. The field is unplayable and that's just the way it ended, 28-0. The old man was in heaven. He had kicked the daylights out of Gillman and he was so happy it was unbelievable. The Gillman mystique was gone—we were a Hayes team.

After the season, we went to the Salad Bowl and we beat Arizona State and then the Ohio State job came open. It's the Gillman-Hayes thing all over again but Woody is riding high now because he'd whipped Gillman and we'd won big in the Salad Bowl. So Woody gets the job.

I'll never forget this. I'm playing handball with him one day. Woody loved handball. I'm still one of his players then but we used to play handball occasionally.

We're out on the court and he says: "All right, Bo, who should get the Ohio State job?

I stop and look at him. "Woody, I think you should get the job."

He glares at me. "You sure about that?" he says.

"Yeah," I say, "I'm sure about it."

He's still glaring. "Why?" he asks.

"I think you're the best man for the job," I say.

He says, "Do you really think so?"

I say, "Yeah, I really think so."

The old codger. . .I think he knew he had it all the time and he wanted me to endorse him, as if my opinion meant a thing.

The man is something else. He thought he could beat me in handball—he was absolutely convinced of it. No way. If we played a hundred times, I'd beat him 99. But that once—that's what he'd talk about. He'd keep bringing it up, so that it sounded like he was the greatest handball player of all time.

When I was coaching for him at Ohio State, he called me one Sunday morning and said: "What are you doing?"

I told him I'd just gotten up. He said: "Come on down and I'll meet you in a half hour and we'll play some handball."

We went down there, without another soul around, and he'd make a bad shot and you never heard such language. I could take him every time. I liked to go down there and toy with him. He could hit well but he didn't have great movement. He had real good hands but he wasn't very quick. I could beat him with quickness. His blood would boil during the games and I don't know how many times he walked off the court without saying a word to me. We had some very lovely Sunday mornings together.

Let me tell you why I respect this man. When I was in school, I didn't have any money. My dad was a fireman and there wasn't much to go around and I was always short of money. Woody came to me once and said since I wasn't playing any spring football, maybe I should go to summer school and get in some of my football work. He said he would take care of the tuition. I didn't need the extra hours—I wasn't having academic problems but he wanted to have a good team and wanted to do what he could to get ready for it.

Later, as I prepared to graduate, they hit me with a bill for two or three hundred dollars. I couldn't pay it under any circumstances and they told me if I don't pay it, I'm not going to graduate. Woody has gone to Ohio State by now and so I go in to see John Brickles, who is the new athletic director.

I say to him, "John, Woody told me he would pay for my summer school. I got this bill and I can't graduate until I pay it. I don't have any money."

He says, "I never made any agreement like that! I don't know what I can do for you."

Don't get me wrong now—John is dead and I love him. He is the guy that hired me at Miami and I love him dearly. But he could be a very stubborn man.

"John," I said, "I'm not trying to get something for nothing. This is what Woody told me and you can check with him."

He said, "I'm not checking with anybody. There is no way I'm going to pay that bill."

So now I'm stuck. I've got only one recourse. I go to the phone and call Woody. I tell him, "Remember you told me to go to summer school so I could work out and everything would be okay. Now they've slapped me with a bill and I can't pay it."

He told me not to worry about it. He said he would come over and talk to me when we went up to Columbus to play the Ohio State baseball team.

So here he comes—just as he said—right to the field where we're playing. I go up to him, wondering what he's going to tell me.

He says, "I told you not to worry about it. I'll take care of it."

I go back to Miami and a few days later I go over to the registrar's office and I ask about the bill. The gal there says, "Oh, it's been taken care of."

Now he didn't have to do that since he wasn't at Miami anymore. As far as I know, it may have been his own dough.

From this standpoint, Woody Hayes is a tremendous man. There isn't anything he wouldn't do to help a player. I respected him for something else—the way he worked. The guys would talk about him and I'd say, "Yeah, he ticks me off too, but he works like a dog and you've got to give him that." I've even seen him tutor players himself to help them with their classwork. He isn't as cold-blooded as a lot of people think. Maybe he has ulterior motives—who doesn't—but I've seen him go to some great extremes to help his players.

About this time I was prepared to be drafted into the Korean War. It was 1951. Bill Arnsbarger had gone to Ohio State with Woody and he called me up and said if I was going to get a masters degree, why didn't I come up to Ohio State and get it there and help out with the coaching. He said they'd give me a graduate assistantship and I'd work with the varsity reserve squad.

At the time freshmen were eligible to play, so we had a reserve squad, and Gene Fekete was the head coach. I was the line coach and since there were only two of us running the show, I got a chance to do some coaching.

I was a general flunky, as all graduate assistants are. I'd help out with the recruiting, I'd run all the errands, pick up things off the floor—jazz like that. I answered to Woody and spent almost all of my time in his office. I followed him around wherever he went. Not just Woody, but his entire staff. I was kind of like their man-servant.

It was a tough year at Ohio State. It was Woody's first season and the team had come off the Snow Bowl loss to Michigan and Michigan had gone to the Rose Bowl. They had a veteran team coming back, led by Heisman Trophy winner Vic Janowicz, but Woody had to take this group of guys and switch them from the single wing into the T formation. The transition was slow, very slow. I could see the same problems that Woody had at Miami were happening to him all over again.

In a way, I was lucky. I saw that first year with Woody. I went into the first year with Doyt Perry at Bowling Green and that first year with Ara Parseghian at Northwestern. I was able to see for myself what happens when a new coach comes into a new setup. There is a fine line between establishing how your program is going to be and trying to gain the respect and friendship of the players.

After my hitch in service and some assistant jobs, I went to work for Woody as a fulltime assistant in 1958. I'd been with Ara at Northwestern. We'd lost every game and I didn't want to leave him but the opportunity was too great to pass up. I don't even remember what Woody offered me. I was single and money didn't mean anything to me then. I wanted to coach.

I was the tackle coach, if you can believe that, but I sort of ran the whole offensive line. We had Jim Houston and Dick Schafrath at the end; the tackles were Jim Tyrer and Jim Marshall; the guards were Ernie Wright and Danny James. We had the most fantastic line you ever saw. We ran nothing but dead T with two tight ends. Dick LeBeau played in our backfield and so did Bob White and Don Clark. Frank Kremblas was the quarterback.

It was a good football team and we should have won the title but one team knocked us out of it. Guess which one that was? Northwestern. My old buddies in Evanston. Ara came up with a quarterback named Dick Thorton and turned his situation right around. They made some big plays against us and finally beat us when Thornton hit Ron Burton with a 56-yard touchdown pass.

The big game of that year—one I'll never forget—was the one we played against Iowa out in Iowa City. Ask Forest Evashevski. He'll never forget it either.

Iowa had won the title. They had beaten Minnesota the week

before and the players were calling themselves the greatest ever—that no one could ever beat them. They had Willie Fleming and Randy Duncan and when the game begins, we match them touchdown for touchdown. We go ahead 7-0 and they make a touchdown. We go ahead 14-7 and they tie it. We scored with about two minutes left in the half to take a 21-14 lead but they come back and hit a screen pass and score with a few seconds and we go in at halftime, 21-21. It is some kind of a horserace.

White is having a great day and so is Clark. Fleming was just as sensational for them but we score and go ahead for the fourth time, 28-21. Again they tie it and we go ahead 35-28. They're marching on us when LeBeau makes a key interception and brings the ball out to the about the 40. We proceed to grind meat and move the ball down to the three yard line, where we kick a field goal to win the game, 38-28.

I'm walking off the field with Woody after the game and somebody throws a pop bottle at us. It sails right over our heads and smashes when it hits the ground. It could have killed us. I'm shaking but Woody keeps right on walking as if nothing happened. I sort of hang back and let him walk by himself.

It was tough coaching under Woody. Some of the players just couldn't take it. He was too demanding in some things. He would argue about ridiculous things and there was no way you were ever going to win an argument with him.

But I learned many things from him. He was an excellent teacher. He had great dedication and I never saw anyone work harder. He also taught me about being mentally prepared each week—to avoid making mistakes.

If you're talking about tricky plays or coming up with a lot of innovations, this isn't Woody. That isn't his type of coaching. He is consumed by whatever he does and when he decides to do something, he keeps at it until he does it right. I mean he just pounds it home and pounds it home. It may not be the best way to do it, but he is going to be so well drilled that the thing eventually is going to work.

Some of our coaches had very little authority under him. As we went along, I got quite a bit of authority. By the time I was through at Ohio State, I was directing most of the offense from the press box, although he sent in the plays he wanted from the sidelines.

We had a 3-5-1 record in 1959 and he almost fired me a couple of times. He wanted to play some guys I didn't and we'd really go around on it. It was just a bad ball club. One day in a fit of anger he picked up a chair and threw it at me. I picked it up and threw it back at him.

He said, "Damn you anyway, I'm going to fire you!"

I got up and walked down to the can. Pretty soon here he comes into the john and says, "Get your butt back in that meeting."

It was always like that. We had some real knock-down, drag-out affairs. Other members of the staff had them with him but ours seemed to be extra special.

I think if you don't stand up to Woody Hayes, he will beat you into submission. I wasn't going to let him do that to me. We got along in our way. I think the fact I stayed five years proved something.

I also admit I was getting a little edgy at Ohio State. I mean, I had a year at Presbyterian, a year at Bowling Green, two years at Northwestern, five at Ohio State and I'm ready to move up to a head job. The only thing that was keeping me at Ohio State is that I had the most responsibility of all the assistants.

Most of the guys were older and they more or less were going to be assistants for the rest of their lives. When I went up to the press box to run the offense, I more or less became his boy.

I ended up being the buffer between Woody and the players. They'd get ticked off at him and they'd come to me with their problems. Woody knew I was the buffer but he also knew I would never put him in a bad position. He knew I would never undercut him or anything like that. I never questioned who was the boss. I never tried to undermine him, and I never want any of my assistants doing it to me.

Don't get me wrong. I'd complain about Woody myself, but I'd do it among the other staff members. I'd never do it in the open, where anyone could hear.

I knew I was being called "Little Woody." But it was a funny thing. Nobody ever said it to my face.

After a while I knew our offense cold. But Woody would put

me in a bad position at times. For example, I'd be out there working with the offense and we'd be having trouble with the defense. Our biggest problem always seemed to be the defense.

So he'd come to me and say, "The defense isn't going at all! Get down there and see if you can get them going!"

Now here are all the other assistant coaches—veterans like Lyle Clark—and I'd go in among them and try to shake things up. I knew I shouldn't be down there because this made the other coaches look bad. This was the roughest thing Woody ever did to me—the worst position he ever put me in.

When it came to the offense, he didn't fool around with me. We ran a lot of half lines and I had a lot of opportunity to coach on my own. The way it ended up, I was coaching the line and he was coaching the backs.

In 1961, we opened against Texas Christian and we had a big drive going with the score tied 14-14 late in the game. I can't give you the exact situation but we were on the nine yard line and we ran down to the six, and so now it's second and six.

They had been honking in there to take the off tackle play away from us and we hadn't passed all the way down, so I called for the belly pass. We would fake to the fullback off tackle and our quarterback would move out while the halfback goes into the flat and our tight end goes down and out. The quarterback either runs or passes the ball to the tight end or halfback. So we get down there and the quarterback pulls up, which is a crime, and instead of throwing the ball out of bounds, he throws it to the backside end coming across and they intercepted it.

I was really sick that night. I blamed myself because I'd called the play. I went into the office to look at the film and who is in there but Woody.

I said, "Dammit, it was my fault, Woody, I shouldn't have called that play."

"You can't look at it that way," he said. "They just didn't execute it properly."

That's all he said. He didn't get on me, when he could have. He showed me an awful lot that night.

Nobody beat us the rest of the year. We ripped them all up. We beat Michigan, 50-20. That game was interesting, but first of all you have to understand Woody before I can tell you about it.

If the game is tight and I'm in the press box and sending in the plays, he will say, "I don't want that" or "Give me this." He will run the show most of the time but he will also accept what I send down. If it really gets tight—I mean hairy—he'll say, "Now, Bo, don't leave me, don't leave me now." In other words, keep them coming. But as soon as we blow them out of there, I can't get the guy on the phone. He is sending in all the plays himself. He is calling them like a machine.

It was funny at Michigan because when we finally got the game blown out, the phone goes dead. I don't know how long it's out, maybe a quarter and a half near the end. I had no contact with the bench at all. In fact, what I ended up doing was sitting and watching the game. Everybody said I called the two-point play to go for 50 but I couldn't talk to anyone down there.

It was a big day for us. Somebody beat Wisconsin and that gave us the title. We're recruiting in Cleveland after the season and I'm at a big alumni banquet with Woody. There are a lot of people there. We had some prospects in the room and we're shaking hands when a guy comes in and calls Woody aside in another room. He tells him the faculty at Ohio State has turned down the invitation to the Rose Bowl.

It is the first time the old man knows it. He calls me in and says. . .well, I can't tell you what he said. I try to calm him down but I'm not getting anywhere. He goes back out to speak and I'm afraid what he might say, but he gives one of the greatest talks I have every heard. He said he did not question the honesty of his superiors, just their judgment.

After we said goodnight, he said he had to get some air. So we went outside and walked. We must have walked all over town. He wanted me with him all the time.

I'll tell you this—I did one hell of a job for him. I worked night and day for him. I probably got along with him as well as anyone. He taught me an awful lot. He is a man who never wants to be outworked. I'm that way myself. Tell me, where did I get it from?

He'd be teaching you all the time. He's a great English major and if any coach would make a grammatical mistake, he'd stop them right there and correct them. Like if a guy would say, "Well, now, if I were him" and Woody would say, "No, No, if I were he."

You wonder why I want to beat him? You beat Woody Hayes and you've beaten the best.

Woody Hayes:

I'll say this: Bo was always a very intense individual and he is a worker. It was even this way when I brought him into Ohio State as a graduate assistant in 1951.

He wanted to continue his education after Miami and I wanted him because he was a doggone good coach even then. I don't bring people into Ohio State to do them a favor. I bring them in to do me a favor. That's why I went after Bo. He was a smart kid. Right from the start we thought he was good. I think his year's background here in Big Ten football was enormously helpful to him.

When I brought Bo back as a regular member of my staff, I needed someone to replace Bill Hess, who was a good coach himself. Bill had been my line coach and that's what I wanted Bo to do. He was also a good recruiter and that's why I went after him. In fact, he still is a good recruiter.

By the time he left me, he was the top assistant on my staff. I guess we had our squabbles. I never fired a coach yet and all I ever said to him was, "If you don't do this my way, I'm going to throw you out of here." Stuff like that.

I want a coach who stands up to me. I get tired of telling a coach something and having him just absorb it. I want a man who if he thinks he is right, I want him to stand up to me. That doesn't mean he's going to get his way but I want someone who isn't afraid to speak his mind.

Bo has a good football mind. He has a driving personality. A good football mind and a driving personality—let's let it go at that. I know he drives his youngsters. I don't know if he learned that from me but he drives the hell out of them. I think maybe he learned some of my bad habits.

When he went to Michigan, he sort of sneaked up on us that first year. We were fat headed. We had won big the week before against Purdue and it's sort of hard to get kids up when they win that big against another supposedly good football team. We scored something like four touchdowns in the first half and it's tough to get them mentally ready for another ball game when they're playing that well. Bo certainly outplayed us and outcoached us. We have never made any bones about that.

We've had some battles. They've been fun. He didn't win the last one in Columbus. I don't know if you can say we upset them. All I know is that the superior team wins and he didn't win. Everybody talks about how we stopped them on the goal line. But remember this: they'd given up only five touchdowns all season long and we went out and got two against them.

It is always extra special when you play Michigan, whether Bo is coaching or not. This is the greatest rivalry in football. So I can't give him credit for the games we've had. You take your other games—Auburn and Alabama, UCLA and USC, Army and Navy. . .they just don't compare.

In a way, I'm proud of Bo. He is a good coach and I selected him first. I brought him to Ohio State as a graduate assistant and I was very instrumental in his going to Miami. In fact, he got the job on my recommendation. . .and don't let anyone tell you otherwise. Without my recommendation, he wouldn't have been hired.

Bo is good competition. He is a better recruiter than any of the other Michigan coaches. But he better watch out about clutching.

The Ghost Speaks:

I guess I have a different attitude about Woody Hayes than most people in Michigan. Certainly most people around Ann Arbor.

I like the man.

I really do.

I think he is beautiful and it's going to be a sad day when he isn't coaching at Ohio State anymore.

Admittedly, I am speaking as a newspaperman. I don't know how Hayes would be to live with, or play for, or write about every day. I imagine it would get to be a pain.

But the way it is now, I see him once a year, maybe twice. Sometimes three if I cover Ohio State in the Rose Bowl. He always stimulates me. He always turns me on. Wayne Woodrow Hayes is one of a kind and I hope he lives forever.

The first time I met him was in the late 1950's when I was making a tour of the Big Ten football camps. I was traveling with that intrepid group of journalists known as "The Skywriters."

This is a wild, weeklong brawl—a test of man's endurance. We'd make two schools a day, morning and afternoon, and then try to drink and dance and play cards all night. It gets pretty hectic.

This particular year, Ohio State was one of the last stops. I was rather taken by the hospitality at all of the schools. I'd never been to most of the campuses and was impressed at the cordial way they treated us. The athletic director usually was at the airport, right at planeside, to meet us. Other school officials were with him. They'd take us into town on a bus or they'd have a fleet of cars to drive us.

The coaches were very nice, too. Some talked well, some didn't. Murray Warmath almost put me to sleep. The important thing is that they were ready for us. They gave us their time and we all came away with an abundance of material. No sports writer could ask for more.

Now it's Ohio State.

They met us at the airport, all right. It was very nice. Very friendly. Very cordial.

They drove us to the Ohio State campus and I was greatly impressed not only by the size of some of those buildings but the size of the football stadium. I'd never seen anything like it. It was awesome.

They took us into the locker room but nobody was there. They went looking for Woody and his team but nobody knew where they were. It was practice time, so they had to be around somewhere.

Finally, somebody said: "They're practicing in private. They won't let us in."

I didn't think much of that. So they wanted to practice in private. I get a kick out of the guys in my business who go out to practice and pretend they're learning things from watching on the sidelines. I could watch football practice every day and never read a single defense.

So we waited.

And waited.

And waited.

"Woody's not going to see us," somebody else said.

Now the fun began.

"What do you mean, he's not going to see us?"

"You heard me. He says practice is closed. He says he is too busy and he's not going to see us."

Well, sir.

You never turn your back on a newspaperman. Least of all a sports writer. Most of all, a "Skywriter."

You should have heard the language.

I've never heard one coach called so many names so quickly by so many writers.

They had a point.

We'd come all the way to find out about his team and now The Great Man wouldn't see us.

Of course I am smarter than the rest of my colleagues. I didn't get upset. I saw a good story. Certainly a different story. So I didn't get excited. I didn't get mad. I sat down and wrote what a shrewd man this Woody Hayes is. I wrote that he's got to figure out a way to draw attention to himself—to make himself more important than all of the other coaches we'd seen on our tour.

How does he do it? By talking to us? By charming us? By filling us with Ohio State lore?

Nope.

He does it by thumbing his nose at us.

Beautiful.

The guys were fuming as we got back onto the airplane. I took out my typewriter and started in on my story. I guess I broke a few of them up when I said, "Is horseradish one or two words?"

That's Part I of the story.

Part II took place the next year when the Skywriters re-

turned to Ohio State.

Now we were ready for him. He wasn't going to turn his back on us. He wasn't going to keep us out of practice. We were going over that fence if we had to.

So what happened?

When we got to the field, there was Woody waiting for us. Smiling, friendly, warm, wonderful Woody.

"Gentlemen, it's so nice to see you!"

He was beaming. He wore a smile from ear to ear. He shook our hands and patted our backs.

Not only were the gates open to his practice field, but beach chairs and tables and umbrellas were set out on the sidelines. Tall pitchers of cold lemonade awaited us.

"Come in, come in," said Wayne Woodrow Hayes. "It's so nice to see all of my friends again."

Another trip to Columbus.

Another Woody Hayes story.

Another flim-flamming.

Long may he wave.

Woody Hayes:
"Long May He Wave"

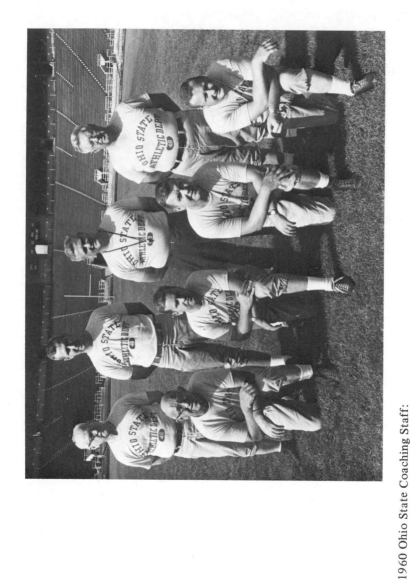

1960 Ohio State Coaching Staff:

Top (Left to Right)—Ernie Godfrey, Gordon Larson, Woody Hayes, Harry Strobel—Bottom (Left to Right)—Lyal Clark, Gene Slaughter, Esco Sarkkinen, Bo Schembechler

Chapter 5

Oh, That Other Ohio State Game
or "Kick the Field Goal, Bo!"

November 25, 1972. . .

Fourth Quarter

Down	Yards to Go	Yard Line	Play
1	5	Ohio 5	Banks option pitch re 1 Colzie hurt-helped off
2	4	Ohio 4	Banks rg 3
3	1	Ohio 1	Banks rt no gain
		time out - Michigan	
4	1	Ohio 1	Franklin's sneak was stopped by center of Ohio line.

I suppose, now, we should talk about this "other" Ohio State game. The one people keep mentioning to me. Our 1972 game in Columbus.

All I've been hearing is: "Why didn't you kick a field goal?" I suppose I'll be hearing it for a long time.

My answer is going to stay the same: "The ball was less than a yard away and if you can't make that, you don't deserve to win."

Let me set it up for you.

This was our 11th game of the season. We went down to Columbus with a 10-0 record. We've got a share of the Big Ten title. If we win. . .or even tie. . .we win the title outright and go back to the Rose Bowl.

Now I've been a part of these Ohio State-Michigan rivalries for a long time. I've been on both sides. I know how intense these games can get. Ohio State was beaten a couple of weeks earlier by Michigan State. That doesn't mean anything. When Michigan plays Ohio State in the final game, nothing else matters. It's a whole new game. A whole new war.

We moved the damned ball all over the field against Ohio State. But it's 14-11 for them in the fourth quarter. We get a break. Randy Logan intercepts Greg Hare's pass and we take over on the Ohio State 29 with about 13½ minutes to go.

We move right down to the five, where it's first and goal, and I figure this is where we do it. They'd stopped us on the one at the end of the first half but now we're going to put it in there on them.

And, if you'll please reexamine that play-by-play, you'll see how we were frustrated.

When most people look back at this game, they think I should have kicked a field goal in three different situations—certainly, this final time, with fourth and one on the one. Their logic sounds impressive. If we kick the field goal, we tie the game. A tie means it all for us—the title and the trip to Pasadena. We'd also have eight minutes left to get on the board again and win it outright.

Well, I'd never go for the field goal, never, because, as I said, if you can't put it in from the one, you don't deserve to win the game. That's how I felt about it then, and that's how I feel about it now.

Remember this: We're not a professional team. There was no assurance that when I put that ball down to kick a field goal that I am going to make it. I don't care if it is from the one-yard line. It doesn't make any difference. I've got a kicker who missed five extra points during the season, and there just isn't that much difference between trying those extra points and trying this field goal.

I'll be honest about it: we were not playing for a tie. We were playing for a win. I mean, we're a running football team and we're in there and we ought to be able to punch it over. If I'm going to second guess myself in any respect, it's on the play I called. I should have run the football again instead of

Joe Falls
Sports Editor

Who Can Doubt
Woody's the Best?

Nov. 26, 1972

COLUMBUS

Is there anyone in the house now who does not believe in the mystical powers of Wayne Woodrow Hayes?

The Fat Man did it again Saturday. Boy, did he do it! He took the second-best team on the field and came out first best with it.

And no matter how any of us weep and wail about the outcome, the fact remains that Woody Hayes is still the teacher and Bo Schembechler is still the student . . . and hold on now, this is no criticism of the Michigan coach.

Bo did a great job of getting his team ready for this moment. His boys played a tremendous game. They could have cracked. They could have collapsed. They could have sat down and cried over what happened to them on this dreary day in Ohio State Stadium.

But the Wolverines showed great poise. They didn't fumble once. They didn't throw the ball away. They came into this cauldron of hysteria and played a game they need never apologize about.

But yet it was Ohio State, under the direction of W.W. Hayes, which made the big plays in the clutch. Twice, they stopped the Wolverines within inches of the goal line. Time and again, they pulled down the men of Michigan when another yard — another foot . . . even an inch — could have turned the whole game around.

It is hard to explain the hold that Hayes has on the game of football in this city of Columbus. But he's got it. It is almost as he is able to will victories for his team.

You just don't come to Columbus for the big games and push the Fat Man around.

He always seems to think of something.

Woody Is a Scary Person'

Imagine winning a game such as this one with only one pass completion. Imagine an Ohio State team running only 44 plays to 83 for the opposition. Imagine the Bucks outgained, 344-192.

You may say these are only statistics, and statistics can be misleading. This is true. But it illustrates that this man can beat you in ways that are just difficult to comprehend.

Frankly, Woody Hayes is a scary person.

This was a terrible moment for the whole Michigan team. Especially for Schembechler. It puts a blot on what has been a magnificent season.

The U-M followers won't talk about the victory over Michigan State. They'll forget the tough one they won on the West Coast against UCLA. Even the last-minute triumph over Purdue will fade into history.

But they'll remember this one and they will chafe at the memory of it. That's because their team came so close, so very close. It was a suffocating setback.

Any second-guessing is really unfair because, in the final analysis, this game was decided on Ohio State's ability to make the big plays.

You've got to give this one to the Ohio State defense. It earned the victory in every sense of the word.

No sooner had Michigan been stopped on the one yard line in the final quarter than the second-guessers began carping in the press box. they wondered why Bo didn't go for what would have been almost a sure field goal. He had said he would play for a tie and this was his chance to go for it.

It could have sent his team to Pasadena.

I Think Bo Made Right Call

But it's hard to buy this criticism. Schembechler, in addition to being a stubborn man, is also a proud man. He had to feel his team could put the ball in, even though the Buckeyes had been playing it tough.

He had to feel his players could negotiate that last yard and if they couldn't, then they didn't deserve to win.

Sorry, I think Bo made the right call. Who'd want to go to the Rose Bowl with a "chicken tie" on your record? The only way to go is with your head high, as men.

Schembechler went at Ohio State with every play in his book. He tried every way to put the ball into the end zone. He used a different formation on almost every play.

Ohio State happened to be equal to the challenge. Don't blame the Wolverines. Give credit to the Bucks.

This Michigan team did not have the offensive punch of last year's team. That's because it didn't have runners like Billy Taylor and Glenn Doughty.

But it had great heart. If ever a team could have folded up, it was the Wolverines after Ohio State's second touchdown. That came in the first three minutes of the second half.

The Bucks had stifled the Wolverines with a great goal line stand to end the first half, and now they moved through the Michigan team with stunning ease. When Archie Griffin sprinted 30 yards into the end zone, it put the Buckeyes ahead 14-3 and a rout could have been on.

But the Michigan players held together. They didn't get rattled. They kept executing. They came right back and kept moving the ball on Ohio State—344 yards they moved it.

That's a lot of yards against a Woody Hayes team.

In the end, they couldn't make that one more yard and that's what it was all about.

Schembechler was crushed by the defeat but his pride also was evident when he told the reporters: "This is the best Michigan team I ever coached. We never dominated a game so much and lost the game."

"We should have won this game because we have come so far, so very far."

Bo then said something else. He said: "Nobody figured we would ever come down to the final game with a shot at the title."

Let's remember that. After all, it is the truth.

trying to sneak it in with Denny Franklin. That was my mistake—not passing up the field goal, running the wrong play.

You'll remember we had them first and goal on the one with 33 seconds left in the first half and didn't score then either. Chuck Heater lost a yard on an option pitch and then slipped on a power sweep while getting the yard back, Bob Thornbladh was stopped at right guard for no gain and Franklin, on fourth down, fumbled the center snap and we wound up back on the three. We made a mistake here, too. It had started to rain and we were playing on that Astroturf, which, to me, is more slippery than Tartan.

But my biggest mistake came with five or six minutes left in the game. That's where I really second guess myself. We had a fourth and 10 on their 37 and I called a pass by Franklin. He threw it low to Heater and they took over in pretty good field position. I should have punted the ball inside the 20 and force them to kick it back to us. I didn't want to lose the psychological edge of being stopped again and so I went with the pass play. I admit now it was a poor call.

We had the better team and should have won. We outplayed them but lost because of our own mistakes. I have to live with it more than anyone else.

The Ghost Speaks:

Well, I sure didn't have much fun this day. But I didn't die, as a lot of Michigan fans did.

The sad thing is that Michigan went into that big stadium down in Columbus and moved the ball on the Buckeyes. They moved it all over the field and, at times, moved it rather easily.

You don't do that very often to Woody in his stadium. Michigan did it and still lost. That hurt.

Now about Bo not kicking that field goal. I have a theory about second guessing. I think you are only allowed to second guess if, at the moment something happens, you make a first guess.

Let me explain.

I covered baseball for a long time and it used to annoy me when writers would second guess a team for making a certain trade, when that trade wouldn't work out.

I think back to the Tito Francona deal.

Rick Ferrell of the Tigers sent Tito to the Cleveland Indians for Larry Doby. The deal turned out brutally bad for the Tigers.

Doby stayed around a very short while. He was through. He'd had it as a major leaguer, and it was evident the moment he put on a Tiger uniform.

Francona, meanwhile, suddenly came to life and began hitting the ball all over the place. Home runs. Triples. Doubles. RBI's. Nobody could believe it. . .and everyone got on Ferrell's back about it.

The day the trade was made, I wrote a story saying I thought it was a good deal for the Tigers. I reasoned that they needed a lefthanded bat and a player of experience and it seemed like they were getting both in Doby.

I stuck with this stand all through those months when Ferell was catching it from all sides.

It is a cheap shot to wait until something happens before you offer an opinion about it.

So, on this day in Columbus, with time out and the ball resting on the one-yard line—fourth and goal to go—I turned to Curt Sylvester and said: "What do you think? Should they kick it or go for it?"

Curt said, "I think they should go for it."

I said, "I think so, too. If they can't put it in from there, they don't deserve to win."

That, my friends, is what you call a first guess. . .and it is the way I've always operated.

The problem is that I write these things after the game—AFTER the fact—and since my stories are read the next day, they come out sounding like a second guess.

No way.

I make my stand there, right on the spot, and live with it.

In this case, I was on Bo's side. I thought he did the right thing.

His detractors, of course, felt he blew the whole deal—especially the trip to the Rose Bowl.

I admit they present a pretty strong case. They argue, "Get the tie first and lock up the Rose Bowl and then go for the win." They point out there was still plenty of time left to score again.

In retrospect, they may be right. I've found it difficult arguing with them. They have a lot of logic on their side.

All I can say is, I thought Bo did the right thing at the time and it would be cheap of me to change my mind now. If we were wrong, we were wrong together.

Anyway, I've always wanted to make a mistake in my journalistic career.

Makes a guy human.

"If you can't put it in from the one, you don't deserve to win the game."

Schembechler with Assistants Larry Smith, (Back Row) Chuck Stobart, George Mans and Jim Young

Chapter 6

Schembechler Is His Own P. R. Agency

Will Perry, Michigan's Sports Information Director:

It's never easy to be gracious when defeat is fresh, emotions drained and a year of work scuttled by a lousy yard. So it was surprising when Bo Schembechler considered the question a second or two, then snapped, "Okay, let them in. Yes. . .right now."

He was allowing the press corps into his lockerroom. . .just 15 minutes after Michigan had lost to Ohio State. That defeat in Columbus was the only one of the 1972 season. And with it went an outright Big Ten championship, a trip to the Rose Bowl and the opportunity to play for a national championship. It was all gone.

Bo and the writers met in a small alcove leading into the main locker area. Questions came fast and pointed—the writers were working against deadlines. "Why didn't you kick a field goal?. . .What was wrong with Shuttlesworth?. . .Did you want a tie. . ?" Finally, it came. "Bo, can we talk with your players?"

Bo never hesitated. "Sure, but they won't be in a good mood. They may not want to talk with you, so be careful." He was opening the Michigan lockerroom, the clothy sweat, the tears, the disappointment, to 'outsiders' who had a job to do. I admired the man for that moment, because I knew what he felt inside.

John Hannen, sports editor of the Toledo Blade who has covered Bo's teams since his first year at Miami of Ohio in 1963, said, "The pinnacle of Bo's press relations came after that defeat in Columbus. I don't think he liked what he had to do, but he realized that game was of national importance. He even let us talk with his players."

Roy Damer of the Chicago Tribune also was impressed with Bo's treatment of the press that day. "If there's any point where I'd say Bo mellowed in his press relations," Damer said, "it would be after that defeat in Columbus. He let us right in. We talked with him, then with the players. They had just lost a game where everything was on the table. But Bo had earned the respect of just about every writer right from the start. He's a helluva guy."

Two years before, in 1970, when Michigan lost in Columbus, Bo had kept the writers waiting. . .and waiting. He finally let them in the lockerroom under the ancient Ohio Stadium stands and answered their questions. By the time he was finished, his players had showered, dressed and left. There were no player interviews that day.

Bo's reactions to the press are never predictable. Writing a book with Joe Falls, for example, is hard to imagine. Michigan won a game 42-0 and Joe ripped Bo's approach to the game as dull and boring. I think Bo likes Joe, but is convinced he knows nothing about football and excuses some of the things Joe writes. I think Bo may be right.

John Hannen remembers Bo in his Miami years as "hard to talk to. If he lost, which wasn't very often, it was an impossibility. He used to throw chairs around the lockerroom. I think he's taken on considerable polish and now accepts the fact that part of his coaching routine is press relations. It's necessary and he's intelligent enough to realize it."

Strangely, for a guy with an intense desire to win it has been in defeat when Bo has shown considerable depth as a person. Take the 1972 Rose Bowl, for example. My job was to make sure Bo got to the post-game press area under the end zone stands, about 30 feet or so from the Michigan lockerroom. I left the press box early and reached the end zone near the tunnel exit to the locker areas well before the game was over. Michigan had a two-point lead with a couple minutes to go and I thought, "This is going to be a lot easier than last time, that nightmare of two years ago. We're going to win."

92

"How about this, Bill, for Bo's next quote?"

Will Perry, Michigan Sports Information Director, and Bill
Cusumano (Standing), Assistant SID

Stanford, of course, messed up everything. Don Bunce was completing passes all over the field and finally the little kicker hit on a field goal and they won. I know how Bo is feeling. Eleven straight victories and this. Another loss in Pasadena after so much had been accomplished through the season. Twenty-five or thirty writers will be waiting for him short-ly—all on Saturday night deadlines—and he just has to talk with them.

I ran to the Michigan lockerroom and waited for the play-ers and coaches. Bo was one of the first in the door. He walked into the partitioned areas the coaches were using, sat on a stool with his head buried in his hands. I waited.

When the players and coaches were all in, the lockerroom door was sealed to everyone. Minutes passed, precious dead-line minutes for the writers across the passage way. Finally, I approached Jim Young, his defensive coordinator, "The writ-ers are waiting. How much longer do you think we should wait before trying to get Bo over there?"

Jim said, "I'll ask him," and he went over to Bo, who's still on the stool. "The writers are waiting, Bo. Do you want to talk to them now?"

Bo looked up rather surprised. "I thought they would be coming in here. Where are they?" I explained that the writers were set up in a special area outside the lockerroom.

"Well, let's go see them," Bo stood up, adjusted his cap and headed for the door. He talked and answered questions for nearly a half hour. Doug Mintline, Sports Editor of the Flint Journal, wrote the next day, "Schembechler may have lost a game, but not his class."

Bo is very forceful in his dealings with the press. I think he gets himself up for this just like a game and it carries over into his post-game interviews. After Michigan had defeated Illi-nois 31-7 in 1972 at Champaign, Bo was still intense, fired-up he calls it. One writer asked him, "What was the turning point in the game?"

Bo fired back, "There. . .was. . .no. . .turning point. We controlled this game from the opening kickoff." In this vic-tory, Bo was uncompromising.

When Bo went into an interview session his first year or so at Michigan, he'd ask, "Now, who's this guy? Is he a good writer?" He doesn't ask anymore. Bo has his own file on writers, especially those employed by Sports Illustrated magazine. I remember one football writer from SI had been here since midweek and talked extensively with Bo. The next week Bo read the guy's story and issued an order: "No more interviews with them. They listen, they agree, tell us how great we are and go back and rip us. No more."

Probably, Bo will relax that order and do more interviews with SI. But he has little patience with writers who are negative about college football, the Big Ten and Michigan.

If Bo had not been a football coach, and there were no openings for tank commanders, he probably would turn to sportswriting. He will ask more questions at his Monday press luncheons than he answers. This makes me nervous. He should be making statements that concern Saturday's game, but instead he talks about the Cleveland Indians or what a great guy Bill Russell is. "I could play for him," Bo will volunteer, and I envision stories the next day talking about Bo and Bill Russell, while Michigan's game with Indiana is buried under some 14-point head on a lefthand page.

Bo regards publicity with suspicion, I believe. A couple of experiences with writers quoting his athletes strengthened that belief. One quote, attributed to his quarterback, Don Moorhead, was obtained during the annual Big Ten sportswriters tour in August and finally printed the week of the Ohio State game in 1969. That one read, "Woody Panics When He's Behind."

Bo envisions these headlines being tacked all over the opposing team's lockerroom, stirring up emotions and possibly triggering a victory against Michigan. Bo wants nothing misrepresented. He will tape a lengthy recording for ABC, replay it and if he's not completely satisfied, he'll do it over. He does not allow a tape recorder in his post-game press conference.

Michigan has a recorder phone, used to tape coaches' comments which are available to newspapers and radio men by merely dialing a confidential number. This is a problem for Bill Cusumano, the Assistant Sports Information Director. Bill literally drags Bo to the phone for the two-minute tape once a week. At one time, when Bo was checking on the counter dial to see how many calls were coming in, Bill told the three oldest Schembechler boys the number and they and their friends were making calls and running up an impressive total. We never told Bo how popular he is in the Schembechler family.

While gadgets like a beeper phone annoy Bo, he's impeccable in the big ones, like the Rose Bowl. The people in Pasadena expect a daily press conference at the Huntington-Sheraton Hotel, live and in full color by the Big Ten coach. The coach of the West Coast team, meanwhile, talks via a telephone hookup from his distant practice location. Prior to opening practice on the Coast, Bo agreed to hold a press conference every day Michigan worked out. This was true in 1969 and again in 1971. Bo missed only one press conference in those two years. That was on Wednesday, Dec. 31, 1969, two days before the Rose Bowl game with Southern Cal.

Jim Murray and Mel Durslag, the syndicated columnists of Los Angeles' two papers, attended that conference along with the regular Bowl press corps. Bo was late and I was nervous. This would be the last press session, a chance for national stories and no Bo. After waiting 15 minutes or so, I walked out of the room and saw Jim Young walking up the stairs toward our mezzanine area.

"Bo won't be here, Will, he had some stomach trouble on the bus coming back from practice. He wants me to handle the conference."

Jim talked quickly and I knew he was worried, not about the writers, but probably about Bo. He seemed anxious to get in and get back upstairs.

I made the announcement about Bo. I thought there was some suspicion among the writers, but Jim took over and the meeting went well.

The next afternoon Bo spoke at the annual kickoff luncheon. Curt Gowdy and his color man from NBC were the featured speakers along with Bo and John McKay, the Southern Cal coach. Bo was not forceful that day.

That night his heart problem became acute and New Year's Day he was in the hospital.

When Bo returned to full-time coaching eight months later,

his relations with the press changed. They seemed less severe. The demands for special interviews, trips, telephone calls fell off. Bo, himself, was not anxious to overload his press duties, while the writers were cautious in their requests. The Michigan Sports Information Department became somewhat protective.

Bo in his first year had attended all Michigan's press smokers, held on Friday nights before home games. Just before the 1970 season he told us, "I want to be with my team so I don't think I'll make those Friday night parties." No one objected.

Still, he does the job. He may not like it at times. But John Hannen says, "Bo doesn't run and hide. He'll answer a direct question and most writers respect him for that. He still takes you down the merry road at his press conferences if you let him, but just ask him 'Why' and he'll tell you why."

Bo Schembechler is his own PR agency. I like watching him in operation—like after the 1969 season, holding a wrap-up press conference and passing out cigars, his tight, sun-squinting grin dominating the room; agreeing to a special radio-television-press conference just two days before the 1970 Ohio State game; personally directing Michigan's annual football team pictures and doing a better job than any sports information director; taking a little extra time with a sports writer from a student paper because he likes kids.

I agree with Roy Damer. He's a helluva guy, even if he's a Cleveland Indian fan.

"I wish I had a job that's a piece of cake like you reporters have."

Joe Falls
Sports Editor

Bo Schembechler: Lean and Hungry

Aug. 25, 1970

ANN ARBOI

U-M is on the way back, all right.

They held the annual Press Day feed Monday and it wa clear to all that the football program around here is definitel' on the upswing.

They served roast beef.

Last year it was hamburgers . . . and you can only wonde what'd happen if Bo ever beat Duffy, as well as Woody They'd probably meet at Maxim's.

But of course food is the last thing on the mind of Glenn F. Schembechler these days. He looks as if he hasn't put any gravy on his potatoes since last Jan. 1, which he probably hasn't.

The guy looks fantastic.

He doesn't look like Bo Schembechler, but he looks fantas tic.

He's down 40 pounds from that blubbery 220 out in Pasa dena and he was standing there looking like a high school sophomore (well, a junior) and telling the members of the media: "I've never felt better in my life, physically, mentally or socially."

And this is bad news for his boys . . because if they felt they were worked too hard at times last year, and some of them did, you can only imagine what Bo has in mind for them now that he is also in shape.

"I'm really confident I can beat this thing," said Bo, speaking of his heart attack. "When I come in from running those three miles in the morning, I feel like there isn't anything I can't do. I feel like going out and running another three miles."

Must Have Incentive to Win

So, suck up your guts, guys — it's going to be a rather testing training camp. The 11 who are left standing start against Arizona.

They asked Bo if the fact the Wolverines couldn't go back to the Rose Bowl would hurt the incentive of his team, and it was a mistake to even contemplate such a question.

Lack of incentive? Nobody gets fat at Michigan anymore, least of all the head coach, and listening to Bo getting cranked about the prospects for the coming season, you get the idea he'd like to meet Woody Hayes, here and now, at anything Woody would like — guns, knives, swords, water pistols, chocolate cream pies . . or the off-tackle slant.

He grinned that ominous grin and said that his team had plenty of room for improvement.

"Do you realize we had a punt blocked last season?" he said. "That's inexcusable."

Schembechler is well aware of the incentive factor, thank you.

"Incentive is the most important factor about our team," he said. "We've got to have it to win and you can be sure we're going to have it."

As for going ito Columbus on Nov. 21, Bo said he couldn't look that far ahead, but then he couldn't help himself and quickly added:

"I think that Ohio State has a little more respect for Mi gan, and if we're going to play for the title that day — 1 out!"

Season Offers Bigger Challenge

Schembechler literally has a lean and hungry look ab him. He acts as if he'd like to go to four-a-day sessions to ready for the 1970 campaign.

That's because this season is an even bigger challenge him than last season. All he had to do last year was rest Michigan's old glory and make the Wolverines the domin team they were in past years.

Now, instead of merely trying to beat the likes of Michi, State and Ohio State, he's got to prove he can beat himself to prove he can overcome his heart attack and produce as fore.

"I can go as hard as I want," Bo said during the pict taking session on the field. "Of course I'm going to take c of myself. If we get into one of our long sessions and it g to be 9:30 at night, I'm just going to go home. I'm not go to hang around all night like I did last year.

"But I'm still going to work as hard as ever. There's only one head coach on this team and that's me and I'm r going to ask anyone to do my work for me."

Schembechler, 41 now, has been given a clean bill of hea by his doctors. All the tests taken on him show no heart da age. They've told him he can resume living as he did bef — with a little less on the eats, please.

That's no problem. Bo may never touch another french as long as he lives.

His only concession to the heart attack which felled k before the Rose Bowl game will be to take some pills to ke his blood thin.

"Okay, we can't go to the Rose Bowl but to me the thing is still the Big Ten championship. You win that a you're going to be ranked nationally and that's what we aiming for — the Big Ten title."

Any arguments?

Chapter 7

Hired by Michigan ("I've Never Cared About Money") for a Thousand Buck Raise

It was wild how they hired me at Michigan. It happened so fast. It was just before Chistmas 1968 and I'd had several calls from Bump Elliott about getting his oldest boy into Miami because the out-of-state admissions were so tough. He called me several times and I checked into things for him. I told him his son had good grades and he had a good chance of getting into Miami.

Just before Christmas he calls again. I say, "Come on, Bump, I told you I'd get your kid in here. . .quit bothering me." I was just kidding him.

He said, "No, that's not what I'm calling about."

I had no idea what he meant. There was no word that he was stepping down at Michigan—no word that the job was coming open.

Bump said, "I wonder if you would be interested in the job here at Michigan?"

I said, "You've got to be kidding. What's going on up there?"

He said, "I'm going to become the Associate Athletic Director and I'm getting out of coaching. Don Canham, the Athletic Director, wanted me to call you."

I'm a little surprised now, right? They don't call you every day in the week and talk to you about the Michigan coaching job. I said, "Sure, I'd be glad to talk to him." I hoped he didn't notice the excitement in my voice.

He asked me how soon I could get up to Ann Arbor. I said, "How about tomorrow morning?" Bump laughed.

So the next morning I'm on my way to Ann Arbor.

Bump came out to the airport and picked me up. He took me to the athletic office. Nobody is around but Canham. School is out and he is sitting there alone in his office.

We shake hands and he says, "Let's go downstairs and get some coffee."

He starts right in by telling me everything about the Michigan job. He says, "What do you think of it—would you like to have it?"

Right away I was impressed with him. He laid things on the table. He didn't play around.

"I'd be very interested," I told him, "But I'm going to have to tell you one thing."

I told him I wasn't interested in going through all that bunk of committees because I'd done it before and it's nothing but a joke. I did it at Wisconsin. I did it at North Carolina. I've done it every place I've gone. It always worked out they knew who they wanted and they were just interviewing guys to be interviewing them.

I told him, "I just don't want to go through all this again. If you want me to be your coach, I'll be your coach. But I don't want to go through a lot of hassling."

Canham looked straight at me. For some reason, I liked him. I liked him right away. That's going to sound funny because I work for him, but I felt there was something special about him. I felt I could believe him.

Anyway, he looks at me and says, "I'm hiring the football coach and I want you to be the coach."

Now that really impressed me. He was being his own man and I liked that. He said he was sure that any recommendation he made to his committee would be approved and there was only one other guy he wanted me to meet. That was Marc Plant, the faculty representative.

Canham and I must have talked for a couple of hours in the coffee room downstairs. I'd heard he was a straight forward guy, so I gave it to him straight. I told him I'd heard some disturbing things about the Michigan program, how they were always trying to save money around here—like if they took a film at a scrimmage they'd have to sneak it out and get the bill through someway to get it processed. Stuff like that. These are things that shouldn't happen and I'd heard about it from the Michigan assistants when they came through Miami on recruiting jobs.

I was really surprised when Bump called me. I'd been to a lot of other places for interviews and, after a while, I refused to go. They offered me the job at Tulane and I turned it down. I was offered the Pittsburgh job and I turned that down, too. Those were the first ones that came after me after I had my first championship at Miami.

Frankly, in the back of my mind I was always thinking about the Ohio State job. I knew if Woody ever left, I'd be tough to beat out for that job. I knew I'd have a real shot at it, so I didn't want to jump into somewhere where I would end up with a mediocre record. When I left Ohio State as an assistant, Dick Larkins, the athletic director, wanted me to stay around. He said I would be in line for Woody Hayes' job but that if I went elsewhere and had a losing record, it might hurt my chances. He put that seed in my mind and so that's why I chose Miami of Ohio. They'd always had the sort of program there where the coach could do well. All you have to do is look at all the great coaches that came out of that school—Sid Gilman, Paul Brown, Ara Parseghian, Johnny Pont, Woody Hayes, George Blackburn and Stu Holcomb.

Anyway, Hayes stayed on at Ohio State. . .an on and on and on. He seemed indestructible. So when the Wisconsin job came open. . .I think it was in 1966. . .I went up there to be interviewed. I really got miffed when I got there.

John Coatta got the job but they brought in myself and Johnny Ray of Notre Dame to be interviewed. This is what I mean about these interviews being a joke. Coatta was all set for the job but they had to go through the formalities of interviewing other guys.

They brought in all the candidates at the same time but put us up at different hotels. Real secret agent stuff. They asked John Ray and I to come down together and he goes in first before the committee. I guess it's about 10 o'clock at night before it's my turn.

You have to picture this. They've got 20 guys sitting around and one of them—a board member, I guess—is sound asleep.

He is sitting there asleep. I mean, how the hell would you feel. I'm mad. Really mad. I don't even want to be there. I don't want to answer any of their questions.

I wasn't going to make a pitch anyway. I never do that. I'm not one to bring along my books and movies and make a plea. I figure they know about me or I wouldn't be there. I'm certainy not going to beg.

What made me sick is that one of the kids on the committee says to me, "What would you do if you had Clem Turner on your team?"

Clem Turner is a fullback from Cincinnati and this kid evidently was from that area. Turner was one of those players who always seemed to be in trouble.

I glared at the kid and said, "I don't know Clem Turner. I only know him as a player. How do I know how I am going to handle him." I guess this was a student member of the committee and I'm hot about the way he is questioning me. I'm in there for maybe 40 minutes and I just don't care what is happening. As soon as I got out of there I called Ivy Williamson, the athletic director, and told him I am withdrawing. I can't get out of there quick enough.

As soon as I got back home, I got a call from North Carolina and I'm really mad. I tell them on the phone, "No, I don't think I will come down." The guy says, "Come down and at least look over the situation." He was the athletic director, as I recall, and I finally give in and tell him I'd come in to talk. But that's all—just to talk. I've really got a negative attitude and how do you suppose I feel when I go before the board—it's on a Sunday—and the president of the school comes in dressed like he's been working out in the yard.

I think to myself: "Here we go again—same thing!"

I have to admit the situation there was pretty good—a lot like Miami, only bigger. Actually it was a good job and they finally gave it to Bill Dooley. This was the only one I ever really cared about.

Vanderbilt called. Kansas State called. But I wasn't going to visit any more campuses. I got to thinking that I'm a Big Tenner and that's what I really want. I decided I would wait for the right job to come along. . .and then here's Bump

Elliott calling me up a few days before Christmas.

After I told Canham I wasn't going through any of that jazz of appearing before committees, he tells me to forget it. He says: "Let's go see Marc Plant."

Now this I could see is a bright guy—not only our faculty rep (how do you like the way I'm already saying "our?") but he's a former president of the NCAA. Marc is over in the lounge at Crisler Arena and nobody is around because it's the holiday. We sit down and talk and he tells me: "You know, I know a little more about you than you think I do."

I say, "Oh?"

He smiles and says, "Yes, my daughter goes to Miami and I've seen your teams play many times—on Parents Day and so forth." So Marc and I talk and I don't know if Canham ever bought me a meal. But I did go to Bump's house.

Looking back on it now, I think Canham always had in the back of his mind that he wanted a "name" guy. I knew I could handle the job. I wasn't worried about some big name coming in and taking the job away from me. Everyone in the Big Ten has great respect for Michigan. Everyone knows the potential is always here—that it is really an ideal spot because of the school itself and its great tradition. The problem was that Michigan had fallen behind the times; it had rested on its tradition. It hadn't been a real progressive outfit in a long while and the head coaching job had been a very, very low-paying job.

Now this you have to believe. I mean about the money. They used to have assistants around here making $6,500 to $8,000 a year and no way can you live on that kind of dough. So while Don probably would have liked to have Joe Paterno or Darrell Royal, you can't get guys like that unless you have good money to offer.

When I was in Ann Arbor, I didn't even look around at the campus. I didn't have to. They didn't have to sell me on anything. I knew what was here—the opportunity.

As I left, I said to Canham, "Okay, what happens next?"

He said, "I'll give you a call in a day or two."

Bump took me back to the airport. We talked about football and we talked about the job. Bump said that Canham

1969 Michigan Football Staff:
Top (Left to Right)—Gary Moeller, Larry Smith, Louis Lee,
Jim Young, Dick Hunter, George Mans—Bottom (Left to
Right)—Jerry Hanlon, Chuck Stobart, Frank Maloney, Bo
Schembechler

University of Michigan 1970-1971 Football Coaching Staff:

(Left to Right)—Larry Smith, Dick Hunter, Gary Moeller, Frank Maloney, Jerry Hanlon, Head Coach Bo Schembechler, Chuck Stobart, Jim Young, Tirrel Burton, George Mans

1972 Michigan Coaching Staff:

Top (Left to Right)—Chuck Stobart, Tirrel Burton, Larry Smith, Jim Young, Gary Moeller, George Mans—Bottom (Left to Right)—Dennis Brown, Jerry Hanlon, Bo Schembechler, Frank Maloney

had really made a lot of changes and that things were so much better than they used to be in terms of getting things you needed in order to have a program. Bump felt the job was going to be an excellent one with the change in attitude at the school, with Canham really wanting to make the football program go.

The word was out on Canham when he took Fritz Crisler's place. Everyone said Michigan was on the move. I wondered what it would be like to have a track coach as the athletic director. Usually that type of thing doesn't work out.

Bump said: "Believe me, he is not an ordinary track coach. This is a business man, and highly successful. He understands his priorities and knows what has to be done to get things moving."

I went back home and told Millie they were going to offer me the Michigan job. I was confident. Really confident. She was thrilled. My Millie is quite a gal.

I couldn't have asked for anything better. You look around the country, at the different jobs, and Michigan just has to be one of the best. Michigan had not been what it used to be and yet it was still there. Schools that have won in the past can win again if they are run properly.

When I took over from Bump, I was extremely loyal to him. I watched what I did and what I said and when we won that first year I made certain I let everyone know I won with Bump's kids. Bump was a man of great class and he showed it to me again and again in that first year, never getting in the way, always trying to be helpful, always trying to encourage me. The night we had our private banquet after beating Ohio State, we gave the game ball to Bump. . .and I don't remember when I felt happier about anything in my life.

When I got back home after talking to Canham, he calls me on the phone—it's the day before Christmas now—and he says: "Bo, I'm offering you the job at Michigan."

Do you know what I said? I said, "Good." That's all. One word—"Good."

But now this will make you laugh. He said: "The salary is $21,000. Is that enough?"

I say, "I don't care about money." I can only imagine what

he thought when I said that.

Now you figure this out—I'm coming from Miami to Michigan. I made $19,000 in my last year at Miami but I'm due for a raise and that's going to be at least $1,000. So any way you look at it, I'm moving from Miami to Michigan for a $1,000 raise—and I don't even care about the money.

I said to Canham, "We've got to take care of the assistants. That's one thing I insist on."

He told me not to worry about it and I have to say he has lived up to his word.

You know, I came here without a written contract. That's the sort of businessman I am. I just trusted him. If you don't have trust, you don't have anything.

I said to Canham, "There's no way I'm going to win anything right off the bat. You understand that now."

He said, "I understand."

I said, "How long do I have to win a championship?" After all, Ron Johnson graduated and so did a lot of other good players. I wasn't sure what they had left.

Canham said, "You can have five years—take my word for it." I took it. If I couldn't win in five years, I'd get out myself.

I said something else. I said, "There's going to be a great transition between Bump's way and my way and anything can happen."

He said, real cool like, "How soon can you get back here?"

I said, "How about tomorrow night?" Now that's Christmas night. I guess maybe I'm tipping my hand, but I wanted to get back so fast and go to work, I'd have left on the spot.

Anyway, I get in about 2 o'clock Christmas night. This time Canham picks me up. We drive to his house and I don't think anybody else knows about it. He gets right on the phone and calls Will Perry, our sports information director, and says, "Will, get over here." He calls Bump and says, "Bump, get over here." He calls Dave Strack and the next thing you know all of us are sitting around talking about what's going to happen.

The next day I was to meet the Athletic Board. I slept at the Hilton that night. They registered me in under the name of Glen Schems and when I got there, I forgot what name I was supposed to use.

The next day, the Athletic Board asked some questions but I didn't mind it. I didn't mind it at all. No siree. They introduced me to them as "our new head football coach."

That Canham's a cutie. I guess what he had done was poll them by telephone, so by the time they showed up they knew all about me.

The amazing thing is how readily I was accepted. I mean, everyone treated me well. The football coach is usually the big cheese in any athletic program and sometimes there is some resentment toward him, especially if he is a new man. But that never happened around here. Never. I never felt any jealousy at all, even a tough so and so like myself taking over from such a quiet, dignified man like Bump Elliott.

Don Canham:

Actually, the first time I heard of Bo was on an airplane going to Indiana. I was sitting with Bob Ufer, our radio announcer. I'd asked a lot of people for prospective coaches and Bo's name was one that kept coming up. Ufer was the first to bring it up.

I had talked to Bump Elliott near the end of the 1968 season and told him I had to fill the job of Associate Athletic Director. Bump was still the coach, but I told him if he was interested in the job, he'd be my first choice.

I asked Ufer if he could give me a list of guys who might fill our job as coach if Bump retired and he mentioned Bo. I also talked to Bob Shaw, who was on Bump's staff and had been down through Miami on recruiting trips, and knew Bo well.

The truth is, I didn't even know how to spell Bo Schembechler. . .and didn't for about six months. I knew he had a great record at Miami—I knew he was respected down there. But that's all I knew—that he had winning teams and a long name.

I can't remember the exact sequence—it was sometime in December, just before the Rose Bowl—and George Allen had just been fired by the Los Angeles Rams. George and his wife were going to the Rose Bowl with us and so when he was fired,

I called him up and during the talk I asked him for a list of people he might suggest to us. I think I kiddingly asked him if he was interested in the job, but it got no further than that.

I talked with several people—I talked with Joe Paterno at Penn State and I had a friend of mine talk with Ara Parseghian. I'd say Bump called three or four other people—men like Vince Dooley and Ben Martin—and asked if they might be interested in moving.

The thing we were looking for was someone who wanted to move enthusiastically. We didn't want to have to buy somebody. We had the feeling we might have been able to get some of these people, but we didn't offer the job to anyone. Bo is the only man I offered the job to. I think you can get people to move for money, but that isn't what we were interested in. We had the money, but I've always believed in enthusiasm first. If you don't have that, you don't have much else. . .and this is what impressed me about Bo when I first talked to him.

Frankly, I decided to hire him in 15 minutes. The first time I met him, he came on that way—a man of great enthusiasm. He knew what he wanted and I could see that he wanted it badly.

When you're trying to hire someone, the tough thing is that everybody charms the pants off you in an interview. You've got to be very careful about initial impressions. Everybody looks good and everybody has an impressive resume of what they did. When Bo impressed me so much with his enthusiasm, I began checking him out every way possible. I checked him out with the people who knew him and with other coaches. I checked with Marc Plant, our faculty rep, who had a daughter going to Miami. I wanted to find out as much as I could about him.

I was really impressed with Bo's organization. The fellow was far more organized than I thought he was. I'm a great one for being able to sort out the important things—at least I think I can—and it seemed to me that he had life and everything else figured out just right. What impressed me is that he said exactly what was on his mind and he told me exactly what his philosophies were. I didn't have to guess what he was thinking.

Some of the things I'd heard about him were detrimental. For instance, the biggest criticism I heard about Bo was that he was a tough guy for an administrator to get along with—that he had been in difficulty with his athletic director because he had to have things his own way. That didn't bother me because that's exactly what I was looking for. I was looking for somebody to run the show and if he's right, he's going to get his way. If he's wrong—well, I'm the athletic director.

Anyway, our relationship has been tremendous. He comes storming in to me at times. I'll listen to him. If he's got something worthwhile and I can do it, I'll do it. He knows that. If it can't be done, it can't be done. He knows that, too.

The big thing is that I have to prove I am right and he has to be logical when he comes to me. We've had this understanding from the beginning and it has worked out well.

I said to him, "Look, I have it from two sources that you're difficult to get along with, and I can tell you right now if we're going to have any trouble it's going to be your fault." We still kid about that. We haven't had any real problems and I have to say in all honesty that he never comes to me with stupid approaches to anything. Everything is sound and well thought out. I have unlimited respect for this man and his judgement.

Now I say we could have bought a coach if we wanted, but I also have to admit we were in a financial bind at this time. Our revenue just wasn't that great. We've increased it by almost a million dollars a year and still it's a continuing fight to meet all our commitments. But it's true—Bo got only a thousand bucks more than he was making at Miami.

Let me tell you the kind of guy he is. He didn't haggle one bit about his salary but one of the first things he said to me was, "You know, Michigan is notorious for the low salaries it pays to its assistants."

He said that was the one thing we'd have to take care of before he'd come here. He said, and I'll never forget his words, "You have to pay an assistant coach a living wage or you get rid of him." Of course he was right about that, and now our salary schedule is up among the top in the Big Ten Conference.

Bo is probably the most intense person I have ever known.

After most games, I go over to his house and we just sit around. It's hard to get him away from football. His wife Millie and I, we try. We try to talk about everything else after a game, especially after we've lost. He allows himself only one evening to relax and I don't know whether he is happy to see me after games, but I enjoy it.

Bo doesn't entertain a lot and he doesn't have those after-game parties. Once in a while, he has some relatives over or maybe a few friends but that's about it. But he's able to relax once he walks into his house.

After the games, he talks a lot to his players and his assistants. It's a funny thing—he's all business except at the press conference. I notice that he sits down then and has an apple or coke and relaxes a bit when he talks to the press. But the moment he goes back into the locker room, he's all business again, and starts working for next week.

Bo is probably the best judge of people I know. I think this shows up in his coaching—the way he moves personnel from one position to another. He does this better than any coach I have ever seen. He has a great respect for Ara Parseghian in this regard. Ara did the same thing at Northwestern and I think Bo probably learned a lot about this from him. I often look at the type of assistants he brought in here with him and hired recently. There is just no questioning their quality. Bo doesn't make many mistakes in judging people.

Before we go any further, I think we should clear up this business of Bump being "eased" out of his job—or whatever it is people have been saying about it. I don't think the true facts have ever been revealed.

Bump and I are close personal friends. Bump is not naive— he knows that when you work at a place for 10 years and you're not winning consistently, it doesn't become fun for anybody—the coach, the alumni, the players or anybody else. We talked about this and we talked about it openly. If Bump had said to me, "Look, give me a couple of more years," I would have given it to him. I mean that. I didn't fire Bump Elliott. My first year as director Bump had an 8 and 2 record. Anyone could live with that.

You have to be realistic about life in athletics. It was early

December when I told him he could stay on as coach if he wanted, but I couldn't promise him that the job of associate athletic director would still be open in another couple of years.

I told him, "I think you should think about it very seriously."

Bump smiled at me and said, "I don't have to think about it." He was ready to get out. I did not force him, and I mean that in all honesty. But the job had ceased to be fun for him, just like coaching track had ceased to be fun for me. It took me a long time to realize it, though. But this business about Bump wanting a long-term contract. . .or that I was putting the squeeze on him—it just wasn't true.

I have great respect for Bump. He admired Bo and I figure if Bump liked a man that much, he was worth taking a good look at. Bump has a lot of high ideals. I mean, what a Michigan man should be—the image he should have. So when he talked about Bo, I listened and listened carefully.

When I spoke to George Allen, he mentioned Ben Martin. I'll admit that—Martin was the first name he mentioned. But he also mentioned this Schembechler fellow at Miami. Allen didn't know him but had seen some of his films and was greatly impressed with them.

Then we were in New York, Bump and I, and we were at Toots Shor's one night. Sonny Werbelin was there. I didn't know Sonny very well—in fact, I'd just met him through an ABC man. He told us we ought to look at Joe Paterno, which we had already done.

He said, "There is a guy coaching at Miami who is pretty good. . .I can't recall his name but you ought to look him up." Werbelin said he had heard nothing but good things about the man.

That, plus what Allen had told us, what Marc Plant had told us and what Bump knew—that got us headed in Bo's direction.

The big thing is that I knew we couldn't hire an unproven assistant for the Michigan job. Secondly, I don't think you can hire a man who isn't familiar with the State of Ohio or Ohio recruiting. If you do, it better be somebody who is familiar with Chicago or the Chicago area. You've just got to go outside of the Michigan area for some of your talent.

I felt Paterno fit into this pattern because he had played a lot of Big Ten teams and he recruits widely in this area. So it didn't necessarily have to be a midwesterner. I did get serious with Joe, but I don't think money blocked it. We never got around to talking money. What blocked any serious discussion with Joe was that he was in a bowl game and I told him we had to do something and do it right away. His reaction was that he couldn't do anything until the bowl game was over. It was one of his early bowl appearances and he wanted to do well. I couldn't blame him for that. I couldn't wait too long, either.

One of the things that bothered me in talking to some of the other coaches is they had southern backgrounds and I didn't know if they were familiar with the great influence the black athlete has had in the Big Ten. That was a real concern of mine.

With Bo, I don't think he looks at his players as being black or white. I asked Bob Shaw if he knew if Bo had any problems in this respect and he said, no, the kids on his team worship him. In this respect, I think Bo is very similar to Fritz Crisler. Fritz wasn't a buddy-buddy coach with the players but he had their respect. Bo is that way, too. He gets close to them but he always lets them know he is the coach, and they have great respect for his knowledge and his ability to lead them.

You know, it is an amazing thing to me that in this era of "freedom" on our campuses Bo can teach discipline to his players and they can accept it.

A couple of things are involved here.

One, I think a lot of young football players want to play professional football—they envision themselves as pros the moment they come to college. They know there is no way they're going to get there unless they have a great coach and play for a great team. Of course there are exceptions but this generally is the rule. Your good teams feed more people to the pros than the bad ones and the kids know this. This is why they're willing to accept discipline.

When we recruit an athlete, we don't say we're going to put you in the pros. We say we're going to have a heckuva program here and if you have 103,000 seats, you are going to have a lot of TV exposure and naturally all the professional people watching Michigan play.

The other thing is that Bo treats all of his players the same way. I think if you asked him how many black players he has on his team, he wouldn't be able to tell you. He tries to help everyone as much as possible but he maintains a strict employee-boss relationship.

I'll tell you this—he is extremely concerned with what happens to a boy when he leaves here. I've seen him bend over backwards time and again to help some kid who played for him. Take our graduate assistants. He could go to Notre Dame or some of the other big schools and hire outstanding young talent. Instead, he'd rather go with someone who played at Michigan. . .and I can't think of a better example of this than the way he helped Jim Betts after he had that eye injury. Bo worried about Jim for weeks.

People have asked me if I'm afraid of losing Bo. Well, that's always a possibility. Maybe this is why I keep extending that five year contract. I know what we have and I want to keep him. That has to be obvious.

Another Big Ten school came to him with a fabulous offer after the 1972 season. They said they wanted him to be both the athletic director and the coach. They offered him a five-year contract. They said they'd fire the athletic director and they'd give him a salary between $50,000 and $60,000, plus a $20,000 television contract and and an insurance policy and a home and who knows what else.

You know something? The whole thing confused Bo. He called me on the phone and told me about it. He couldn't understand why they would fire the athletic director. That really bothered him.

Do you know what he told them when they made him this offer?

He said, "Okay, I'll deal with the athletic director." That ended it right there. It was a beautiful answer on his part. He figured if they had so little ethics—to hire him behind the athletic director's back—he didn't want to pursue it any further.

The big thing is that he didn't use this to hold me up for more money. That tells you the kind of man he is.

Bo is one of the people I really enjoy being with. I don't know how he feels about it, but I feel we're very close. I enjoy him. I hope he enjoys me. He is unique.

The Ghost Speaks:

This may sound strange, but I've known Don Canham for only a few years, and not too well, at that.

I used to think he was a pretty pompous guy and felt I could live very nicely without him.

Don was the track coach at Michigan and who cares about a silly sport like track? They're running and jumping all over the place but who really knows what's going on? Except for a few Olympic events and maybe a Jim Ryun mile, who cares?

I'd see Don down at Cobo Arena at the NCAA Indoor Track and Field Championships every March. He'd be walking around the floor in one of those tuxedos and looking very important and very sure of himself. Also, very handsome. That bothered me a lot. Nobody should be in the position he was in—the athletic director of a school with the tradition and heritage of The University of Michigan—and look like a leading man in Hollywood.

Anyway, I never cared to meet him because I figured we had nothing in common.

That's what you call your old prejudice in action.

I've gotten to know this man over the past few years, especially since we started putting this book together, and I have found him not only to be one of the most intelligent men I have ever encountered, but a decent person on top of it.

While he wants to put Michigan on the top in athletics and keep his school there, he is also a man who cares about the people who work for him and he has helped many of them with their personal problems. He defends his coaches tenaciously when the luck of a season has gone against them and public criticism is running high. So don't tell me Don Canham is all business. Mostly, but not all.

115

What I like about him is that he's a doer. He gets it done, now. That's his strongest trait—one I wished I possessed.

I proposed the idea for this book at the back of the Michigan press box. It was the next-to-last game of the 1972 season. I didn't have to sell him at all. I just mentioned it and immediately he saw the potential. A book on Bo. Who knows Bo? Let the world know about this man.

Canham said, "Let's talk about it after the Ohio State game."

He paused for a moment.

"I think we'll do it," he said.

I knew we would do it. He couldn't resist the temptation to promote Michigan. It is the thing he lives for. Isn't that right, Don?

"Just think, Bump, with Tartan Turf, our laundry bills will be cut in half."

Former Michigan Assistant Athletic Director Chalmers E. "Bump" Elliott (Now University of Iowa Athletic Director) with Michigan Athletic Director Don Canham in 1968

Bo Has Returned Michigan's Pride

Nov. 24, 1969

IT WAS ON A WARM AFTERNOON late last Sepmper that Don Canham, the Michigan athletic direcr, was sitting behind the desk in his office and slowshaking his head.

"We've played only two games and already people 'e telling me that I've got a genius on my hands," was saying. "I don't know what to think."

Canham was a track man in his coaching days, a outstanding one, but the intricacies of football leave m a little confused, as it does the rest of us. But 'o games into the season and his Wolverines had ored a pair of smashing victories over Vanderbilt d Washington and it seemed to leave everyone—including Canham—a little restless.

When Canham took over for Fritz Crisler and made e big change—moving Bump Elliott behind a desk d hiring Bo Schembechler to be his football coach it was done with one purpose in mind.

Canham wanted to win, and win big.

He wanted to win big enough to put the pressure Michigan State and fill his 101,001 seats in Michin Stadium. Everyone at U-M was tired of being cond best.

But nobody, not even the astute Canham, had any tion that Schembechler would become such a dominnt force in such a short time.

He moved in, this new man from Miami of Ohio—is man with the long name that can't fit into anye's headlines—and took a team that was entirely w to him and led it to the heights.

In less than a year's time, Bo Schembechler has stored the old pride and prestige to the University Michigan . . . and he's done it only with his coaching.

Hard Work Pays Off

YOU CAN ONLY WONDER WHAT it's going to be ke when he starts recruiting his own players. He is football coach 24 hours a day, seven days a week, ur weeks a month and 12 months a year . . . and om all the reports about him he recruits as zealously he coaches. Duffy Daugherty may have to hire mself a jet.

Schembechler has no real secrets, and it's not much a story to say he attained the heights with Michigan mply by hard work.

It's no story at all, except it's the truth.

Bo Schembechler believes you can run the counter ay well if you practice it 500 times then you can do so much better if you practice it 501 times.

He's very much like his old boss, Woody Hayes.

Schembechler believed there was only one way to at Ohio State and that was for the Wolverines to exete their plays better than the Buckeyes. That's exy what they did.

He knew he had two psychological weapons but he ed them judiciously. Also, craftily.

He knew the players were still seething about the way Woody Hayes tried to rub it in last year but he didn't try to inflame them with the memory of that humiliation. He knew he didn't have to.

But he did mention the Rose Bowl and what people were saying about Michigan, that the Wolverines were second rate representatives. Yes, Bo found time to mention this quite often.

But more than this, he stressed the fundamentals he had been teaching all season. He is primarily a fundamentalist, not a psychologist, and when he studied the films of the Ohio State team and then appraised his only personnel, he felt he could win. His job was to convince the players of this. "You could see it in his face right after the Iowa game," said a Michigan official. "You knew right then he felt he could win."

Players Respect Bo's Work

SCHEMBECHLER PREPARED NO complicated offense or defense for Ohio State. He merely wanted his players to execute what they knew better than ever, which of course they did, almost to perfection.

Note that the Wolverines incurred only one serious penalty, had only one pass intercepted and didn't drop a ball all day long.

To be sure, the Michigan players have gathered in their frat houses at night and grumbled about Schembechler's taskmaster tactics. But they knew their complaints were weak ones because the boss was working harder than anyone else.

Capt. Jim Mandich put it this way: "When you'd go into the office early in the morning and Bo would be there watching films or you'd see him watching films on Saturday night, when the rest of us are off . . . well, you'd say to yourself, 'If he can do it, then maybe I'd better start doing it.'"

He asks no more of his assistant coaches or his players than he asks of himself.

But he also gives them Thursday night off.

"It's a funny thing about the coach," said Mandich. "He'll go and go and go and get everyone higher and higher and higher, but then, suddenly, he'll break into a laugh or tell a joke . . . and then we can start all over and go at it even harder."

Don Canham can relax. Until somebody can prove otherwise, he's got a genius on his hands. What other coach in the Big Ten has never lost to Woody Hayes?

That's real genius

Chapter 8

Player Relations: "How Do You Tell Them About Pot When You Never Smoked It?"

I hear coaches say it's tougher than ever to coach these days because of this new attitude among the students on our campuses. I don't know if it's any tougher. . .maybe it is. . . but I can tell you it is more enlightening.

Years ago all a coach had to talk to a player about was football. Now he has to deal with other things—other aspects of life. I think the secret of coaching today is the ability to sit down and talk with a player about subjects and problems other than football.

I think the football players of today have many more interests outside of football than they had years ago. In the past, football was the single most important factor in their lives. Today they are aware of other things.

We are not bringing in a group of narrow-interest youngsters. All you have to do is consider how many we have in engineering, medicine, and the more difficult programs in literature, science and the arts. Naturally, when you play football of the caliber we play at Michigan, you are bound to get the type of youngster who is greatly interested in the game. We have players on our team who are so football-oriented that football is still number one with them and some are majoring in physical education, but not as many as in the past. Frankly, I was the type of player who considered football number one in my life, and of course I like this type of player—interested in other things but letting nothing interfere with his football.

I used to generalize about young people but I don't anymore. How can you? They're all different. I've had an opportunity to talk to these kids and it's interesting to me that while they may have a lot of radical ideas, they're interested in our football program and enjoy the games and go out and cheer for Michigan.

A psychologist could probably explain this better than I, but I think it's because they appreciate excellence, no matter where they find it. Take the down-and-out ones who are rebelling against everything. I don't have a whole lot of feeling for them because what they're doing is not constructive; it is destructive. I don't think we have nearly as many of this type today as we had two or three years ago because the students may have realized that destruction is no way to effect change. All they will do is upset people by rowdyism and rioting. The more mature youngsters are changing things with sensible, constructive criticism carried through the proper channels, and they feel that a lot of things are wrong in this world, but not everything. Our campuses have been reasonably calm and I think this is a good sign—a positive approach toward solving some of today's problems.

I try to help my players in as many ways as possible. Take the problem of drugs. They don't talk to me about it, but I bring it up to them. My attitude about drugs is the same as it is toward drinking, smoking or anything else that is harmful to the body. If it affects your physical performance or your mental alertness, I'm against it.

I don't think a man can be a competent football player if he smokes marijuana frequently. I'm like so many other coaches. I preach against it, talk against it, and hope that I have some effect on them.

Now I'm not naive. Any coach who believes drugs are not a problem is putting his head in the sand. I think almost every youngster in college today has tried some sort of drug, just out of curiosity if nothing else, but I also think there is a tremendous difference between trying it and using it.

I talk with my players more on an individual than a collective basis about drugs, because if you do it collectively it comes out sounding like a speech and there is no quicker way to turn your players off than to stand there and give them a speech—especially coming from a 44-year-old coach who knows little about it, has never had it or even seen it.

The kids know this and so they say to me, "How can you tell me it's wrong when you don't know anything about it?"

They've got me cold and they know it. I grew up in the days when you were breaking training if you drank a beer. Nobody ever heard of marijuana. All of a sudden it came on the scene, and we're confronted with something we don't know anything about.

I try to get to them by saying, "Anything that will hamper your performance can't be good. If you've got to take something to make you feel good, you have a problem. I just can't see a football player doing that. I think it's a cop-out and I can't accept it." You have to get to them eyeball-to-eyeball. One-to-one. Otherwise, they're going to back right off.

I've never really had many kids taking drugs at Michigan, but I've had some evidence of our players trying it. It never got to the point where I had to make a major decision on what to do about it. Usually the kid would eliminate himself and drop from the squad on his own. You have to consider it a problem and treat it as a problem.

Since my players know I'm no expert on marijuana or hard drugs or alcohol, I just tell them, "Why hurt yourself and your performance?" They will argue that marijuana is no more harmful than several beers, and you don't get a headache or hangover. It is pretty compelling logic, if true, but I tell them they would be a lot better off without the beers OR the marijuana.

If my players touch drugs, they're not listening to me and they're breaking my rules, which has an important psychological effect on them. It has to weigh on their consciences, and this is one more diversion from what they're supposed to be thinking about.

I think it's bad for a football player to be seen smoking in public, not only because it's harmful to him physically, but obviously if someone sees a player smoking, the observer can think the worst about what is being smoked.

I admit I am very adamant about cigarette smoking, but I can't help it. I have never seen a single player of mine here at Michigan smoke, and I'd better not because I just won't accept it. Smoking is bad for your health—it says so right on

"Mrs. Jones, I'll tuck your little boy in every night."

"Just because you're wearing shorts, don't think you're on some beach."

the package. If a player is going to be efficient, he'd better be healthy and no way is smoking going to help him perform better.

Take Paul Krasula. He is coaching at the University of Toledo. He was the captain of my 1967 team at Miami, a real tough guy. He came into my office here at Michigan one day, sat down and lit a cigarette. You must understand that he had been out of school for five years.

I looked over at him and barked, "Krasula! Get that cigarette out of your mouth! Throw it in the toilet right now!"

I'll be darned if he doesn't get up and throw it away. Now I was only half kidding, but I just can't take it to have my players smoking in front of me—even my former players. Poor Paul was embarrassed, but he understands me.

Drinking beer is a little different. I still don't like it but I can understand it. That's because I did it and still do. I like an occasional beer. I am not concerned about it if a player goes out on a Saturday night with his girl and has a few beers. But suppose we're losing? Suppose he isn't playing well? How can I defend that player if somebody comes up to me and says he saw so-and-so drinking it up on Saturday night. It's the old story of moderation and sense, and it doesn't make sense when performance or health are affected.

You have to guard against so many things when you're a head coach—even this business of people passing around petitions among your players.

There are people on campuses today who want football players to come out and make a stand for or against something. They're no dummies. They know football players are a little special.

I tell my players one thing: Don't sign anything unless you know what it is. I tell them they're representatives of the football team, but not the whole team. If they sign anything without telling me, I am part of that team and I have nine other coaches who are part of that team and we have a right to know what they are signing in our names. They can do it individually if they want to, but they can't go around my lockerroom getting signatures for something I don't know about. That I won't tolerate.

124

As for girls, they aren't the problem they used to be years ago when you would have to talk to young men about pregnancies maybe two or three times during the year. You have to keep this in its proper perspective. You're talking about nearly a hundred people—a hundred young men—and the incidence of "girl problems" just isn't that high.

I have seen players who wanted to get married while they're in school, and in some cases they chose the right girl and it helped them on the field and in the classroom. I've also seen cases where it's been a disaster. I don't like to generalize, but it seems that it is best for a player to wait until he has completed his final season of football and his education before he gets married. When I first came here, we had as many as 15 married players, but most guys today are more interested in getting their educations and playing football than in getting married.

The black-white question? This is going to sound high-minded, but I don't consider it a problem. I don't even know how many black players I have. Or white ones. I never count them.

I know you're going to have some dissatisfaction among your black players. You are going to have some who think they probably weren't given the right opportunity and maybe they are going to say being black is the reason why. You are also going to find some white players who are going to say the black players had better opportunities than they did. Now what do you do?

This is going to happen on any team. There is no way you are going to please everybody or you would never get anything done. It is just fundamental that some kids are bound to be disappointed about different things. When they're not playing, they've got to have some excuse for it and they have to find a scapegoat. They have to blame somebody else, and naturally it's going to be the coach. You may as well face up to this fact and make the most of it.

I think too many black students have polarized themselves from the whites. I try to avoid this on our team. The only way I can do it is to treat them all alike. I don't go out of my way to mix them up in my dressing room or separate them. If it

125

happens that when we're traveling a white kid is rooming with a black kid, well, he is. I've had certain players with similar backgrounds ask me if they could room together. Fine. I don't object to that. But we just have to go down the line and match them up in order.

Maybe the black players are having different problems than the white players. Maybe it's because they are black, but they still have basic problems and I figure that's my job—to help them solve problems.

So many times I see coaching staffs use a black coach to recruit black players. We don't do that here. We have one black coach on our staff, Tirrel Burton. Tirrel played under Ara Parseghian at Miami and he coached in high school. I had known him for several years and was very impressed with his work. He's a nice guy and a good coach and when I had the chance to get him on my staff, I hired him.

I will never pull Tirrel out of his area to help me recruit a black player because he is black. That would be an insult to him. He goes into white homes and black homes and he recruits players the same as we all do. I don't ask him if his prospects are black or white, but I do say to him the same as I do all the others, "When you bring a kid in here, you better get a kid with good character."

The one thing I'm proud of is that I'm ready and willing to help anyone with his problem. I make this very clear to all my players. Whether it's a black group on campus, a fraternity group, part of the administration on campus, I tell them, "We will solve our own problems. I don't want anyone coming in here talking about our problems."

I don't know how much a football coach can do to help the young people, but I have one policy here and it is that although I help the players as much as I can, the most important people in my program are my assistant coaches. My assistants come first and then come the players. I care very much about both of them.

When you talk about your assistants, you have to be realistic in that you're dealing with men who are directly tied up with your success. They simply have to mean the most to you. You may demand loyalty but you have to give it back to them.

126

It is a two-way street. You work the daylights out of them and they will determine more than anyone else whether you are going to be a success or a failure. They help you make decisions and they do the bulk of the work on the field. You just can't be aloof from them. You have to listen to them when they make suggestions, no matter how far-fetched they may be. You have to believe they are trying to do the best they can to help you have a better program.

Almost all of our recruiting is done within a 300-mile radius of Ann Arbor, so we're able to find out an awful lot about the kids. We talk to their coaches and counselors and people in the community. I learn a lot when I go into the homes of the players. You can tell right away what kind of disciplines they've had in their homes. I've made my share of mistakes but I feel that I can judge young people pretty well. I try to find out about their attitudes about school and football.

To me the first criterion in recruiting is character. You want to get the right type of kid. If you get a kid with good character, he is going to do whatever is necessary to get his degree and remain eligible.

When I go into a home, my assistants have usually been there before me. They've filled them in on all the basic stuff about Michigan. But the kids and parents want to talk more about the schooling than the playing. I've got a great edge because when I tell them about the quality of academics at Michigan it is all true.

I know they're looking at me every minute I'm in their homes, but I don't perform for them. I really don't know what I'm going to say to them. I think it is better to just be honest and say what I feel. I'll get fired up over certain topics, or I just might put my feet on my desk if they come into the office to talk to me. It is just whatever I feel.

Nobody but me gives a grant-in-aid for football around here. I think that's important. The head coach should have the final say on all prospects because he is the man who will have to answer for their performances, both in school and on the field.

I always let my players know I'm the boss. There has to be a boss. But the one absolute rule I have is that I will take time out to talk with a player any time of the day or night if it is important enough to him.

The players are so vitally important. I think a coach today will lose his touch if he becomes too aloof from his players and pays too much attention to things other than coaching. Sometimes being away from the campus can be important because speeches and clinics can mean money to him. But you still have to get your priorities straightened out. But you still decide what is the most important thing to you. With me, it's being here working with my coaches and players.

Say I'm in a staff meeting, and you come by unannounced and my secretary comes in and says, "Joe Falls is outside and he'd like to talk to you." I might come out, but I might not. It all depends on what I'm doing. But if a player comes by, no matter how low he is on our team, my secretary has instructions to tell me if it's important and I will go out and talk to him.

My players know the most precious thing I have is time and if I am willing to give it under any circumstances, I think they know this is the highest compliment I can give them. I can't give them anything else that's worth a nickel, but I can give them my time.

I am probably not what you'd consider a great alumni coach. I understand the importance of alumni and what they can do for you—in fact, what they've done for Michigan—but I put my coaches first and my players second and everything else follows.

All I hear now is how the young people are rebelling against discipline. We give them discipline here and not only do they accept it, they seem to want it. They seem to understand what it's all about—why you have to have it or else you're going to fail.

I have highly disciplined football teams and it's a funny thing, but the players like it. They actually like it. They're proud of it. When we go up against another team that's a little bit loose, they make remarks about it.

Leadership from the seniors helps a great deal. The first point I make with my players is that our leadership has to come from the seniors. They are first here. If they play great football, we are going to win. I tell this to my whole squad. My seniors know they have to produce. They know me by now and they know what I demand. They also know what I think of them. When we fly anywhere, for instance, our seniors sit in the first class section. The rest of us, including Don Canham, sit in the rear of the plane. I wouldn't have it any other way.

I don't think there's been a football player who's come out of Michigan to become successful who can say our program is wrong because it is too tough or too disciplined. If you don't have discipline, you're not going to make it in life.

A football player has to give to get. When you're dealing with numbers as a coach does, you must have certain rules and regulations for everyone. When a meeting is called, you're there on time. When a practice is called, you're there on time. I don't want any player coming late to a meeting who isn't shaking like a leaf. He knows I'm liable to stop the meeting right there and explode on him in front of the whole team. I don't care about his excuse. I want him there when it's time to be there.

I will not hold a bus for anybody. When the time comes to leave, we leave. I will take an airplane off. I will do anything but I will not wait on guys who are straggling in late. If I'm putting a certain amount of fear into them, okay. That's discipline, too.

Tyrant? I don't buy this description of myself because a tyrant really isn't interested in the people around him. I am. My players know I can be tough, but they also know they can call me by my first name. I'm interested in everything about them. When I'm mad, I can turn it on, but I don't stay mad. I just go on the next thing and forget it. If the coach doesn't have discipline then he can never teach it to his players.

I like football players. I like being around them, and if you don't enjoy them you'd better get out of the business. I would ten times rather stand around in a corner talking to four or five of my players at an alumni dinner than shake hands and make small talk with people I don't know.

You see, football is a very special kind of game. It brings different people together and exposes them to one another like few other things in life ever do. Everyone has to bare his soul because you are in such a competitive situation. There is no hiding on a football team, no cop-outs. It's a different challenge all the time; it is tense, it is pressure—and you must try to know everything about every player so you can help him react to these things. You know what you've got to do. Here it is, and all you can say is, "Let's get it done."

Some players may think they're fooling the coaches, but they're not because the coaches know the players like a book. They know who the dedicated ones are and who the groaners and gripers are. It all comes out.

I don't know whether the players like me or not. I think some do and some don't. But I hope they all have respect for the fact that I am trying to better them as individuals and players so that we can all have a better football team. What it boils down to, I guess, is that the guys who are playing the most like me the most.

I'm aware of the other ones—the ones who aren't getting the time they feel they deserve. I know. I was one of them myself when I was a player, and practices are tough on them. They're used as demonstrators, running the opponents' offense or setting up the defense. It's a tough way to go, especially if you're a junior or senior. I try to recognize what these players do. I mention it in our meetings. I try to make them feel as important as I possibly can—because, in their way, they are very important. When we win a championship, we get a championship ring for everybody. The lowest sub—I don't care who he is—is going to get one.

We try to recognize their efforts in practice. We have a "champion of the week" on offense and defense. We also have a "scout champion of the week." This is something I believe in. Everyone, no matter who, has to feel a part of the team. I'll give a sub as much time as I'll give a regular. I know they grumble. I know they gripe. I can't solve all of their problems but I do what I can and I think they all know that I'm a player's coach. I've always been a player's coach.

I will talk with every player on our squad on a personal basis twice a year. After spring practice, I will interview every one. I'll ask them what kind of semester they had academically. I'll evaluate their performances on the field. I'll project how they will contribute in the fall. I'll tell them exactly how I feel about them. I want to know where they'll be in the summer—where they'll be working or what they'll be doing. I write down their addresses so I can find them if I want them. I take a notebook with blank pages in it and I fill it out for each kid. Nobody else is involved. Just myself and the player. We go over everything we can think of. We also do this at the end of each season. It is especially important with the seniors because that's when they need you the most—when they're getting ready to graduate.

You can't even forget about them after they graduate when they can't do you any good anymore. If you did that, you'd be cheap. None of the things you tried to teach them when they were playing for you would mean anything.

One of my favorite players here was Jim Betts. He taught me more than I ever taught him. When I came here, he was a sophomore. He had missed freshman ball because he'd had a knee operation, and then he missed spring practice. Denny Brown was ahead of him as a quarterback and so was Don Moorhead. Jimmy was third and because the Big Ten did not have a red shirt rule, we couldn't hold him out for a year until his knee got stronger. So Bump Elliott played him as a tailback behind Ron Johnson and as a split end and things like that.

When I came here, we put him back at quarterback. He didn't look good since he hadn't played there since his high school days. He was rusty and awkward. Moorhead moved ahead of him.

Jimmy kept plugging away all through his junior year and by the end of the season there really wasn't much to choose from between the two, except Moorhead had more experience.

So now it's his senior year and what it boiled down to is that he would have to go through the same routine of being the second team quarterback or he could try his hand at safety on defense. He wanted to move so he could play and he turned out to be an excellent safety man. This is with no experience, mind you. Jimmy was a class guy, a tough guy, and he wasn't afraid to give. He was respected by the other players. He had a

Bo Reflects About Former Player Jim Betts: *"I love the kid."*

lot going for him.

He was drafted by the New York Jets in the fourth or fifth round and it seemed like he had a bright future ahead of him.

When he was getting ready to graduate, he was a student teacher at one of the schools in Ann Arbor. The kids loved him. Everybody loved him, especially his swimming class. The last day they were going to throw him into the pool, as a going-away present, and when they picked him up, one of the kids grabbed the whistle which was on a stretch band around his neck and when he let go of it, it hit Jim in the eye and he lost the sight of it.

So that's how he went to the Jets' camp—with vision in only one eye. He couldn't run, he couldn't keep his balance, he couldn't do much of anything. Here was a very gifted athlete and something like this had to happen to him.

When the Jets dropped him, Jim came back to campus. He was one player I really enjoyed talking to. He'd come into my office and we'd talk for hours.

Well, he didn't have his degree. I don't know if this is legal or not, but I called the alumni club in Cleveland and said, "Hey, here's a kid who needs help." They went right out and came up with the dough so he could get his diploma.

Jim worked for me on the freshman team and did a fine job. In fact, he worked with Denny Franklin and I used to love the way he'd get on Denny to make him put out. They had a great relationship too.

Jim is married now and he works for Goodyear. He got into their training program and I always kid him about being the first black president of Goodyear. Imagine that, a black, one-eyed president. I love the kid.

Jerry Hanlon:

There are some things about Bo which I don't think people are going to believe—like this business of him being so hung up on his players.

Well, let me tell you one thing. It is true. Absolutely, positively true.

We'll be sitting in a staff meeting trying to get something organized and trying to get ready for the next game and a young man will come by with some problems. Bo will drop everything and go talk to that kid and so there we are, twiddling our thumbs, waiting for him to come back into the room so we can get on with our business. I've seen him do this time after time.

He has a great feeling for young people. He cannot bring himself to lie to them, even if it means losing them when we're trying to recruit them. He just won't do some of the things other coaches will do.

We get on him in the staff meetings about this and say, "Gosh, Bo, these guys are telling this kid he can play as a freshman". . . stuff like that. . .but he won't lie to them. He won't make any promises he can't keep. I guess this is one of the things I admire about him—his absolute honesty.

Of course you must understand that I may be more than a little prejudiced when it comes to talking about Bo. I've been with him for eight years, ever since he hired me out of high school. I've had chances to go elsewhere. I like to think I have the kind of ability that other schools could use, but I've never wanted to leave Bo. We just—well, get along.

He has an intense desire to be successful. But I think you already know that. Coaching is his life and he wants to be a leader in his field. Most successful coaches have this great desire but it seems to be a little more with Bo. I don't know how many of us would do the things he does to be successful. I've often thought about the sacrifices you have to make to be a head coach, the pressure you have to face. Of all the things I have ever said about Bo, the one thing that makes him great in my mind is that he loves his job so much that he will sacrifice a lot of the pleasures of life so he can be successful. I don't know whether I could do it.

Bo's desire is so great that he influences everybody around him. The greatest tribute I can pay him is that I never worry about doing any more than anybody else on the staff. When you get into a situation like that it only reflects one thing—good coaching. If he can get his staff to think that way, then he has done a tremendous job. I think we have one of the strongest staffs in the country, individually and collectively, and it takes an extremely strong person to handle this kind of staff.

He's a funny guy. He's a great organizer but is terrible on details. He forgets things. He'll forget what time it is or where he put something but he'll know exactly how many times we've run the halfback draw in the past week. He loves to meet people and has a great sense of humor. A lot of people don't realize this until they are around him a lot. If you have ever heard him speak at banquets and make the statements he does on the spur of the moment, then you realize the wit and humor he has. Of course, I've been around him so much maybe I notice it more than most people. But he has the capacity to feel what other people feel. Take our assistant coaches. He has a feel for us that I don't think most head coaches have. It's like he never forgot he was an assistant himself.

He gives us responsibility and allows us to carry through with it. He tells you to do something and you do it. He doesn't ask how you are going to do it—only that it gets done. Every little step isn't laid out for you. This gives you a sense of security in your own position and I think is important to a man in any business.

I'm really not surprised he can get the kids to produce for him, I mean, that he can get them to take all that discipline. He gets us older guys to do it, so why shouldn't he be able to do it with the kids? I don't know if I could ever define leadership, but Bo has it.

I know some people think Bo is stubborn. To a degree he is, though I really don't think that's the right term for it. For instance, I'll get into it with him. Maybe it'll be over a bit of strategy—how we should block a certain play. It'll get pretty hot and I'll be pounding on the table and he'll be yelling at me. Sometimes we'll do it his way, sometimes we'll do it my way. The big thing is that we can have these arguments and when we walk out of that room, that's it. It's over.

Bo has calmed down a lot. I don't know if this is because of his heart attack. But he is still intense about his coaching. I think part of his success is that he has changed so little over the years. I've discovered this in talking to the high school coaches. When we were at Miami, he'd go into a high school and sit down and talk to the coaches and spend time with them. Now that he is the coach at the University of Michigan, he does the same thing. I think the coaches really appreciate that in him.

I'll just never forget his heart attack. I was completely shocked. I was probably the first one to recognize it. I think I was.

We were at the monastery the night before the game and Bo always liked to watch the movies with the kids. He liked to sit down with them and be close to them. I happened to be sitting in the back of the room and he kept getting up and leaving. That was unusual. He never did that.

Usually Bo and I sit down in his room and talk a little about what we're going to do the next day. But now when I go into his room, I've got my notebook with me and I open it up and I start to go over some things, and I look up and he's already undressed and he's in bed.

I say, "What's the matter? Don't you feel good?"

He said, "I don't feel too good. Can we talk in the morning?"

I know that's not Bo at all. The next morning I went to Mass with Dr. O'Connor and as we were coming out of Church, I told him I didn't think Bo looked very good.

I said, "He's just not acting like Bo Schembechler."

I'll tell you, it was really rough without him at the game. We tried to figure out what we would do—I mean, offensively and defensively—and we decided we would keep it as much the same with Bo as possible. That meant me going to the press box and calling the plays and Chuck (Chuck Stobart) working with the information on the sidelines.

I don't think we really called that bad a game. It was a heck of a football game—a tough one all the way. I don't know if the play calling influenced the final outcome, but the big thing was that without Bo being there we didn't have our guiding influence. We didn't have anyone saying, "All right, we're going to do this or we're going to do that." Not that we were arguing or anything—oh, how can I put it?—but there was more indecision that you'd normally have in a situation

136

like that.

I would say on the phone, "Let's try such and such a play." Chuck would say, "Good, let's try it." Then I would ask him, "What do you think we should try?" It was a matter of communication and you know if they ask you enough times what you are going to do, you begin saying to yourself, "I don't know for sure." I mean, you can't give them any written guarantees that a certain thing is going to work or not. That's how we missed Bo.

I know his absence really affected the mental attitude of the kids. I have never seen so many of them cry at the same time. We had to decide what to tell them. We didn't know how to approach it—to say he was just taken ill and wouldn't be at the game or what. But we knew the kids knew Bo and if he wasn't there, they'd know it was something very, very serious. We'd never been in a situation like this before, so we tried to explain that Bo had been taken ill. I think we said there was a possibility he'd had a heart attack. They were completely stunned.

We were all in a meeting room at the monastery and as we left to get on the bus, some of the kids broke into tears and some walked across the walkway to the chapel to say a prayer for Bo.

It had such a sobering effect on everyone. Here were the kids and they should have been doing one of the most joyful things in their lives—to play in a Rose Bowl—when all of a sudden they are hit with something like this. It was like saying, "Your father is ill."

You could see the change in them. It was difficult for any of them. . .any of us. . .to keep our mind on the game. Everybody had said that this should have been a great inspiration to the team—to go out there and try to win the game for Bo. But it happened at the wrong time. If it would have happened the day before the kids would have had a chance to digest it and say, "Hey, Bo's ill. Let's go out and get it for him." Then maybe it would have inspired them. Now, just two hours before the game, it was an entirely different situation. They couldn't digest what was happening and it had a very bad effect on them.

You see, we didn't want to come right out and say that Bo had had a heart attack. For one thing, we weren't completely sure of it—although all the signs pointed to it. But we were concerned about his family, that they might hear the news on the radio or television as they were coming out to the game. That would have been too much for them to take.

The guy had to go through an awful lot—more than many people know. You know when he had those pains in his chest when he got back to coach—well, they lasted into the fourth game of the season and I know he was getting very frightened by them. It was that hernia which was causing the discomfort but I guess Bo couldn't be absolutely sure and I'd see him in the dressing room sitting there sipping on that skimmed milk.

But along about the fifth game, he started barking at me when things were going wrong. I loved hearing it. I knew then he was getting better and was going to be fully recovered.

The Ghost Speaks:

This chapter gave us the most trouble of all. Bo touched on many subjects, and many of them were touchy subjects. Drugs. Girls. The black-and-white question. Smoking. Drinking. Protesting.

He said: "I don't like this chapter at all."

I said: "What don't you like about it?"

He said: "I just don't like it."

Bo was being a big help at this point.

I knew I would have to rewrite it, so I sat down with him a second time and we went over all the same subjects. He said almost the same things.

I didn't let him know that—that he was repeating himself. I just let him talk. I tried to incorporate some of the new things he said but it still wasn't working to his satisfaction.

He began complaining to other people about it—like to Don Canham, who, in turn, mentioned it to Gail Green, the gal who runs School-Tech Press.

The truth is, Gail, a frustrated journalist, rewrote this chapter. . .because one of the most difficult things to do in the writing business is to rewrite yourself. You see things one

138

way and it's hard to convince yourself this is not the right way. But Gail—bless her—took the time to do it herself.

I mention this for one reason.

I am convinced that Bo didn't dislike the chapter so much for the way it was written but because of what he had to say. He did not feel in full command of himself when he got around to talking about drugs.

Smoking, he could understand. He's done that himself. Drinking, he could understand. He has an occasional drink. Even the black-and-white question he could get with.

But he'd never tried any drugs, and when he attempted to speak to his players about it, he knew he was not speaking from strength.

He finally admitted to me one day: "The players know I've never taken any drugs. They know I really don't know what I'm talking about because I've never tried them myself. Dammit, that bothers me."

Bo is a man who likes to be in complete control of everything he does. This is one time when he has to go by the book and not by his own personal experience.

It kills him, but at least he is honest enough to admit it.

Bo Asks Tight End Jim Mandich, *"If that looks so easy, why didn't you do it last Saturday?"*

"We don't run the ball ALL the time", says Quarterback
Dennis Franklin.

Chapter 9

Mr. Schembechler,
Why Do You Run the Ball All the Time?

One of the big words in my profession is "philosophy." With me, I guess it means: Why do I run so much?

My buddy here, Mr. Falls, thinks I'm a stubborn man—that I fix my mind to run the ball and nothing is going to change my mind.

Well, I have some very definite reasons for doing what we do. You see, our whole strategy is a little different than some people's.

We are going to base our football first on a strong defense. That's number one. The second thing we are going to do is move the football on the ground. By moving the football on the ground, we can have a better opportunity to maintain control of the ball.

I can't build a defense unless I can attack that defense where it is the most vulnerable. What I'm saying is, the toughest thing for a defense to stop is the run. Now if I am a passing team, there is no way I can build a successful defense unless my own team can attack my defense by running the ball. We play against each other far more than we play our opponents— spring and early fall. That's where you put your team together.

Alright, so my thinking is—strong defense, strong running and passing third. We don't think we can live without passing. But if you don't have a good passing attack, you can get by. Take 1971. We lived without a passing game and lost only once—by one point to Stanford in the Rose Bowl. We were so good that year that we sat right here in this office and said this is the first time we are going through a season without passing.

I don't believe you should try to do something that you can't do just because this is what you ought to do. We stressed defense first and running second. We had two of the three. If we couldn't get that third one, why try for it and make yourself mediocre in the other two departments? So we said the hell with it.

My assistants didn't hassle me about this. I listen to what they have to say because they're a bunch of sharp guys. But what we did in 1971 was the culmination of all our thinking.

We started out that fall by throwing the ball some. We just squeaked by Northwestern, 21-7. We felt, why kid ourselves—if you can't do it, you can't do it. It isn't like pro football. If we needed a passing attack, we would have traded for it. But this isn't necessary in college ball.

Basically, I would like to be the type of team that is ⅔ or ¾ running and ⅓ or ¼ passing. But if I can't achieve this balance, I can always fall back on my running.

Here's the thing about passing in college ball: Let's say I have a super dropback passer and he is hitting receivers all over the place. We develop a great passing attack. Now he graduates. Unless we have another dropback passer with a good throwing arm, I am going to have a tough time with my offense. I cannot attack my defense in the spring or fall because I can't run. I can't stop the option play—and that's the toughest thing about college football, containing the option play.

Secondly, I have to go to my backfield men and my linemen and say, "All right, you guys. We have been sitting here dropping back and protecting the passer. Now you've got to get down there and knock them off the line of scrimmage."

You don't do this overnight. This is something which has to be inbred in your system. The first thing an offensive lineman at Michigan knows is that when you get down there in that three-point stance, you get your weight forward and you go on the count and you fire out. You blow them off there—you hit them in the middle. You get your legs up and you go. You get tough and you go and you go and you develop this technique until you can move the other team out of there.

But you can't do this if the ball is being snapped and three-fourths of the time you are dropping back chicken fighting some guy.

I am coaching a system of football I think you can win with. I can change from the Wishbone to the Power-I to the I formation or even to a split back option attack. The basic theory is that those linemen up there are blowing off the line of scrimmage and attacking the defense.

The most demoralizing thing you can do to another football team is to first-down them to death. That kills them. It is one thing to get a quick touchdown—you can explain that away and come back to play again—but when one team is methodically jamming the ball down the other team's throat, that has a great demoralizing effect on that team. Physically, you have moved the football on them. That's a shattering experience.

Actually, our offense is lots more complicated than most people envision. You see, much of our variations are in blocking. Why kid about it. How many fans understand blocking technique or even want to find out about it?

We have a very intricate blocking scheme which is even hard to teach. It takes a lot of time to teach our system. One play may look like another play, but the blocking is entirely different. So what looks simple, isn't. Our offense isn't what you would call simple at all. It is very complex.

Our defense is the same way. That's why we always have to be on our toes and doing a lot of coaching. We have to make absolutely sure everybody is carrying out their own assignment.

The key is defense and I don't think you can win championships without defense.

If we have the skill to pass, we'll pass. We did it when Don Moorhead was here and look how many of the Michigan passing records he broke in the two years he played for me. So don't tell me I am afraid to throw the ball.

It is not easy to run the ball. It takes a lot of effort. We run a play until we reach near perfection. I want perfection but I know we're not going to get it so we try to come as close as we can. You can run a play for six weeks, a hundred times a week, but when it breaks out of there and gets you a first down or a touchdown, you are happy and it is worth all the effort. You have accomplished something.

One thing I really get uptight about are fumbles. You've seen me pull players off the field when they fumble the ball. This isn't done indiscriminately. In 1972, I pulled one of our players when he dropped the ball early in the game. But I knew he was a super kid and it wouldn't hurt his confidence. I was trying to prove a point to some of the other players. But you take someone like Chuck Heater—he dropped the ball but I kept him in there. I didn't want to hurt his confidence. It all depends on the individual.

Fumbles can be physical but we don't accept that. We accept fumbles only as mistakes and carelessness. You check it. Most of your fumbles are carelessness. I'm not saying a guy can't be hit as he's taking the handoff and drop the ball. That happens. But there is no way you can tell me that if you carry the ball properly. . .and concentrate on carrying it properly. . .that you should be dropping it all over the place. Winning football is the achievement of near perfection.

Not only do you have to teach your players, but you have to motivate them. That's a big word in my profession—motivation. I've read books on it. But you've got to get them to do the job—you've got to keep them interested and striving for that near perfection.

What we do here at Michigan is set goals in every manner possible. We have individual goals, team goals, offensive goals and defensive goals. In fact, we have a pretty intricate awards system. I got most of them when I hired Jim Young out of high school. I never coached in high school but he came in with his awards system and I like the idea. It is not exactly the way we do it now, but the basis of it is there.

Take our Victors Club, for instance. A player earns the right to be in the Victors Club on a week to week basis as a result of his performance on the practice field and in the games.

For example, he can't miss three practices in a row for any reason. A linebacker will have to make so many tackles and so many assists—we're talking about the game now—and if he reaches that number, he earns a place in the Victors Club. We determine this every Sunday—who goes in the Victors Club and who comes out. We put a huge board up in the dressing room with their names on it. We have the names printed up in plastic. When the players come in on Monday, that's the first thing they look at—to see if their name is on the board.

"I told you a million times, Slade, if I wanted a pass, I'd call for a pass."

We have another board next to that one and it's called Champions of the Week. We've got three categories on that one—the outstanding offensive player of the week, the outstanding defensive player and the outstanding scout team player. That last one gives the down-the-line guy a chance to get some recognition for himself. All these players get a certificate of merit from the coaching staff. I also give them a trophy and they get to keep the trophy. No steak dinners or anything like that but if you are in the Victors Club eight out of the eleven weeks, then you receive a very large trophy indicating you are a member of the Victors Club.

If you think this sounds a little silly, I should tell you about some of the players who come storming into my office wondering why their names aren't up on the board or why their names have been taken down. It's very important to them. That's because everyone can see who we think is doing the job and who isn't.

I've seen 'em come in on Monday and say, "I gotta keep my string going on the big board." Or they'll say, "I've got to get my name back up on that board."

Another thing we do is that the guys who are in the Victors Club get special jerseys to wear in practice. It has a Wolverine on it and the words "Victors Club" are written on it. The rest of the guys wear regular jerseys.

We had a fellow named Pete Newell who played defensive tackle for us in the 1969 and '70 season. He played in 21 football games at Michigan and made the Victors Club in every game. He is the only guy who has ever done that.

I think the merit system is good. We all like to be recognized for what we do and this is our way of letting the players know what we think of their efforts.

So this is my philosophy. I suppose you can question what we do since we lost our last game the first four years we were here—two to Ohio State and two in the Rose Bowl.

I look at it this way: I lost to Southern California, 10-3; I lost to Ohio State 20-9; I lost to Stanford, 13-12; and I lost to Ohio State, 14-11. I was in every damn football game I played, and with a little more, I could have won all of them.

I don't want this to go into the book, but we may have to

finesse them a little more in 1973. We may have to open up a little more but we have the guy to do it with—quarterback Denny Franklin.

Denny Franklin:

People are always asking me, "What's it like to play at Michigan?" I don't remember how many schools were after me, but it was a pretty good number. My final decision was between USC and Michigan. I remember coach Schembechler telling me I had a scholarship to Michigan and I could go beyond the first signing date to make up my decision. He was the only coach in the Big Ten to tell me that.

I think Ohio State was rushing me a little. I think I can relate more to Bo than I could to coach Hayes. He is younger and I think he knows a little more about my lifetime. If you have a problem, you can go to coach Schembechler and talk to him about it. He will give you advice and help you out.

We got along right from the start. He knows he had power and he was trying to instill that power into me. He is powerful and down to earth and I think that is important. He is the type of person who can inspire you.
Coach Schembechler made no promises to me—no guarantees. All he said is that I would get an opportunity to show what I could do. I believed him.

I was afraid of USC. They had Pat Haden out there, a quarterback from California. He and Coach McKay's son made All-America together. That isn't what scared me. It was their relationship. McKay's son was a receiver and Haden was the quarterback and they were living together. I figured how can I go way out there and try to beat out somebody who not only is good but already is tight with the coach and the coach's son. That'd been ridiculous.

Here, at Michigan, I didn't even know who played quarterback. I didn't care. Coach Schembechler promised me a chance and that's all I wanted. You won't believe it, but he talked first about my schooling, then about football.

Coach Schembechler expects a lot out of you. But that's the only way you can win. He keeps you on your toes and I guess he'd pick on me more if I wasn't so inexperienced.

I've been yelled at a couple of times—a couple of times when I thought I was right, too. I remember once at Iowa I was running an option play where I was supposed to read the defensive end and decide what to do. Well, I flipped the ball back. . .because that's what I read. . .and I could see him jumping up and down over on the sidelines.

When I got to the bench, he said, "You're supposed to keep the ball." I told him I didn't read it that way but he kept yelling.

When we looked at the film, he kind of said, "I could see what you were thinking"—no outright apology or anything but he let me know he could see my way.

I would like to pass a little more and sometimes I question this run-first, pass-second theory. You see, I don't know football like he does, so I don't know if my opinion means all that much. But I always thought you passed the ball first because you are trying to establish a score and take control of the game. If you pass early and get a couple of touchdowns, then you can run the ball to eat up the clock. But if you run first, which takes time, and don't get anywhere, then there isn't much time left to pass and you are left in a pressure situation where they know you're going to throw the ball.

I never said any of this to Coach Schembechler, but. . .

The Ghost Speaks:

Yes, I think Bo Schembechler is a stubborn man. He will do things his own way, and if you don't like it, that's too bad.

I would like to him pass more.

I would like to see him open up more.

I think sometimes he traps himself with his own stubbornness. I don't think he should back himself into a corner where his hard-headed ways hurt his career.

In other words, if he's got to throw a little razzle-dazzle at them to get the job done, he ought to be able to do it. Why let the other coaches ever get an edge on him?

But look at his record.

I can criticize his methods but not his results.

That's what Bo Schembechler is all about. He is his own man. For this, I admire him.

Joe Falls
Sports Editor

Win Over Purdue
Is Michigan's Best

Mid-November, 1971   LAFAYETTE

It'll seem chintzy to the rest of the country — mighty Michigan restorting to a dinky field goal in the final minute of play to remain among the nation's unbeaten football giants.

The pollsters certainly aren't going to be impressed with the Wolverines' last-minute victory over Purdue. Give them scores like 61-7 and 63-7. That's what makes them go ga-ga. Points, points, points . . . and more points.

It matters not how you win the games but how you make the scoreboard lights blink.

Yet, when this whole ordeal is over with and Bo Schembechler is sitting around the fire in his den in Ann Arbor this winter . . . you do sit down once in a while, don't you, Bo? . . . He may reflect back on this afternoon in Ross Ade Stadium as the finest moment his team knew all season long.

Michigan had to play football on this bright autumn day, hard, tough, demanding football. No adding machine this time. Just muscle and blodd and guts and poise . . . plenty of poise. A break, too, a colossal break, but that's part of the game.

The Wolverines had to have all of this to win and the big thing is that they had it when they needed it. It is one thing to frolic into the end zone against the hapless Hoosiers and Hawkeyes but it was something else trying to get it done against these Boilermakers.

Itis no great accomplishment for a team to roll in the early going, when bodies are strong and minds are fresh. But only the good ones can get it together at the end of a contest that was as roughly played as this one.

This is the mark that Schembechler has put on this team. The Wolverines did not get the touchdown they wanted to win it like champions. They had to settle for Dana Coin's field goal from the 15-yard line with just 43 seconds to play.

Bo's Kind of Football

But don't overlook the fact that the Wolverines had to go 60 tough yards with the clock running against them o put the ball in position for the winning kick.

As they moved with poise and power, you could only think of all those dark evenings on the practice field with Schembechler screaming at his players and running his offense plays over and over and over, until stomachs hurt, bodies ached and dark mutterings could be heard from the players.

This is Bo's kind of football and it is a tribute to the coach and the players that they had the strength and the savvy to put it together and keep it together in those final four minutes. These things don't happen by accident. You get them only one way — by hard work.

It can be a frightening experience playing Purdue on its home field. Traditionally the Boilermakers are not one of the great teams in the Big Ten. But they have had the ability to rise to some fantastic heights here and pull off stunning upsets. Just ask Duffy Daugherty about it. Or Ara Parseghian. These men have known the grief of playing Purdue at Purdue.

And so it seemed that another upset might be in the making. The Boilermakers, who yielded 698 yards to Michigan State only two weeks ago, were a very inspired football team. They broke takcles, they smothered Billy Taylor in the early going and they forced the Wolverines to earn every yard they gained.

They had the scoring touch and they had the crowd behind them. The place was rocking and reeling all afternoon.

The fans were smelling blood, too.

The Wolverines were sluggish at the start. They seemed overconfident. They were tackling poorly and making uncommon mistakes on offense. If you can believe it, they were even throwing the ball in an effort to get something working.

The Purdue band was playing: "Who's Afraid of the Big, Bad Wolves?" And when the teams left the field at halftime, with Michigan holding a slight 10-7 lead, the fans gave the Boilermaker players a standing ovation.

They had done a tremendous job against the No. 3 team in the land—a team picked by 21 poonts to win this game.

No Panic for U-M

But there was no panic, no alarm-sounding, on the Michigan side of the field. Schembechler kept calling the plays that had worked all season—the fullback drive by Ed Shuttleworth, sweeps by Glenn Doughty and then, finally, Taylor slashing over the tackles, breaking free and making important yardage.

The Wolverines had to survive a startling 66-yard touchdown pass by Purdue and a 34-yard field goal which tied up the score early in the final period.

But look back on the whole game and there were the Wolverines hammering 49 yards in 14 plays, 83 yards in 10 plays and, ultimately, moving from their own 38 to the Purdue two to get into range for the winning field goal.

Who is this Tom Slade who plays quarterback? He is a sophomore who doesn't play like a sophomore. He plays with the control of a seasoned senior.

Bo calls the plays but this young man gets them going.

It was a game of s h a t t e r i n g breaks and late in the day Schembechler al but turned blue over one of the decisions. He slammed his cap to the ground and screamed at the officials . . . and anyone who remembered Pasadena two years ago had to hold his breath as the Michigan coach ranted on in such anger.

But the fire went out quickly. In moments Bo was back on the phone to his agents in the pressbox, plotting and planning the final drive which resulted in victory.

When it was over, a final thought occured. You wondered what might have happened in Pasadena two years ago if this man had not been stricken by his heart attack.

The Wolverine team could have gone either way that day. It could have played inspired football without its leader or it could have fallen apart. It fell apart.

That's what this man means to this team. He is the boss, ruler and dictator. You may not approve of his ways but it is hard to argue with his results.

149

Joe Falls
Sports Editor

U-M Games Dull?
Not This One!

November 19, 1972   ANN ARBOR

It wasn't dull. And it certainly wasn't boring. What it was was scary.

Scary and exciting.

Just like a year ago, the Michigan football team was pushed to the limit by Purdue before winning on a last-minute field goal . . . and again it makes you wonder about the way football is played around here.

In fact, it's almost like we're seeing a taped replay of the 1971 season.

For two straight seasons, Michigan rolled over everyone in sight through the first nine weeks, winning by scores of 56-0, 61-7 and 63-7 one year and 41-7, 42-0 and 31-0 the next year.

And, for two straight seasons the Wolverines ran into Purdue and had to huff before they could pull the game out.

So you have to wonder:

1—Are we being fooled by Michigan playing so many soft teams early in the year?

2—Or is this a team that does what it must to win?

It is probably a little of each. We probably have become deluded by the way the Wolverines run over patsies. We probably expect too much when the Wolverines run up against a team with the talent of Purdue.

But let's never lose sight of the fact that the important thing is not how you play the game but whether you win or lose . . . and so far you have to be impressed with the results Bo Schembechler has been getting around here.

Even though he may try men's souls with his conservative approach to the game of football, he has been a master in the games played in the Michigan Stadium.

The 9-6 squeaker over Purdue was Bo's 22nd straight victory at home and not even Woody Hayes can make such a statement.

The problem is — the point Bo still must prove — is that his brand of football can win all the games, and coming up now is another test in Columbus, and, possibly, the ultimate test in Pasadena.

Boilermakers Were Daring

Bo hasn't made it all the way.

But, for this season, you have to say so far, so good.

Purdue was the best team the Wolverines have faced this season. That was evident right from the start, the way the Boilermakers came out with such abandon and starting moving the ball around on the Wolverines.

Purdue was passing on first down. The Boilermakers were, hitting dangerous sideline passes. They were running Otis Armstrong on some smart delays and, in general, paying little regard to Michigan's reputation.

The Wolverines just couldn't seem to get going. It got as frustrating as last year's game in West Lafayette, or the Ohio State game here, which the Wolverines squeezed out, 10-7, or the Rose Bowl game, which they lost to Stanford, 13-12.

They just didn't seem able to adapt to the conditions. They kept trying to punch it out and couldn't.

Schembechler changed his tactics at the start of the second half. He had to. His ways weren't working.

So his team came out and threw an end-around at Purdue. It didn't work, but it was an admission by Bo that his other strategy wasn't working either.

In two plays, quarterback Denny Franklin put the Wolverines in business. He hit Bo Rather for a 20-yard gain in a tough third-down situation and then, in another touchy third-down spot, he lofted a long one to Clint Haslerig which carried 52 yards.

It didn't exactly prove that Michigan has a passing game because after Franklin's 11-yard strike to Paul Seal for the touchdown, the Wolverines had trouble when they tried to go back to the air.

U-M Got the Big Break

However, the point is that these Wolverines had it when they needed it—maybe not a whole lot, but enough, and don't overlook the fact they were up against a very good football team. Even though Purdue's record is no better than 5-5 for the season, the Boilermakers are as dangerous as most teams around today. They have an awful lot of talent.

When it got near the end and the Wolverines needed a break, they got it when Randy Logan picked off Gary Danielson's pass to give Michigan the ball on its own 42 and set the Wolverines in motion to drive back for the winning TD.

So they were favored by 13½ points and won by three, but they made the plays when they had to. There was Logan's interception, then a great run by Franklin for 19 yards and another brilliant effort of 22 yards by Chuck Heater.

These were clutch plays, made when the Wolverines had to have them, and until somebody can prove otherwise, it makes this a pretty good football team.

Schembechler gets credit on this day if for no other reason than the way he called the play for Michigan's only touchdown.

It was a pass play off an unbalanced line which completely fooled the Purdue team. Seal was all alone in the end zone when he caught the ball. The play was an example of Schembechler's thoroughness.

He put the play in during fall practice and they practiced it nine straight weeks without using it. He set it up for just a situation as the one which arose against Purdue.

And — most important — when his players tried it, they made it work.

"I promised them it would give them a touchdown one day," Schembechler chortled with understandable pride.

Now Bo is down to the end again and again his whole season hangs in the balance of what he does against Ohio State and possibly Southern Cal.

That might not seem fair. When a man wins 10 straight games that should insure him of success. But Schembechler has spoiled a lot of people by setting such a high standard around here.

He has been winning so much that he is expected to win everything. Anything less is a disappointment.

Remember when an 8-2 season or a 7-3 season was considered a success at Michigan? No more. Bo has created a monster for himself and he must keep feeding it . . . or else he'll be devoured.

*"Well it's just too *%@†$! windy to pass today."*

Bo Checking Wind Currents Before Game

"Neither sun, nor rain, nor snow, nor gloom of day shall keep this currier from the swift completion of his appointed rounds."

Billy Taylor (42) Heads for Winning Touchdown Against Ohio State in 1971 as Larry Cipa (13) Blocks and Fritz Seyferth (32) Runs Interference

152

". . . Nor did they."

Billy Taylor Triumphantly Dances Down the Field After Scoring Winning Touchdown

Our Boy, Bo Schembechler's ingrained German Stubborness almost did him in Saturday.

Almost.

But in the end. . .the very end. . .he bent just enough and Michigan pulled out a 10-7 victory over Ohio State in probably the most emotional game played in the big stadium since. . .well, what year was it that Ron Kramer got kicked out of the game and the Michigan followers pelted the Ohio State team with a barrage of snowballs?

Or was it the year—Bump Elliott's first as coach—when Woody Hayes blew his top over losing and began throwing chairs, kicking the down markers around and tossing his baseball cap all over the place?

No matter.

For absolute frenzy, this one topped them all.

Hayes was a raging madman at the end of this one. Scarlet and Gray? He turned Scarlet and Purple. The Ohio State coach, who has been known for some rather volatile sideline behavior, lost complete control of himself and had to be restrained by his own players and coaches.

Maybe he had good reason. It'll be interesting to find out what the films show on Tom Darden's interception. Did he climb all over the Ohio receiver's back? Did he interfere? As sure as God made Little Brown Buckeyes, Hayes will have a word or two about the play after he looks at it in his screening room.

Or is that "screaming" room.

It'll all be academic, however, because it's not likely they'll change the call. It would be difficult to get the 22 players out on the field again, not to mention the 104,016 spectators in the stands.

Woody Had Half a Team

It'll stand forever in the books as a three-point victory for Michigan—possibly the toughest three-point victory this shool has ever attained.

It should have been no contest. Woody came here with half a team. He came in with a defense and Tom Campana. That was all.

But it was almost enough to turn it all around and pull off one of the most shocking upsets in the history of this long and heated rivalry.

Michigan made mistakes, many mistakes. The Wolverines were favored by 14 points and hoped to run it up on Woody for past favors bestowed on them in Columbus. But they just didn't look like a team of great power.

Not like the No. 3 team in the land.

And certainly not like the No. 2 and No. 1 team, either.

Bo kept playing it straight. Straight ahead. Bang. bang. bang. bang. bang. He kept trying to ram the ball down the Ohio State throats.

Shuttlesworth up the middle. ...Taylor off tackle. . . Doughty over the guards.

It was dull, drab football for 55 minutes—not wh you'd expect from a team which had displayed the aw some power the Wolverines had in some of their earli games.

The big crowd watched silently, restlessly. Murmu began in the press box. "Come on, Bo. . .open it u Come on, Bo, get it going."

It was an amazing performance on the part of t Michigan coach. He kept calling the fullback smas Stubborn? Yes. He'll always be stubborn. But—and th is what it was ultimately all about—he also displaye great confidence in his team.

He felt that somehow, some way, his players wou summon the strength to pull this one out, just as they ha the previous week in Lafayette.

And he was right.

But he had to bend a little.

Finally, the Razzle-Dazzle

After staying on the inside through almost all of t first 55 minutes, he ordered some razzle-dazzle—or what razzle-dazzle in his play book.

He actually began going to the outside. He even put t ball into the air. It was not exactly a case of panic, b even Bo was admitting that his conservative style wasn getting the job done.

So, in their finest moment of the season, the Wolve ines went 72 yards in 11 plays to win it. Billy Tayl cleared the end (behind a tremendous block by Fritz Se ferth) with the winning touchdown with just 2:07 to play.

Four of the 11 plays went to the outside, and twice th ball was put into the air. It was Bo's boldest moment—an his best.

His detractors—and there'll be more than ever now will point to all the problems Michigan had in its last tw games. But don't overlook one item:

These games are still 60 minutes in duration. Thos final five can be more important than the first 55.

Or as Bo was saying in the tumult of the dressing roon "An 11-0 record isn't bad."

It is a tribute to the man's ability that his team had again in the clutch. They pay him to win, and that what he has done in these three short years at Michigan.

Maybe these aren't the Mad Magicians of old, but a long as you keep scoring more points than the other tear not too much else really matters. It's not likely there wa an unhappy fan in the house.

In his time as the boss, Schembechler has won 25 game and lost only four. He has outscored the opposition by walloping margin of 1,047 to 308. And, most importan he is now 2-1 against Duffy Daugherty and 2-1 agains Woody Hayes.

All that is left—and can there be any real doubt abou it now—is a victory in the Rose Bowl. It's hard to se how Stanford, which couldn't handle San Jose State, ca offer too much of a problem to Bo's boys.

He won't be No. 1, as he'd like—not unless Nebrask and Oklahoma play a scoreless tie on Thanksgiving Day And even Bo isn't looking for that.

"It could be a tie, but it won't be scoreless," he said.

Actually, Bo can thank Tom Campana for that stunning 85-yard punt return which put Ohio State into the lead Imagine what his critics would have been saying if he had come up with no better than a 3-0 victory.

Now they all have a comeback victory to savor. It'l be a nice, warm winter around here.

(This Column Reproduced)

Chapter *10*

Bandages, Bruises and Bluegills

Lindsay McLean:

I've been the trainer of the Michigan football team since 1968. Bump Elliott hired me before the start of his last year, so I've seen the transition from Bump to Bo. It's been, shall we say, a unique experience.

You know Bump. He was a very relaxed person. He had that nice-guy image and it carried right into the training room. He was always at ease in here with us, and we were at ease with him.

Now Bo Schembechler takes over. It's a whole new deal and, frankly, it scared the pants off me.

For example, in one of our first scrimmages, Jim Mandich gets hit late on a pass play and he gets up slugging the guy. It was Barry Pierson. I guess this story is well known around here but Bo runs over and raps Mandich on the helmet and throws him off the field.

I shuddered when I saw that. I didn't think our guys were ready for this kind of discipline. I thought there might be some kind of rebellion against Bo. We didn't have that much depth and I was nervous. I knew we couldn't afford to lose any players for any reason.

Bo was so different from Bump. He wanted to know the exact details on everything, and I knew he was questioning my ability as a trainer. Why kid about it. He was wondering if I had the ability to decide whether a guy should play or not. I knew he was greatly concerned about this because at that time Michigan had the image of soft, rich guys who weren't very tough. Bo was tough. He was that hungry, hardnosed country-type of guy who pushed hard all the time. I remember people telling me he was never going to work out at Michigan.

The players were scared of Bo, especially the freshmen and sophomores. He intimidated them with his go-go-go ways and he was so tough that we actually had some guys who weren't reporting injuries or were afraid to say they were hurt. They knew that would create a touchy situation between the trainer and the coach and they didn't want to get into it.

I remember once Reggie McKenzie had a pinched nerve all through spring practice. He had a muscle weakness in his neck and Dr. O'Connor said he wasn't supposed to practice. Reggie was one of those sophomores who was wary of Bo. He was all excited about playing here and he would go out on the field every day. Bo knew he wasn't supposed to practice but all of a sudden he calls over to him one day and says: "Are you all right, Reggie?" Reggie says, "Yeah, coach, I'm okay". . .and with that he snaps on his chinstrap and rushes out on the field.

I go right out after him. He is getting into the huddle and there I am behind him grabbing him. I tell him, "Get off this field, you hear me!"

This is the first time I'd had any direct confrontation with Bo. I didn't know what to think. I didn't know what to expect. But Bo didn't argue with me. He let me take McKenzie off the field.

I think that's where it turned around between us. I think Bo had a little more respect for me after that. As time passed, he began coming into the trainer's room and talking to myself and Dr. O'Connor about our injuries. He asked about McKenzie's injury and Dr. O'Connor explained to him, very carefully, why Reggie shouldn't be playing. Bo listened just as carefully, and then went along with the doctor.

We have certain rules here at Michigan. Some schools will let some players play with certain injuries, such as pinched nerves or certain fractures. Dr. O'Connor will not allow that. He doesn't want any of our guys suffering permanent damage.

So now you should see Bo. If we get any of these injuries he is right into the trainer's room and he's looking at the x-rays and studying the charts, just like he is a doctor himself. That's

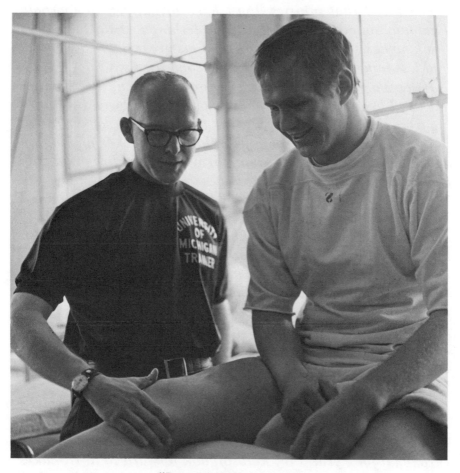

"Does BO think it hurts?"

Trainer Lindsy McLean with 1969 Team Member Bob Baumgartner

really great because he wants to learn as much as he can about injuries. You might even call him a "trainer's coach." He is forever calling his "summit" conferences—Dr. O'Connor, our equipment man, Ron Pulliam, and myself.

I've worked with some coaches who consider injuries as freaks of nature and let it go at that. They figure nothing can be done about it. Not Bo. He questions every injury we have and he is convinced that injuries don't have to happen in football. That may sound strange but it is something he truly believes. I think he has something. Because of his great interest we have had less injuries in the past few seasons than we've ever had.

He puts a great deal of emphasis on equipment. I remember one day I heard this awful racket out in the hallway. It is coming from the equipment room. It's the freshman locker room. Bo is in there and he's going from locker to locker picking up shoulder pads, examining them, throwing them down in a pile. He is saying "I don't want this junk on any of my players!" What can the equipment man do? He tells Bo he is on a limited budget and is doing the best he can with it but Bo isn't ready to accept any of this. He stands there and keeps pitching the stuff into the pile. He wants the best for his players—the very best. From this standpoint, he is ideal to work with.

Bo conditions his players far more than any other coach I have ever worked for. You look at it and say he is doing too much—that he's overdoing it. In fact, he is almost sadistic in his off-season conditioning programs. That's one of the things that scared me in the beginning. I thought he was going too far with it.

But you talk to the athletes, the ones who have been involved in his program, the ones who have programs at other schools, and they come to appreciate Bo's ways. Once they've been through it for a year, they kind of look forward to it. It makes them feel better and they know it makes them better ball players.

In the beginning, they feared him. There may have been even a little hate in there. But there was always respect. They came to understand what he was trying to do, and they even began to feel superior to other teams who weren't in as good a shape.

Bo is a unique guy to work for, all right. One fall we had a rash of the flu. . .temperatures of 101 and 102 and 103 and sore throats and things like that. It happened at a critical time, just as Bo was putting the team together, and so we had one of our summit meetings. This time it was Bo, myself, Dr. O'Connor and Dr. Anderson. We sat down and talked it out. Bo said he wasn't letting anybody out of practice just because they had the sniffles or because they weren't feeling well.

He said: "That's been done here in the past and we're just not going to do it anymore. They're going to have to learn to play with a little discomfort."

He said he would leave it to us what constitutes really being sick and so we decided if there was any swelling in the lymph glands, chest congestion or temperatures over 100 degrees, this would automatically rule a player out of practice.

Bo said: "Okay, the three-point figure is our guideline—a guy has a hundred degrees and he is out."

Well, that's when we had this rash of viruses. It hit all of a sudden. First it was Bruce Elliott. Then it was our tackles. They were calling me in the middle of the night. They were calling me in the morning. It was spreading everywhere.

I kept reporting these ailments to Bo and he was very amiable about it. He said he appreciated me letting him know what was going on. But he said something else. He said: "You know, we can't lose many more of these guys or it's going to ruin our practices."

Finally, we had six or seven guys in bed at one time, and the thing was still spreading. They were thinking of calling off the practices. It was getting that bad.

Unfortunately, one more player came in to see me. He'd got it, too. He was just as sick as the rest of them. He had 101-102 degree temperature and was really sicker than a dog.

By this time, Bo had sent word into the trainer's room that if there were any more ailments or injuries, we'd have to check with him. In other words the rules were off because we were getting so low on manpower. I was still following the three-point figure we agreed on and I told the kid he'd better go back to bed.

Tom Coyle was also sick at this time but he was able to practice. Bo was saying what a magnificent man he was—that nothing was going to bother him.

Anyway, I took one look at Coyle and sent him back to bed, too.

Now I go out on the field to report this to Bo. He sees me coming out of the door and he piles through the people on the field and stomps right towards me. He gets about three inches from my nose and he starts screaming.

"I am the only doctor on this team!" he is yelling. "If I say a guy is not sick, he is not sick! You can pack your bag and leave this afternoon if you don't like it!"

I mean, he's really hot. He's yelling loud enough to where everyone could hear him. Everything just stopped on the field. All of the players just stood there and looked at us.

I looked at him straight in the eye. You see, I'd learned something about him. I learned that when he acted this way it was just because he was excited.

So I stood there and said: "Bo, this guy is definitely sick. I'm doing the best I can to keep as many guys on the field." With that, I turned around and walked off.

After practice, I had a dozen guys come up to me and pat me on the back and tell me I was just magnificent out there standing up to Bo. It really wasn't that, though. I wasn't standing up to him. I knew how he was and I just let him have his say. Then I just told him what the situation was. And do you know something? Guess who was in my room after practice talking to me? He was saying we had to do all we could to get these guys well. He spoke very easily. Very softly. I think he'd even forgotten he'd raised his voice to me out on the field.

I respect Bo because he is interested in what is going on in the training room. A lot of coaches say the training room is your area and just go ahead and handle it. I'd much rather work with the coach. Bo gives me complete authority on treatments now and I know he respects my opinion. The thing about him is that he has to have facts—concrete facts. You give them to him and he'll listen. Actually, he's the best coach I ever worked for. . .and you can imagine what I felt—his trainer—when he had his heart attack.

He had me scared out there, too. I mean, I could see when he took his clothes off in the locker room how out of shape he was—how heavy he was. I knew something was bothering him in Pasadena. I could tell he had suffered some kind of attack, I didn't know what. As I said, he's got that image of being a hardnosed competitor and he didn't want to show signs of physical weakness to anybody. But I knew he was in distress and I couldn't believe it that day when he came charging out of the dressing room and picked up the football and began runing all over the field with it. I thought he was going to keel over on the spot.

When Bo had his attack going up that hill at the monastery, I was walking behind him. I saw him stop for a moment but I really didn't know what was going on. That was the day before New Year's. I was upset about it all through the evening and I waited up until 1:30 in the morning until Dr. O'Connor got back to the monastery and I told him I saw Bo stop going up that hill and that he definitely wasn't feeling well.

Bo kept trying to fool us. He came down for breakfast the next morning as if everything was all right but all you had to do was look at him to know something was wrong. He looked awful. Not like Bo Schembechler at all.

The players were stunned when they were told about his attack. I think Jim Young said he thought it was a mild heart attack. You could see the tears in the eyes of the players. It got so quiet in that room. You could just see all the spirit go out of them. They looked washed out. I watched them when they went out on the field for practice. I knew that there was no way they were ready to play football.

I think Bo's cardiologist was shocked by his interest in his heart. You know, the first thing Bo did was get every possible book he could find on the heart and read them from cover to cover. That's the way this man is—he has to know as much as possible about the things he is involved in.

It was funny at spring practice. Bo wasn't allowed to work but the doctors let him come out for the practices. I didn't want him walking around, so I got this golf cart for him.

He'd look at it and say, "No way am I going to ride around in any golf cart. I will walk, do you hear. I will walk. A golf cart? That's plain ridiculous."

I'd say, "Well, you really don't have to use it. We'll just keep *it behind you so you can sit down any time you feel a little tired."*

Bo glared at me.

I said, "I promise I'll keep it out of the way."

He kept glaring.

I'd have a student drive it out there every day. He'd park it near Bo. It was funny. He'd try to ignore it. But he knew it was there. He'd walk around for a while and then, with a disgusted look on his face, he'd plop down in it.

Sometimes, when the play would go to the other end of the field, he'd start it up and drive down there. But I never said another word to him about it. We'd just go out at night and bring the cart back.

We were truly concerned about him. I had my oxygen on the field everytime he went out there. I don't think he knew that either. Everybody was fearing the worst.

I remember the night before his first game back. We were in the hotel and I knew he was feeling very nervous about himself. He was having some chest pains again. It was that hernia he had but you could see it was preying on his mind.

You know Bo, though. He tried to figure out things himself. You could see him setting there thinking about it. He finally got up and said he knew what it was. He said, "I didn't eat anything yesterday. That's why I've got these pains."

From then on, we always made sure he got a little breakfast—even a little skimmed milk in the dressing room. That helped to relieve the pressures in his chest.

I was always worried about him but what can you do? Most people who have medical problems want to ignore them and figure they will just go away. That's like most football coaches—they think that most injuries will go away in time. In fact, some even want to forget that they ever happened. They don't even want to talk about injuries.

Not our man. The way he read about his heart and planned his own rehabilitation program—it was something else. I never saw anyone so intense about anything in my life.

The only time I could even talk to him during that winter was when he was out walking around the track. I'd go out there and walk with him. I had to set my pace to his pace. . .

and there'd be the two of us walking around and around, me giving him the injury report, him listening, and both of us walking, walking, walking.

It was crazy. I'd be reading from my report and all of a sudden he'd start jogging in the middle of my conversation. He'd bolt 20 yards in front of me. I had to run to catch up to him. I'd start in again and he'd be saying, "Yeah, yeah, I got it. . ." and all of a sudden he'd be 10 yards behind me because he was back on his walking pace again.

After our second Rose Bowl trip, I felt that Bo had completely recovered. We went through the whole procedure out there again and I felt good about the way he handled it all. I quit taking the oxygen to the hotel with me. I kept it in the car but didn't take it to my room.

I think his heart attack has slowed him up. He is not as intense as he used to be—not as strained. He doesn't go at that all-night feverish pace in his office. He relaxes more with his family.

But I'll tell you. I wish it would change him more. He still has that temper. . .oh, my, does he have it. He can still get pretty hot and when things start popping, you know it.

Frank Gusich:

They called me a "Wolfman" at Michigan. Some Wolfman. I weighed 185 pounds and a lot of days they'd push me all over the field.

But I'll tell you, it was something else playing for Bo Schembechler.

You hear a lot of things about football coaches—how so many of them really care about their players. I mean, after the players can't help them anymore, after graduation. Sometimes this is true, but sometimes it isn't. I can only say this: Bo Schembechler has been on my side ever since I quit playing for him, and if I've got a chance to make something of myself in life, it's because of him.

Okay, he got me my job. I'm working for his friend, Joe Hayden, in Cincinnati. I'm married now and I've got a future. Maybe Bo felt sorry for me. I don't know. Maybe it's because

I was so light. All the other guys seemed to be drafted. No pro club wanted me. Bo saw this. . .and I'm convinced he went out of his way to get me to work for Mr. Hayden.

I'll tell you something else, though. There was a time when I wasn't all that sure of Bo Schembechler—I mean, whether I liked him or if we'd ever get along.

My home was in Cleveland. Bo was coaching at Miami then. I was in high school, a pretty fair player, but Bo didn't recruit me. It was obvious he didn't want me. All of a sudden I'm at Michigan and he is named the coach and now I'm really wondering about my football future. If he didn't want me at Miami, what would he want with me at Michigan? They were uncertain days, believe me.

We heard that Bump Elliott might be stepping out. Bump was the one who recruited me. I liked Bump. I related to him. We were on the same wave length.

I tried to get enthused about the change because any time you have a change, you have to believe things will be better. But I talked to a lot of guys in Cleveland, non-players, and they were telling me that when you play for Bo Schembechler you will hate football by the time you are a senior. Right off the bat, I thought things were going to be very rough. I tried to keep my mind open but I was pretty wary.

We had a meeting in the beginning. Right away he came off as being a tough guy. He had all kinds of restrictions, like he was against fraternity living. He wanted the guys living in dorms, not in houses. I said to myself, "Uh, oh, here we go."

I'd watch him closely in the workouts. I knew he didn't have an eye for me. He had some great players, guys like Jim Mandich, and he just didn't pay any attention to me.

I thought maybe if I worked extra hard, he'd notice me. One of my biggest thrills is when I busted my wrist but told him I was going to play anyway. That's when he called me "Blue Twisted Steel." That gave me a tremendous lift. What he was doing, of course, was psyching me. But I didn't know it then. I just thought to myself: "This guy is all right."

Bo can get a little upset when things don't go right. Remember our loss to Missouri that first year. They blocked a punt on us and Bo was still seething about it when we went to

164

practice the following Monday. Oh, Mondays. Beautiful Mondays. Whenever we lost one—and thank heaven we didn't lose that many—I wanted to disappear from the face of the earth on Monday. Bo Schembechler is a man who never forgets when you lose a football game (and if the players at Michigan have had one break, it's the fact that four of their losses came in the final game of the season. . .two in the Rose Bowl and two down in Columbus. . .and they did not have to face Bo on Monday.)

Anyway, Missouri blocked this punt on us and now Bo has us lining up on punt plays. But it happens again. We mess up another punt play. Now there's Bo running down the field at Brandstatter and he goes down there and kicks the daylights out of him. We're all standing there laughing. The offense is laughing. The defense is laughing. The funniest part about it is that it wasn't Brandstatter's fault and Bo is giving it to the wrong guy. But that's how he could be—pow! He'd blow sky high.

Every day he'd call me a lollipop. Sometimes he'd do it in anger, sometimes—the worst times—with no expression on his face. Just "lollipop." It used to grind me. I'd be out there getting beaten up because of my size and he'd be calling me "lollipop."

I remember we're at the Rose Bowl. We don't have that many players out there, so I'm playing in behind Tom Darden and I'm getting a lot of work in practice. They're coming at me again and again and I'm getting some good licks in on Garvie Craw, our fullback.

I'd rip the plays apart and I'd destroy the whole outside sweep. You know what Bo was saying? He wasn't giving me any credit at all. He was saying the plays didn't go because Garvie wasn't doing his job. He said I was still a "lollipop" and you can imagine how that got under my skin.

It seemed like I couldn't do anything to please him.

Now I feel the man is n ʼ friend. I can't do a thing for him anymore. But I feel close to him. People have called me a loner. That's true. I am ha ʾ to get to know. But as time went on under Bo, I could see that all he was trying to do was get 100 per cent out of me. He seemed to understand me.

Sure, some of the guys got disgruntled because of all his rules. We thought some of them were just plain stupid. But why kid about it. We liked to think of ourselves as free lance liberals. We didn't want anyone telling us what to do, not even the head football coach. But he made us bend to his ways. . . or else we couldn't have played for him and that would have been the worst fate of all.

The truth is, I never went to Bo with anything. I mean, personal problems or anything like that. I'd stop by his office once in a while and we'd chat but it was never anything serious.

I'll tell you what sort of person he is. We had this player on our team, a defensive back, and he used to hang around with the wrong guys and he was always getting into trouble. They were stealing a lot of stuff and getting into it with the police. Finally, Bo just gave him the axe and told him he couldn't have that kind of player around.

You really couldn't trust the guy. You couldn't turn your back on him. But he came back the next year and asked Bo if he could have another chance. It was my feeling that once Bo gave you the axe, you've had it.

But do you know what he does? He not only takes the guy back, but works him, so that by the time the Ohio State game comes around, the guy is playing quite a bit and really contributing to the team. I think Bo was afraid that if he didn't take him back, he might ruin the guy's chances in life. I think this is an admirable trait and Bo does have feelings for other people.

Look at his assistants. Look at the way they kill themselves for him. Why do they do it? Because they want to get ahead? That's part of it. They do it because they have respect for him. They do it because they know he's a good coach. Bo is eminently fair. In the years I was on the team, I don't think there was ever a time where a better guy wasn't playing.

I liked playing for Bo. It may sound icky, but I just knew we were always going to win. That made it all worthwhile. Bo would come into the meetings. He'd be pessimistic, like all football coaches are supposed to be, but he also was the eternal optimist. He'd be completely honest with us and if he felt

166

we should beat a team by 40 points, he would tell us so. Then he'd tell us why.

The heart attack? I suppose everyone in this book has his version of that day in Pasadena. We were getting taped at the monastery and we were watching part of the Rose Bowl parade and the Cotton Bowl game.

We looked around. . .and Bo wasn't there. Somebody came in and shut the TV off and everybody turned their chairs around to face the front. I think it was Jim Young who spoke to us. Funny how so much of it is hazy now.

He said something like Bo wasn't feeling well and was being taken to the hospital with a chest pain and they think it was a heart attack. We were stunned. We sat there and listened but I know I couldn't believe what I was hearing.

Some of the guys got up and went into the chapel across the way. My first reaction was: "We'll kick the hell out of them." But it wasn't what I felt. I felt down. Cold. Like the fire had gone out.

You know, when you play football there is no in between— either you think you're going to win or you're not. I'm an optimist, too, but the moment we went out on that field, I could tell that my mind wasn't on the game and nobody else's was either. We were going through our drills but it was like the guys were looking up into the air instead of thinking about what they were doing.

We looked around when the game started. No Bo. It's like. . .well, say, you have a report to type up and you have a girl type it for you everytime. Then, all of a sudden, she isn't there and you've got to do it yourself. It's just not the same. I could tell immediately that we were going to lose.

It's funny but you'd live to see a smile on Bo's face. He usually didn't say much if everything was going right. But he'd smile. You'd look for that smile and when it was there, you knew everything was rosy.

The guys used to mimmick Bo. I guess players do this to all coaches. But they'd make that angry Bo face and the rest of us would crack up.

I remember once we had a guy who started to goof off and he went to Bo and said he was quitting. Bo, as you know, is

167

big on signs and slogans. When he first came to Michigan, he had one that he plastered all over the place. It said, "Those who stay will be champions."

Well, on the day this guy quits, he goes up to one of these posters and writes underneath it: "And those who don't will be lawyers, doctors, bankers, industrialists, judges. . ."

You know what I'd like to see? I would like to see Bo dance. I don't know why but I'd like to see him out on a dance floor and I would like to see him play golf. Maybe it's because he never does these things, but I think deep down he would like to try them, and I'd like to be there when he does.

I'll bet he'd be a good dancer. And, of course, a great golfer.

G. Preston ("Chappie") Chappelle:

I've known Bo since he was a freshman at Miami University. I am now a manufacturer's representative, but at that time I was a scout for the Cleveland Indians—a bird dog—and I scouted Bo as a pitcher during his years at Miami. We became good friends. Few people know it, but he was a good prospect until his senior year when he hurt his arm. I think he had good possibilities. He was a typical lefthander, fast enough and yet wild enough to keep everyone loose.

In the late 1960's, I was in the hospital and there was a "No Visitors" sign on my door. Around noon one day, I looked up and there was Bo. I looked at him and said, "Bo, Bo, what the hell are you doing here?" I was so dumbfounded I couldn't talk. Here it is the middle of his season, the middle of the day, and he's standing there in my hospital room. I was happy and pleased that he was there. I knew he didn't have time for this sort of stuff.

He looked down at me, with that Dutchman's drawn lip face, and he said, "Well, what the hell are YOU doing here? Come on, what's going on? What's happening here?"

We talked for a while, and he told me that if I was going to get well, I'd have to do it myself. He told me that's where it starts—with one's self. He showed a great deal of confidence in me.

You see, Bo is a very stern person. He is very direct. He has a way of getting things across to you. I don't mean with big words. I mean with his innate honesty. I've seen him this way with athletes. I think this is one of his great strengths. He never has to back off anything he says.

I know it is this way when he's out recruiting. He will never promise a boy something he can't deliver. A player will never be able to say that Bo Schembechler lied to him.

Some people remark about how tough and hard Bo is. That's true. He has to be that way in order to be successful. But I've seen him around his family. I've seen him around his children. You can't tell me this is a tough, hard man. However, in football it is a different game.

I have had the pleasure of going on a few fishing trips with Bo and, believe me, he attacks fishing just as enthusiastically, with the same intensity and excitement as he coaches football. As a lefthander using an open bail fishing reel, he does a creditable job—at least he thinks so to hear him brag about his fishing exploits. You feel you should take a "group picture" of him. We usually fished for walleyes, but Bo came up with more bluegills than walleyes, and he'd catch more fish accidentally than intentionally.

Bo Schembechler is a winner, and when you win as much as he does, people are going to be out gunning for you. The more he wins, the tougher it gets, not only in winning, but also in recruiting. That's why he has to keep pushing himself the way he does.

Obviously, I am one of his great admirers. But I have found this in Bo: He is a man who is not interested in suspects. He is interested in prospects. He is not interested in possibilities. He is interested in the person who can get the job done. That's Bo Schembechler and who can fault a man for that?

Gusich: *"I'd be out there getting beaten up because of my size and he'd be calling me 'lollipop'."*

(Left to Right)—Jim Betts, Tom Darden, Bruce Elliott, Frank Gusich, Michigan's 1970 Secondary

G. Preston "Chappie" Chappelle

Chapter *11*

Press Conference With the Ghost

I think we should have one chapter devoted to my relations with the press—especially with Mr. Falls, my Ghost-Author Reporter.

How about it, Joe? We'll call it: "Michigan Football, Dull and Boring."

Falls: Let me ask you some questions about your philosophy. How does it effect you when I come out on a Saturday. . . as I did a couple of times in the 1972 season. . .and was critical of your whole philosophy of football? I did call it "dull and boring." Remember?

Schembechler: I'm getting used to it now. It's like you coming out to the Minnesota game and putting the rap on us. The week before Minnesota bombed out Iowa. That really scared us. We said, "That team gives you some problems." We knew they could run the option to the sideline. We knew they'd have two tight ends. We knew they'd put a flanker out there. We knew they'd run the triple option. They were running up yardage left and right, and at the time they were leading the Big Ten in offense. So you tell me not to worry. They were also leading the Big Ten in rushing and that's nothing to laugh at.

Falls: But you still killed them, 42-0. It wasn't even a contest.

Schembechler: So we killed them but they came in all fired up. They were going to play Michigan and Ohio State back to back and they were ready for a big effort against us. So the game begins and they kept giving us good field position. We're in fourth down territory so often in that first half it

171

wasn't even funny. So, without making mistakes, we methodically put it to them. We fall in the end zone every darn time we get the ball and we go in at the half, 28-0. Midway through the third quarter, it's 42-0. When it's 42-0, I'm not going to bury the guy. But you went ahead and wrote we didn't play a very exciting game.

Falls: That's right. I thought it was very dull. All you did was pound into the line. You got the job done but I don't think it excited anyone. That's all I said.

Schembechler: Well, it's true. . .we didn't play an exciting game, but we beat the daylights out of them. Defensively, we kept getting field position and kept taking advantage of it.

Falls: Then it must have made you angry when you picked up my paper and read what I wrote because you accomplished what you set out to accomplish.

Schembechler: Absolutely.

Falls: Did you throw the paper across the kitchen. . .or what did you do with it?

Schembechler: I said to Millie, "You know, if Joe really knew what our defense did. . .I mean if he realized how it kept setting up field position for us so we could methodically cut them down, he would have never written what he did." I mean, no other team did it to them and they played Nebraska and Colorado and they went down to Columbus and almost beat Ohio State.

Falls: What would you have written?

Schembechler: I felt there were two great performances that day—by Dave Brown, our sophomore safetyman, and Denny Franklin, our quarterback.

Here was Brown, our little safety. . .and a safety has to be a super guy—a great pass defender and he's the guy who has to stop the long gainer all the time. . .he has to run punts back and now he has to come up on all option plays away from our monster— and he did one heckuva job against Minnesota. He had to come up and make every hit and he did. He had twenty some tackles in that game. His performance was something else. It was beautiful. Yet, not a word in your column about it.

Franklin was something else, too. If I had left him in, he would have cut them, 80 to 0. After the game, Cal Stoll, the

Minnesota coach, came up to me and said. "You've got the best quarterback we've seen all year. . .and that includes Humm at Nebraska and the guy at Colorado."

Falls: Does it bug you then when you see writers take super-ficial views of these games?

Schembechler: Yeah, but I can't tell you what to write. If you come in with a preconceived idea, there is not much I can do about it."

Falls: Wrong there, coach. I come in with no preconceived ideas. I'm not that smart.

Schembechler: Well, the same week you wrote what you did some guy from Sports Illustrated comes in here. . .he sits right there in that chair in my office. . .and he is going on and on about our organization—what a great program we have here at Michigan. All the time in the back of my mind, I am saying to myself he is going to cut the hell out of Big Ten foot-ball. Wait and see. . .and darned if he doesn't go ahead and do just that. He was a Minnesota graduate and I can't remember his name but it's the same thing every time they come in. They're an odd bunch. They'll tell you how wonder-ful you are and what a great coach you must be but as soon as they leave here I tell my coaches we're about to be cut to ribbons and we usually are.

Falls: What do you think of sports writers in general?

Schembechler: They're no different than coaches. There are a lot of coaches I don't think are worth a thing and there are a lot of sports writers I don't think are worth a thing either. There are a lot of sports writers who are very good friends of mine.

Falls: Do you think we are a necessary evil?

Schembechler: Yeah, but you have a hell of a problem in my opinion. That's because you can't write about the games anymore. I mean, isn't it true that back in the old days before TV not too many people saw the games? But now almost everybody sees what happens. . .or they know what happened . . .and you can't come along with a play-by-play account of the game. I don't even read articles like that. I won't read a story that goes first period, second period, third period and so on. It has to be something interesting to hold my attention. So you have to dwell on personalities and that can be tough to do. In college football we don't have super stars that stay and stay so you can write about them all the time. Our stars are here and gone. What it boils down to is that you have to have a coach who has some charisma—a coach you can write about in a colorful way. He has to be a guy who does something different all the time—somebody who is going to cause some controversy.

Falls: We write about the players.

Schembechler: Yes. . .but you have to understand that these kids aren't pros. You are a professional writer and you are accustomed to dealing with professional athletes. You go right in and start talking to them. Here, in college ball, you don't know what this kid may say or what that kid may say. They may be only 17 years old. You can say if he is old enough to compete, he is old enough to speak for himself. But that isn't always the case. Some players just aren't matured enough to stand there and carry on a conversation that's going to get into hundreds or thousands of newspapers.

Falls: I felt it was an affront to your players when you wouldn't let us in to talk to them after they lost at Ohio State in 1970. Nine straight games they won. . .and nine straight Saturdays we went in to talk to them. When they lose one—and I admit it was a tough loss—you kept us out. You were saying they couldn't handle defeat.

Schembechler: Well, I let you in this last time when we lost in Columbus. Both dressing rooms were similar. They were very emoitonal. Players were in there crying. They were broken. I didn't think they wanted to talk to you after the 1970 game. I let you in this time to see what would happen. I have to admit that I thought they conducted themselves very well.

Falls: I've always felt you should trust the press until it gives you some reason not to trust it.

Schembechler: When I kept you out in Columbus, it was nothing personal. I just felt the players weren't up to it.

Falls: Some of them talk very well, you know.

Schembechler: Too well at times.

Falls: What do you mean?

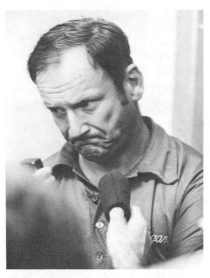

Falls: *"Don't you think that 'dull and boring' is a fair assessment of Michigan football?"*
Schembechler: *"If you knew anything about football you'd never say that."*

Falls: *"Well, you have to admit that 28-0 is not a very exciting score."*
Schembechler: *"For you or for me?"*

Falls: *"Well, what about your fans?"*
Schembechler: *"Are they demanding refunds?"*

Falls: *"But what do you do with your team when you're leading 28-0 at halftime?"*
Schembechler: *"I coach up a hell of a storm when I'm leading 28-0 at halftime!"*

Schembechler: Take Don Moorhead. He was around a long time and he'd say anything. That's why the writers were always going to him. When we beat Ohio State in 1969, I said to my players, "If we get on top of them, we can beat them." Well, Don made a remark and it came out like, "Bo's got Woody's number." I never said any such thing or even hinted at it. Then somebody out on the West Coast asked Denny Franklin why there were so many Ohio boys on the Michigan roster. He said something like, "Only the good ones." It was a good line, but you've got to treat it like a line from a college kid and not give any great importance to it.

Falls: I guess we're always looking for something to write.

Schembechler: I can give you something every day. All I have to do is act like Woody Hayes. You'll have something to write. But that's not my way. Now let me ask you a question—what do you think of Woody Hayes?

Falls: I admire Woody from a distance—but I wouldn't want to live with him every day.

Schembechler: The prosecution rests.

Falls: Hey, that's me not you.

Winning at U-M:
It's a Big Bore

Oct. 28, 1972   ANN ARBOR

With exactly two minutes and 16 seconds left in the third quarter of Saturday's game, the crowd started filing out of Michigan Stadium. The time of day was 3:20 p.m.

This had to be the earliest walkout in the history of football at the University of Michigan.

Boring?

Well, we tried the word "dull" a couple of weeks ago but nobody around here would accept it. So how about "boring?" Does that fit better, Bo?

When the third quarter ended, a writer from the Minneapolis Tribune came by and said: "Do you realize we still have another whole quarter to go? It seems like I've been here my whole life. In fact, it seems like I was born here."

Isn't that beautiful? Here they had the annual battle for the Little Brown Jug, a confrontation that used to light up the skies and make the grounds tremble, and people were walking out and others were making sarcastic remarks.

It wasn't the best of days—foggy and wet with a light drizzle falling. The game was a complete mismatch. Michigan-vs.-Minnesota? It seemed more like a Tuesday afternoon workout at Ferry Field.

What we have here now is a quandary. Everyone, including myself, moaned and groaned in the days when the Michigan football team couldn't get out of its own way. Now all the Wolverines do is win and it's still not very exciting.

I know exactly what's going to happen when all the U-M fans —including Bo Schembechler—read this column. They're going to say: "What does he want from us? We're winning, aren't we? Isn't that what this game is all about?"

This is true. Winning precedes everything else. But they're still playing pretty drab football out here and let them try to deny that.

Big 10 Is Near Bottom

Now they can also add: "Would it be better if we lost a few?"

Nope . . . and that's where the quandary comes in. Schembechler is doing what he was brought in to do—put Michigan back on the football map—but he's putting a lot of people to sleep in the process.

You can blame much of it on the quality of football in the Big Ten. The old conference is at an all-time low. Right now there are only two teams in the conference — Michigan and Ohio State — and it's getting so that the entire Big Ten season boils down to the final game between these two schools.

Take the Minnesota team which absorbed the 42-0 pasting on Saturday. It had to be the worst Minnesota team to come into Ann Arbor in a long time. There was a time, even when the Gophers were down, when they were so physical you never knew what to expect from them, and you knew you had played a football game when the afternoon was over.

This time they looked like a team out of the MIAA, and let's not have any nasty letters from the Albions, Adrians, Hopes and Olivets. The Gophers weren't remotely close to matching Michigan in manpower. It's that way on most Saturdays around here.

It would be easy to say, then, that it is not Michigan's fault that these games are so boring. Can Bo and his boys help it if the other teams are so inept? Again, this is true . . . but that's not the entire answer either. The Michigan team is just unexciting the way it performs.

Schembechler is a percentage player. He plays the percentages right down the line. You certainly can't argue with the results. In his four years at Michigan, he has won 35 games and lost five. That's a remarkable record.

But it just isn't very exciting to see his team move relentlessly from one end of the field to the other.

This is the old Woody Hayes c r i t i c i s m and Woody has laughed at his critics for years. Bo can laugh now—and will—but his brand of football just isn't stimulating.

The quandary becomes compounded when you wonder what might be going through the mind of Don Canham, the architect behind this plan to rejuvenate football at Michigan.

Right now you also can't argue with his results. He brought in Bo and Bo is winning and the fans are turning out in big numbers. There were 84,190 sitting out in the muck Saturday and there's a chance Michigan may even top Ohio State in the national attendance race this season.

Canham was commissioned to merchandise this whole package and he has done a brilliant job of it. But if he is honest with himself, he must be wondering how long the fans will buy this sort of entertainment.

In Saturday's program, Canham was quoted as saying: "The excitement, fun and relaxation surrounding college football make it a very special athletic event and we at Michigan want your visit here to be an afternoon to remember. We are trying to make it just that.

"We are continually trying to make your afternoon more enjoyable. Parking facilties are being increased with more areas for those tailgate picnics. Michigan's Tartan Turf playing surface has added a new dimension to watching college football. And those twin electric scoreboards, among the largest in the nation, were installed with our fans in mind."

Again, all of this is true . . . Canham and Schembechler have done their jobs very well. But you also have to wonder about some values when Whiskey, the little pooch who pushes the beach ball round with his nose at halftime, gets a bigger reaction from the crowd than the football team does.

I suppose I shouldn't complain. The way Bo plays it, keeping the ball on the ground, the clock keeps moving and the games end early and I can make my deadline with ease.

It just doesn't seem like much fun, that's all.

RIP

Bo Schembechler's
Favorite
Column

MAY IT
REST IN PEACE

Former Cleveland Indians Scout "Chappie" Chappelle: *"He has good possibilities."*

Schembechler as Miami of Ohio University Pitcher as a Sophomore in 1949

Chapter 12

In the Beginning, It Was Baseball

Background? It's a funny thing but not many people have ever asked me about my background. I mean, where I come from—where I was born and what I did as a kid. I was born on April Fool's Day—April 1, 1929, in Barberton, Ohio. If you know Barberton, you know it's a tough town. It's an industrial city with every ethnic group you can think of living there. Schembechler. That's German. I guess that's why people think I'm stubborn. It's my German name and Germans are supposed to be stubborn. Right, Mr. Falls?

I have two older sisters—Virginia, who is approximately five years older than me, and Marjorie, who, I believe, is 13 months older. You know how it is with sisters. You grow up and you never really find out how old they are. It just isn't important.

Anyway, my dad, who is dead, was named Glenn E. I'm Glenn E., Jr. and my youngest son—Shemy—is Glenn E. III.

Until I went to college we lived in the same house . It was a rented house on the East side of Barberton. My parents rented it from a fellow who owned a grocery store and I guess they had some kind of a deal because his store was on the Northwest side of town and we used to buy all our groceries from him.

After I went to college, my dad decided to build his own home. So we cleared out a field behind a city park and my dad had a fellow build a small house with two bedrooms and attic and you can guess who got the attic.

We were of modest means. My dad was a fireman. He started out working for the Babcock and Wilcox (B & W)

Boilermaker Company in Barberton. Then the depression came and so he took a job as a fireman because he figured that would insure him of work, which it did, and so he was with the fire department for 30 years.

Because he was a fireman, my dad was home a great deal. He used to moonlight with a friend who had an electrical contracting shop. My dad was frustrated because he hadn't moved on further in life, but you must understand that neither my mother or father had a high school degree. My mom, now she is something else. She's a dynamic old girl. She's over 70 now and she's a doer. My mother is a dynamo for church. I mean, you're talking about 40 years in the church—Episcopalian. My dad was Catholic but all the kids went to Episcopal Church. That's how forceful my mom was. She gets in on everything—alter guild, mother and daughter banquets, the whole works. I really like and respect my mom—she's a great woman.

My mom is not educated but she has read a lot which means she's pretty smart right now. People like her. Like if my friends are coming into Ann Arbor for a game. They'll call and ask me if my mom—her name is Betty—is in town. They'll take her out after the game and they'll put away two or three martinis and have a good time for themselves. Mother really doesn't understand football but she knows me like a book. If she calls me after a game, she'll say, "What the heck did you do that for?" I mean, it wouldn't be, "Oh, forget it, honey, everything will be all right." She's not that way. She says what is on her mind and wants to know what is happening. I love her dearly.

My dad was a super honest guy. Of all the people I've ever known, I've never known anyone as honest as my father. He'd never lie to you or do anything that's illegal, crooked or shady. When he was with the fire department, the job of fire chief came up and the guys down at the Elks Club told him to come down to the club one night. That was his hobby. He liked to go to the Elks Club and play cards.

When he showed up, one of the guys said to him, "Glenn, we want you to have this job." He looked at them. They offered him the answers to the Civil Service exam so he could compete with the other guy who was going for the job of fire chief. My dad came home that night and he was crying. I remember him sitting there crying.

He said, "I just can't do it. I just can't do it."

The poor guy was shattered. I felt sorry for him. Here he wanted this job more than anything else in life and they wanted him to cheat to get it. He couldn't believe they would do that to him.

I really respected him for what he did. The only thing I said to him was, "Dad, did you ever tell that guy how he got the job?"

He said, "Yes. . .and it doesn't bother me at all."

Instead he took a job as fire inspector. It wasn't the big job and he always knew it. But he kept it to himself and I admired him for that, too.

My dad died in 1962. He was 60 years old. He died of a stroke. I was an assistant coach at Ohio State then and he came down to Columbus for our game against Northwestern. I remember we lost the game, 18 - 14, when Bo Scott intercepted a pass and ran for what should have been the winning touchdown but we failed to score later on when Paul Warfield was caught for being illegally in motion. Why do you remember such things? I remember we went out to a spaghetti place that night and the next night, at about 10 o'clock, my mother called me while I was in a staff meeting. She said dad was lying on the couch watching television and he started gasping. He was gone in 30 seconds.

It's odd but I never considered my father a hero. I mean, I never asked him for a lot of advice. He was what you'd call a non-athlete. He didn't follow sports. He didn't read the sports section. When I played high school football in Barberton, he never came around to the practices or anything like that. It didn't bother me because I'd see so many of the other dads sticking their noses in.

My father started getting interested when I went to Miami. When I became a coach, especially at Ohio State—man, that's when he started prancing. He'd go down to that Elks' Club on Friday nights and tell them all about me. I could just imagine what it was like. Ohio State was pretty big in Barberton and I can just hear him laying it on the guys.

One summer when I was at Ohio State he asked me if I wanted to go fishing up in Canada. We went with this dentist and his boy. I realized then, for the first time, what kind of man my father really was. I knew he wasn't educated but he was a smart guy in his own way. He was interesting and he was fun. We'd sit around and drink beer and we had a good time. We finally got to be good buddies. This is the summer before he died and I felt bad I never got to know him better but at least I had that summer with him and I've always been thankful for that.

I was a sports nut as a kid and baseball was my first love. I loved the Cleveland Indians. This was back in the days of Hal Trosky and Earl Averill. My mom was crazy about them, too. I'd listen to every game on the radio and I remember even when I'd sit on the toilet, I'd sit there and announce those Cleveland games just the way the big announcers did: "There's a hot shot down the third base line, Kenny Keltner comes up with it, over to first—he's out!" Stuff like that. I was really nuts.

My favorite football team was Notre Dame. This was when Angelo Bertelli was the quarterback. Back in those days I could name you every player on the Notre Dame team. I'd never been to South Bend but I listened to every game on the radio and I could picture every play—what South Bend was like and just what the stadium looked like. One of the biggest disappointments of my life was the first time I walked into that stadium in South Bend. It was nothing. It wasn't as big as the stadiums I'd been accustomed to at Columbus or here at Michigan. It was a tremendous letdown for me.

I don't follow any baseball now. None at all. But as a kid, it was my game. One of my close friends was Hal Naragon, who used to catch for the Indians and later coached for the Detroit Tigers. I remember he introduced me to Bob Feller and I didn't get over that for a long time. I was a pitcher myself, a pretty good one. I was a short-armed lefthander. I'm ambidextrous.

When I was at Barberton High School, we made it to the state finals in Columbus one year. That led to one of the

Bo Schembechler, Barberton, Ohio Sophomore, 1944

"If I had considered recruiting myself, I'd have said, 'Ain't no way that kid's going to make it. No character.'."

Schembechler as Miami of Ohio University Offensive Tackle
as a senior in 1950

toughest days of my life. We had a pretty good right-handed pitcher named Don Smith. I was the lefthander. We played Upper Arlington in the semi-finals and we were supposed to beat them easy since they had a record like 15 and 6 and then we were supposed to play Cleveland Heights for the championship. Smith is pitching the semi-final and I'm supposed to work the final. They've got me at first base now and it's a tough game. We load the bases twice and I'm on third base each time but we can't score and so it's 0 - 0 after seven innings and we go into extra innings. They load the bases against Smith and so they bring me in to pitch and this guy, a right-handed hitter, hits a blooper down the right field line and all three runs score and we lose, 3 - 0. That's it. I never get to pitch again. No finals. No nothing. We're eliminated and that's as close as I ever came to the championship. One batter.

The greatest football game I ever played in high school was the day we played Alliance. Again we lost. Alliance had a tough team and so did we. I think we were both undefeated. I was playing offensive tackle, 190 pounds and wiry. We took the ball inside their 30 yard line and kept it there all day long but couldn't get it into the end zone. You know how mad I can get. I was completely frustrated. The longer the game went, the madder I got. I was making hits all over the field—big hits—but we wound up losing, 7 - 0. I remember walking back to the dressing room feeling sick. I sat down and started to bawl. I mean really bawl. It's a funny thing, but I looked up and I was the only guy crying. I wasn't ashamed of it. I didn't care who saw me. I knew I'd played a helluva game and I didn't care if anyone saw me crying.

I've cried here at Michigan. My players have cried. When this happens, I just let them cry. It's nothing to be ashamed of. Right now we've played two games at Columbus and we cried after both of them. Like our 1972 game. Everyone cried after that one. Everyone. I stood there in the middle of that room and told them they were a helluva football team. I said, you've got nothing to be ashamed of. I used some tough language. I didn't care. I wanted them to know how I felt. Football is an emotional game and if you don't let your emotions show, you can't be much of a football player.

I remember once, as a kid, we were playing in the corner sandlot. My dad gave me a football but we really didn't have any equipment. I tried to tackle this guy but he dragged me right through a tomato patch. He wouldn't go down and I wouldn't let go, so he just kept dragging me. I ripped my knee open but I wouldn't cry. I didn't want anyone to see me cry. Now I don't care.

I played all kinds of ball—football, baseball, basketball. We'd play games with tennis balls. I liked that. You could really spin a tennis ball. We'd play morning, noon and night.

I first started in with organized football when I was in the seventh grade at Oakdale grade school. Word got to us that we could play on the high school freshman team so I went down there and got a uniform. I had to go three or four miles a day to practice. I had to cross a canal and run almost all the way. I did this for two years and soon football became more important to me than baseball. I could see the challenge in it. I saw how rough it was and I would see these guys hitting one another and I would respect a guy who would go in there and hit. I wanted to be that way myself.

I got into basketball because of a tough guy named Clarence Cox. He was the Superintendent of Schools in Barberton and he started me in the game. I became a big scorer on the team. I'd take left-handed hook shots—anything left-handed. I couldn't shoot right-handed worth a darn. Our coach was Carl Harter and he was a tough, honest, straight guy. Will I ever forget the day they called a technical foul on me and what he did to me.

He calls me over to the side and starts chewing me out. I said, "I didn't say anything!"

He screamed at me, "You get off this floor, hear!"

He chased me all the way across the floor, took me into that locker room and grabbed me by the hair and said, "Don't you ever. . .don't you ever do anything like that again!" The technical was on a guy named McCoskey. He had cussed out the referee. But he turned around when he said it and I am standing there and because of my reputation of being. . .ah, somewhat gregarious. . .right away the coach thought it was

Bo—(Top, Far Right)—and Childhood Friends—(Top, Left to Right)—Bob Christianson, Chuck Price—(Bottom, Left to Right)—"Peanuts" Price, Chuck Schenz

187

me and he's out there screaming at me. I'm mad because he's accusing me of something I didn't do and—boy, he sure hit me. Not with his fist—he sort of slapped me. He grabbed me by the hair and slapped me. I was afraid of him. He was just a little guy but he was strong and I was afraid of him.

I think back to that now and, yes, I have to admit I've put some guys up against the wall in my office, I've been so mad at them. I had some fights as a kid, but no fight is a good fight. The only fight I really had I'm not proud of.

It was down at a dance. I think it happened when I was a sophomore. Remember Bob Toneff? He was a tackle at Notre Dame. He was my buddy and they had these raps on Friday night. There were guys there from Kenmore and Barberton and some of the other suburbs and you know how those things can get.

I don't know whether the guys figured I was a fighter or not but there was a guy in there from Kenmore who came in with a gang. He was an ex-Marine or something and I ask which one is it. This guy comes out and I say, "Hey, I hear you caused some trouble at our dance." He says, "Yeah, so what!" I say, "I'm going to take you on right now. You just let me get this coat off." Well, he starts taking his coat off and I don't give him a chance. I deck him right there. I put him up against the wall and bloody my knuckles all up. I think I hit the wall more than I hit him. I don't think I really hurt him. The chaperone came by and we got out of there as fast as we could. I wasn't proud of what happened. It was just one of those things. I sure wasn't a fighter. The big rumor was that he was coming down the next week to get me. I had to go back, of course. I went back with the guys but he never showed up.

Girls? I wasn't very good with girls. I was always bashful. I sure wasn't a ladies man at all. We'd go to parties. . .yeah, we'd do some kissing. . .but I was so wrapped up in sports I just didn't have much time to do any chasing. I was a straight A student in grade school but when I went to high school I didn't do a thing. I never studied, I never opened a book—I never did anything. I didn't cheat but I might have copied a few papers. I took four years of math and don't know why I did. All I got were C's and D's. I took English but I wouldn't take chemistry or physics. I just took a lot of junk. I just wasn't interested in anything. There was a guy who wanted me to go to Michigan but there was no way I could have gone to Michigan. Ohio State recruited me but I wound up going to Miami of Ohio. At mid-year they sent home a report to my parents and said my chances for success weren't very good because I wasn't studying. I was having kids congregating in my room and making noise and stuff like that and when my parents heard about it, I started getting scared. My mom still has that report. I don't know if she is going to blackmail me with it or not but she has kept it all these years.

It was then I decided I'd better shape up. I started to study and I guess I graduated from Miami with a B average. Actually, I was a pretty good student from then on. Don't get me wrong. I didn't study a whole lot but I did what I had to do. I got a natural science and physical education degree and later, at Ohio State, I got my masters in physical education.

But, without my mom, well, who knows. . . . . .

Mrs. Betty Schembechler:

It sounds silly but Bo never gave me one bit of trouble. He and his sisters squabbled a little bit, but that was only natural. I was never called into the police station or the school or any place else. Not that he was a saint. I imagine he did things that I never knew about. But he just didn't do much running around. When he was in high school, he played in three sports and he just came home tired every night. He didn't have a car, so he stayed pretty close to home.

I'm so happy he is a football coach because this is what he has wanted to be for such a long time and so often so many men in life become sidetracked and do things that they really don't care to do. I used to go to Miami a lot and watch him coach. I didn't know that much about football and so I'd watch him down on the field. Now I watch the games. He was a lot more intense at Miami than he is now. It was even that way when he worked for Woody at Ohio. When he'd lose a game, you wouldn't even talk to him. I'd have his meal ready for him—I'd do the cooking for him on Saturday night—but he'd come home and he'd be tired and he might lay down for a while before dinner to take a nap after dinner. He wasn't much for conversation. I don't try to give him advice anymore. After all, he is old enough now and Bo is a real good boy. He's got good judgment about most things and I think he's done a wonderful job with his wife and those three boys.

The Ghost Speaks:

This wasn't a great chapter. Just a necessary one. Background on Bo. But I enjoyed listening to him talk about his childhood because when you are around this man and listen to him talk football all the time, you forget he has ever had other interests in life.

Don Canham let it slip one day. We were talking about Bo and he said, "I never met a man who had a more single-purpose mind than Bo Schembechler."

I buy that. Bo's life literally begins and ends with winning football games. Little else seems to matter to him. Believe me when I say he goes at his job 12 months of the year. That's one reason why he is so successful. Not only does he like what he does, he is consumed by it. I couldn't imagine Bo doing anything else in life but coaching a football team.

This may make him appear to be a one-dimensional man, but I don't think so. That's because he has to deal with so many people and this presents him with an eternal challenge since everyone is different. He seems to relish this challenge, thrive on it.

I remember one of the first days in his office when we started putting this book together. He came out to talk to Lynn Koch, his secretary, and he was saying something like, "See if you can get me a flight to Chicago at about three or four in the afternoon"—when suddenly he looked up at the window behind Lynn and said: "Get that window cleaned!"—and then got right back into his conversation ". . .because I've got to be in Chicago tomorrow night for a seven o'clock meeting."

Click, click, whirrrrrrrr, hummmmmmmm, click, click,

hummmmmmmmmm.

Please do not disturb. Football coach at work.

Bo with Gil Chapman (24), Chuck Stobart, Larry Smith to His
Left, Dennis Brown Behind.

*"The nice thing about football is that you can learn any-
where—even in the army."*

Football Team at Camp Rucker, Alabama in 1952—Bo is
number 57

Chapter 13

Presbyterian: Bibles, Servants, Mansions and Chicken Sandwiches

The nice thing about football is that you can learn anywhere. Even in the Army. I learned to connive in the Army—to take good care of old Bo Schembechler out on that field.

I spent two years in service—1952 and 1953—and I played one year with the 135th infantry regiment at Camp Rucker, Alabama. We were undefeated and won the championship—the Regimental Championship at the post.

I was an offensive lineman in college but I always had this yearning to play linebacker. I always dreamed I would make a great linebacker.

The coach of the team was a lieutenant who really didn't know much about football. I'd go over to his house and we'd go over the plays and I'd coach the defense. I set it up so we used a six-man line with me the middle linebacker. Theoretically, with a six-man line you keep the guards from getting out on you and the tackles and ends from getting out and that leaves you free if you're the middle linebacker. All you have to do is beat the center and then you can knock the tar out of everybody. I had a lot of fun at that position.

I got along pretty well with everyone. I mean, it wasn't that tough to take all the discipline then as it is now. The only time I ever really got mad—and you know about my temper—was when this guy from Louisiana, a sergeant with an IQ of about 75, made us all fall out and take butt cans and get down on our hands and knees and pick up all the pebbles on the parade ground.

I get the most upset when I'm accused of doing something I

didn't do and I didn't do it and I didn't like it and I told him so. He got smart, just like you'd expect him to, but I told him, "You just don't make everybody get down on their hands and knees because of what a couple of guys did and you know who did it."

I was down there on my hands and knees picking up rocks. There was no way I was going to win the argument. He won it, but there was no way I wasn't going to tell him what I thought. It is just bad strategy to make everyone pay for the mistakes of a few.

Anyway, they wanted me to play again in my second year but I'm in my middle twenties by now and I just don't want to play any more football. I had my fall plans all laid out. I had the type of job that would give me weekends off and I was going to catch the biggest game in the South every week. I had an old car and I went to Atlanta to see Duke play Georgia Tech; I went to Auburn to see Auburn play Old Miss; I went to Mobile to see Alabama play LSU; I went to Talahassee to see Florida State play Abilene Christian College and this last one is one game I'll never forget.

Florida State came out—there were 75 to 80 beautifully dressed guys—and—this is no joke—here comes Abilene Christian and they've got no more than 25 players. It was the wildest thing I ever saw—guys were playing both tackle and guard and everything else and I'll be a son of a gun if they didn't beat them.

I usually had a couple of buddies who liked football who traveled with me. We'd get there early enough so even if there was a sellout, we'd stand outside the stadium looking for tickets. We always got in. There'd always be some guy peddling tickets. I never traveled in uniform but we always managed to get pretty good seats.

I got out of service in the summer of 1954. June, it was. I got out three months early and I'm driving North as happy as a lark. I want to coach but I don't have a job and my first stop in the old Chevy was Lexington, Kentucky, where Bill Arnsbarger was working for Blanton Collier.

I told him I was looking for a job. I'd been a graduate assistant but now I wanted a job where I had some real responsibilities. I was single and so I didn't need a whole lot of dough. I played with Bill at Miami and he said he knew a guy who took the coaching job at Presbyterian College in South Carolina and needs a line coach.

I didn't want to turn around and go back to the South again, so I continued on to Columbus. I stopped in to see all of the old coaches—Doyt Perry and Bill Hess and all the rest. I asked Woody if he had a job but there was nothing available. When I got home I got a call from a guy named Bill Crutchfield. He was the coach at Presbyterian—that's in Clinton, South Carolina. . .it's a boy's school at the time, 500 boys, no girls. I'm single, as I said, and I figured what the heck—a job is a job.

I took my separation money from the Army and bought a Chevrolet coupe and I'm on my way back to Clinton, South Carolina. This is a town of about 10,000 people—you're not going to believe this story—and it is run by the Bailey Cotton Mills. It is the kind of town where you lived in houses built by Bailey, shopped in stores run by Bailey—the Bailey bank, the Bailey mill. . .that sort of thing.

When I get there I've got to find a room. I'm looking around town when word gets down to me that Mrs. Bailey—this is the elderly lady whose husband is dead—she's looking for me. She wants to see me. She lives up in this big mansion, the Bailey mansion in Boxwood Gardens, and she lives with her daughter, who is about 40 at the time, and her grand-daughter, who is about 18. Three gals in one house.

It seemed that they always had somebody from the university living with them. Even though they had servants, they wanted a man around and they asked me to come up and see them.

It's just like you'd imagine—they had tea and crumpets and the whole thing set out for me. . .and that's got to be some kind of picture: Bo Schembechler sitting there eating tea and crumpets and saying, "Yes, m'am," "no, m'am," "thank you, m'am." They had a black servant and his name was "Man" and he'd bring all the stuff around. They had a gardner and a maid and now the four of us—me and the three ladies—are sitting there eating and talking back and forth and they tell me they've got a room upstairs that they'd be only too happy to have me use.

I'm wondering about this whole thing—I mean, my car is parked out in their driveway and it looks like the Grapes of Wrath. It's just stuffed with junk and now they're talking about me moving in to this big mansion.

They took me upstairs and showed me the room and they said it would be $30 a month. Mrs. Bailey smiled and said, "Of course that includes breakfast. Mind you, you don't have to eat with us all the time—just when you wish."

I'm standing there listening to all of this but I'm not believing any of it. Room, breakfast, servants, maids, mansions—all for thirty bucks a month. I was a little embarrassed and I said, "Well, I promised I'd look at a couple of other places, so maybe I'd better go there and check those out first."

So I'm walking out on the porch and one of them—Mrs. Marshall, who is Mrs. Bailey's daughter—she comes out and says, "You know if you would like the room, you really can have it for twenty-five dollars."

I say to myself, "Why not, they're nice people and how many times am I ever going to get a chance to live in a mansion."

I think what would the guys back in Barberton think if they could see me now.

"Okay," I tell her, "it's a deal" and she runs back inside to tell everybody. I don't know how this is coming out so far—I mean how it is sounding—moving in with three ladies—but to keep the record straight they were ladies every day I stayed with them and, this you won't believe, I was a perfect gentleman.

It was really something else. "Man" starts unpacking my car for me and Mrs. Marshall comes out and says, "Let's have some milk and sandwiches."

I said, "I think I'd better unpack the car."

She said, "No, Man will do that."

When I go up to my room later, I can't find anything. The place looks empty. I think maybe he put the stuff in the wrong room. But there it is—my pants hung in the closet, my drawers in the bureau. . .even my shoes are shined.

In the morning I'd come down for breakfast and there'd be Mrs. Bailey, Mrs. Marshall and the daughter waiting for me. I'd sit at the head of the table and every morning they had a passage from the Bible that I was to read. I'm the man of the house—so every morning I'd come down and I read the passage from the Bible and we'd have a little prayer and then we'd eat breakfast. At night there was always a note on the door to my room, telling me what to look for in the refrigerator—chicken sandwiches and milk and cookies.

Now this is the absolute truth: After a while Mrs. Marshall decides I should have a social life.

She says, "I think we should have a party for you."

Me, the dummy, says, "For me?"

"Yes, we could invite all of your friends."

I say, "I really don't have any friends here—I wouldn't know who to invite."

That's no worry to Mrs. Marshall. She brings them in from Spartanburg and all over the State of South Carolina—it's my party and I'm standing there shaking hands with people I'd never seen before and saying, "How do you do? It is nice to meet you."

As I said, I've got this Chevy coupe but Mrs. Marshall goes out and buys a Chrysler Imperial. She says, "Now Bo, I want you to drive this car and break it in."

So now I'm driving around in a new Chrysler Imperial, I'm living rent free, they make me breakfast every morning, they've got goodies waiting for me every night and for the first time in my life my shoes are always shined. I would like Don Canham to read this part, if he thinks he's taking such good care of me. He never once has shined my shoes.

About the football at Presbyterian. Crutchfield is the coach and there's me and Norm Sloan, who went on to become the basketball coach at North Carolina State. Norm knew nothing about football and didn't care about football—basketball was his game. So it's actually Crutch and I coaching the football team. They never had a winning season in over 10 years and we start out opening with Clemson and they beat us, 33 to 0. The second game was with Furman and they beat us, 27 to 0.

Now we're 0 and 2 and we haven't scored a point yet.

Our third game is with Davidson. Davidson has won three in a row and they come down to play us for homecoming and we upset them. Now we are 1 and 2 and we play the most unbelievable football game I have ever seen in my whole life. I'm talking about the Wofford game. At Wofford.

We go up and they're kicking the dickens out of us—the score is 19-7 with about six minutes to play and they're driving on us. The ball goes to our one yard line and we pull out the first team and put in the second team since the first team isn't stopping them. Well, the second team does the job and now get this: We stop them on our one-yard line. . .five or six minutes left. . .19-7 behind. . .the first play we run off tackle and the second team fullback goes 99 yards for a touchdown and we kick the extra point and it's 19-14 with five minutes left in the game. We short kick them and get the ball and now it's our turn to drive down the field. We go right to the goal line and by this time Wofford. . .now when you play at Wofford the whole stands come out around the end zone where you are driving and they stand there and scream at you. It is something else. When you come out on the field, you have to go through about 50 yards of Wofford students. They line the freshmen up and they're all wearing beanies and here our guys are filing through this narrow path for 50 yards and all the freshmen are screaming at them: "Terrier Meat! Terrier Meat! Dog food! Dog food!"

You just know it's incensing our guys—so now we're driving down in there, right to the one-yard line. We drive off tackle and now they're going to measure for the first down, inside the one. The old guy—the old official very astutely comes in and holds up his hands to show the crowd we missed it by inches.

So the next play our quarterback takes the ball and drives forward and our guys think it's a touchdown. There is no big pileup, there is nothing—he just dived into the end zone for the score.

Now here comes the referee or the umpire—I can't tell you which—he jumps in there and picks the ball up. He assumed the head linesman was marking the forward progress of the

"For the first time in my life my shoes are always shined."

Bo while Coach at Presbyterian College, Clinton, South Carolina

ball. But where is the head linesman? He's got his back turned on the play and he's going over to the stakes. The guy with the ball runs over to him but sees that his back is to him and he stops in his tracks. Now you have to understand there are all these crazy kids around the end zone. They're screaming and yelling and carrying on. The guy looks at them, then looks at the ball. He puts the ball down—so help me—and says, "First down Wofford!"

I could have killed him in cold blood. Right there I could have killed him. Bill Crutchfield is a very wonderful football technician—he knows his football all right but he doesn't get very emotional. Now he is trying to pull me off these guys and I'm screaming, "I'll kill you!. . .I'll kill you all!" I have never been robbed, totally robbed, like that in my whole life. I went crazy out there. That night, I understand, even the officials themselves almost got into a fight over the way they bungled the thing.

We went on to win our next five in a row. We beat the Citadel, Catawba, Appalachian State and a few others. Our big star was Kenny Webb, who later played for the Detroit Lions. He was our star. He'd run the flip 8—he'd take that pitchout and go with it. He was only a freshman but he was some player.

When I went to Presbyterian, I had a choice of two deals. I could either take a flat $3,600 a year or I could take $3,400 and have free run of the cafeteria. I took the $3,400 with free run of the cafeteria and with the meals I got at the Bailey mansion, you know I didn't go hungry that year.

Chapter 14

Barry Fitzgerald Was My Coach

After my year at Presbyterian, I coached one year at Bowling Green. It was a beautiful year. That's because I worked for Doyt Perry.

Here is a man who is really something. He's the Barry Fitzgerald type. I mean, he smoked a pipe and he was kind to everyone but he was tough in a Barry Fitzgerald way.

I met him when he worked for Woody Hayes at Ohio State. I guess he was on Woody's staff for about four years, from 1951 through 1954. Doyt was in his 40s then, older than most of the assistant coaches you'd see. That's because he was such a great high school coach. He was the kind who coached, let's say 10 years at Lorain Clearview. Everytime he was about to get a better job, they'd come up with a little more money for him and he'd stay.

He finally left and went to Upper Arlington in Columbus and it'd be the same thing there—every Christmas they'd come around and give him some money and presents and stuff like that. He was a very popular guy. He must have been there another 10 years, so here's a guy who must have spent 20 years in high school football when he could have been a great college coach.

When Doyt got the job at Bowling Green in 1955, I was the first one he called. I liked my year at Presbyterian but I knew I had to move on. It wasn't for the money either. I was making five thousand at Bowling Green. . .or maybe it was fifty-five hundred. I think it was five thousand. It didn't matter. Money didn't mean much to me. I was a bachelor and didn't need much to get by on.

Doyt Perry, Bowling Green Head Coach

1955 Bowling Green University Football Coaching Staff:
Top (Left to Right)—Forrest Creason, Lloyd Parkson, James Ruehl, Robert Dudley, Jack Taylor—Bottom (Left to Right)—Bo Schembechler, Doyt Perry, William Gunlock, Bruce Ballard

1955 Bowling Green University Coaches:
(Left to Right)—Doyt Perry, Bob Dudley, Bill Gunlock, Forrest Creason, Bo Schembechler

What I liked about the job at Bowling Green is that we didn't have many coaches, maybe four or five, and I could really get a chance to do some coaching.

I moved in with Doyt in an old house on Ridge Street, down near the athletic office, and what we did is we got a lot of bunk beds and put them in the back of the house. We would recruit on weekends and we'd put the kids in those beds and Doyt and I would sleep out in the front room. We didn't have any dough to house the kids but we could put them up for a weekend and feed them over at the student commons.

Sundays were always the best, especially in the summer. Doyt would sit up on the porch smoking that pipe of his and he'd philosophize about everything in life. The guy has had open heart surgery and he's in his 60's now and living down in Florida but there isn't a player who ever played for him if you mentioned Doyt Perry's name that he wouldn't smile.

Doyt could be a tough one all right. I remember one night we're walking up the steps to the house and I'm in a big argument with one of our coaches about something or another concerning football.

Doyt turns around to us and says, "I know that both of you guys think you can coach this team better than I can. I know that but I'm going to tell you something else. You are not the head coach. I am the head coach. If you don't do things my way, I am going to fire you."

You know something? I think I said, "Yes, sir" to him.

We went in there that spring and really pushed them. Bowling Green had never done anything. When I was at Miami, we'd always beat them 40 or 50 to nothing. But now we had them hustling and when we opened against Defiance, we were scared because we didn't know what he had. We beat Defiance 40 to 0—imagine that!—and went on to beat everyone else until we went over to Oxford to play Miami.

Ara Parseghian was the coach at Miami and he had some kind of team. This was the team which upset Northwestern and probably got Ara his job at Northwestern. Bill Gunlock was on our staff and he's a friend of mine. We played together at Miami and so now that we're going back to play Miami, we're both so fired up we can't even see straight.

Doyt sees this and on the day of the game he says to us, "Okay, I know what this game means to you guys. Do you want to say anything to the team?"

I blurt out, "Yeah, you betcha. I want to talk to them."

So what do I do? I'm so fired up I get up and can't even speak.

We did a great job defensing their offense. Miami called almost all of their plays from the line of scrimmage, so we set our defense so that we could jump from a defense that was strong inside to one that was strong outside, and vice versa. The Miami quarterback would be "automaticking" a play against one defense and then we would jump to another. All day long they were running plays in a stacked defense.

We did a great job. We lost our quarterback on Thursday of that week and also our No. 1 tailback. Our best running back, a sophomore, was also out of the game but we're giving them a tough time of it on defense. They finally break a trap on us near their own goal line. They go all the way to midfield with it and go on in to score. We lost, 7-0. . .our only loss of the season. . .but we played a great game that day.

When the season is over, Ara goes to Northwestern and he asks me to go along with him. I guess he wanted to find out what I knew about defensing his offense.

1957 Northwestern University Coaching Staff:

(Left to Right)—Bo Schembechler, Paul Shoultz, Dale Samuels, Head Coach Ara Parseghian, "Doc" Urich, Bruce Beatty, Alex Agase

Chapter 15

How Could Anybody Quit on Ara?

Let me tell you something about Ara Parseghian. He is one of the great minds in this game of football. I don't know of another coach who has more imagination than Ara. It's not that he just designs plays—he designs them where you can use the skills of the players involved to make them go. So many coaches try to make their personnel adapt to their style of play. Not Ara. He builds his attack around the type of personnel he has. For example, he was a success right off the bat at Notre Dame because he knew how to utilize his quarterback, Johnny Huarte. This plus the fact he can stimulate his players makes him a great coach in my mind. I've always had the highest respect for Ara.

After my year at Bowling Green, I got a job offer from Kentucky. But when Ara came along and asked me to coach his freshman team at Northwestern I went with him. I knew Ara a little at Miami.

When I was a freshman, Ara was playing his last year of football at Miami. He was elected captain the following year, when I would have been a sophomore. I don't know what the rules were then but he had come back from service and instead of playing one more year at Miami, he went up with the Cleveland Browns. He spent two years there and got hurt. He'd had a bad hip, so that in my senior year at Miami he came back as a freshman coach. That's when I got to know him. We were friends, but not that close. I'd visit him and we'd talk football and that's how I got to know his offensive strategy.

When I took over the freshman team at Northwestern, Dale Samuels was my assistant. The next year I moved up as line coach on the varsity and that season we went 0 and 9. We lost every single game. I couldn't believe it. Every single game. As the season went along, you could see what was happening and pretty soon you knew there was no way we were going to win any games.

We had that little conference room under the stadium and that's where we did all our work. We'd sit in there until twelve or one in the morning trying to figure a way we could pull one out. We never did. That's when I really got respect for Ara.

No matter how badly things were going, he never got on us about it. Now when you're the head coach, you chew off some heads once in a while. But he never said anything to us. He never blamed us for anything.

I could see what the trouble was. We had some guys who were playing only for themselves and that's one thing I've always emphasized here at Michigan. There is no way anyone will ever play for themselves on my team. If you're going to be a success, your seniors are going to have to come through for you. They've got to have their greatest years. No matter how good the younger players may be, they are going to perform on the basis of what they see the top guys do. In other words, if they can look up to the seniors for the way they're working and hustling, then they are going to work and hustle, too. If the seniors are dogging, you're in trouble.

This is what happened at Northwestern. We had seniors that were almost totally concerned with their own achievements. Can I make All-America? Can I make All-Big Ten? We had guys who were concerned about that more than anything else.

I'd watch them walk by the office and go back to see the publicity man. They'd want to find out what went out on them that week. Are you kidding me? What kind of way is that to play football? They weren't concerned about winning—only what happened to themselves. You can imagine what that was doing to Ara.

I probably learned more in that one season under Ara than I have in my entire life. It is one thing when everything is going along well and you are winning. But when you're losing week after week, you find out some things about this game and the people who play it.

Those seniors let Ara down. They let the whole season go down the drain. I thought we might be in trouble when we went out to play Stanford. They didn't have that good a team but they beat us. There were numerous situations—and you could see them during the game and especially on the film—where there was a lack of effort on our side. You could see where a guy could have made a tackle if he would have run harder—if he had pursued more. Stuff like that. It was awful.

I felt sorry for Ara because there wasn't much he could do about it. Complicating matters was the fact our athletic director, Stu Holcomb, was upset with Ara because he wasn't playing his kid, Chip, at quarterback. I know this: There is no way any athletic director or administrator or anyone outside of my coaching staff is ever going to come to me and tell me who to play. I'll listen to my coaches, but that's all. No one else tells me what to do.

I can go out on the field and see some beautiful players running around, but as soon as you put them into a game they start making one mistake after another. They drop the ball, they miss a block, they run the wrong way. That guy shouldn't play. A guy with lesser ability should be in there if he is the soundest player.

I was still a bachelor, so I could go hard at my job. Ten, twelve, fourteen hours a day—it made no difference. I had nothing else to do and I loved what I was doing, even though we were losing. It was a chance to learn.

I got to know Ara pretty well. If he had a banquet or something, I'd usually drive him. But if you're talking about socializing, the one guy I really liked—and still do—was Alex Agase. He was on the staff and if you're ever talking about a square shooter, it is this man.

I mean, if I wanted to know something I'd go to Alex. He'd give it to me straight. No hemming or hawing. That's why I like to compete against his teams. You know you're always going to get a straight deal.

I might be out scouting on Saturday but I'd always wait on the front steps for Alex to come home. He was the only guy I could really level with. I could always find out what was going on from him—he was the guy I always waited on.

Ara Parseghian:

I knew Bo when I was a freshman coach at Miami under Woody Hayes. I also knew him when he was playing his senior year at Miami. I was impressed even then with his enthusiasm in relation to what he was doing. He was intelligent, he was an excellent student in school—he had a lot of the qualities you look for in a coach. He was an offensive tackle and he wasn't overly large but he was a great competitor. That impressed me, too.

Bo is one of the most intense people I have ever known. He is always striving for perfection. He not only is able to analyze the strategy of an offensive line but he is such a technician that he can take apart blocking techniques and put them back together again so that the people he is working with can understand what he is doing and can benefit from his knowledge. You might say he is very much like Bob Toski, who has a tremendous reputation as a golf teacher because he is able to disect the golf swing. I think Bo has the ability to analyze exactly the physical movements involved in blocking techniques and the ability to teach it to others.

He knows, for instance, the best way to attack a defense. He understands line play. I mean, the evaluation of talent and the development of that talent. He can judge individual talent as well as the total concept of offensive line play.

I was always impressed with him. The one reservation I had was about his temper. I didn't know if he could control it in order to become a head coach. But he has learned this with maturity. When he was with me, he was such a perfectionist that he wanted things done right and he wanted them done now. Now he has learned to exercise some control over himself.

Actually, Bo and I are pretty close. We talk an awful lot on the phone. We talk recruiting, we talk strategy, we talk football. He is a stimulating man. He knows how to put things together.

Chapter 16

"You...Are...Going...To...Be...My...Quarterback ...If...We...Both...Die...Doing...It!"

Coaching the quarterback is usually the responsibility of the head coach and most of the success or failure of a team is determined by the ability and the type of young man that performs at this most critical position.

As I arrived at Oxford in January of 1963 to attend the press conference that was to name me the new Miami of Ohio University head football coach, I stopped by the cloak room at the student union where a young football player was working who was a sensation as a sophomore at quarterback for the Miami Redskins. His name was Ernie Kellermann.

When I was introduced to Ernie, he asked one question: "Coach, I hope that we'll pass more than you do at Ohio State."

I said, "Ernie, the first thing we're going to have to find out is just how well you *can* pass."

As it turned out, Kellermann was probably the most exciting player Miami ever had. He was the All-Conference Quarterback for three years. He was the all-time leader of the quarterbacks at Miami in almost every category—passing and rushing. He was a dynamic little guy about 5'11" tall, and he weighed 170 pounds. He was one of these great little athletes probably overlooked by many of the major schools, and he ended up at Miami.

Ernie naturally was our most outstanding player in 1963. Midway through the season we were playing Northwestern of the Big 10 in Evanston. It was the last Northwestern team coached by Ara Parseghian. Midway through the third period trailing 19-7, Ernie had driven our ball club down inside the 10 yard line, but unfortunately on the ensuing play he sustained a hip pointer that took him out of the game. It also took him out of the following week's game against Ohio University in which we had an opportunity, by winning that game, to win the Mid-American Conference Championship.

The following year in 1964, we again played Northwestern. This time, Ernie put on one of the greatest offensive quarterback displays I have ever seen. He passed and ran beautifully. Northwestern was an exceptionally fine defensive team, but Ernie had that knack of avoiding the blitz and getting the ball out to the receivers and scrambling for first downs. He led us to a 28-27 upset over Northwestern.

For his three years in college, Ernie was by far the most outstanding player in the Mid-American Conference. Professional football scouts who would come by our Miami practice sessions would marvel at his ability, and then in the same breath shaking their heads, say, "It's too bad that he doesn't have the size and speed to be a professional football player."

Ernie had one ambition in life and that was to play pro football. He was an exceptionally fine golfer. He could play baseball. He was an exceptional basketball player. He was a great all-around athlete, but for some reason he chose football for a professional career, which is rather odd because that would be by far the most difficult sport for him to play professionally.

He was drafted late in the draft by the Dallas Cowboys and he reported to their training camp at Thousand Oaks, California to be converted into a defensive back. Now, you have to understand that Ernie had never played defense at all during his college career. The only tackles he ever made were when there was a pass intercepted or a sudden exchange of the football.

Midway through the exhibition season the Director of Player Personnel of the Dallas Cowboys called me, and he said, "Bo, I'm not sure whether Ernie is going to be able to make it, but I just want you to know that he is the most enthusiastic, dynamic young player in our training camp, and although he has never played defense before, he tackles aggressively, he learns quickly and has a tremendous desire to make our team."

I told him then that that was nothing more than I would have expected to hear from him. Ernie was always that kind of player at Miami.

When the team broke training camp and went back to Dallas, just before the opening of the season, I got a call from Ernie and I could tell he was quite shaken by the tone in his voice. He said he was the last football player cut by the Cowboys and that under the rules of professional football he could not be kept in Dallas as a "taxi-squad player," meaning a player who practices with the team but is not allowed to play with them unless one player is deactivated on the regular roster and the "taxi-squad player" is activated. There are usually six or seven of these players who practice with the teams but do not play in the games.

So Ernie was without a job, and he said to me, "Bo, you've got to get me another chance. I know I can make it. I just know I can if you can get me another chance."

Now I want you to know it is darn difficult, with the season just a few days prior to opening, to get a youngster an opportunity with a professional team when most of the squads have already been picked. But I felt I owed him so much that I would do everything I could to possibly help him.

After thinking about it for a while, I started to call Blanton Collier who helped me get my first coaching job at Presbyterian College. Rationalizing, I said that since he did me a favor, I would do him a favor. So I called Blanton, the head Cleveland Browns coach, I asked him how familiar he was with Ernie Kellermann and of course he remembered his outstanding career at Miami. I told him that Ernie had just been cut by the Dallas Cowboys and he said that he had not yet heard of him being placed on waivers. I told Blanton that if there was a chance that he could use a defensive back on his "taxi squad" and that if he took Ernie I would guarantee him that Ernie would evenutally worm his way onto his regular team. He had always been very much impressed with Ernie and so he said to me, "You send him up here tomorrow to our practice and I will have Art Modell, the President of the Cleveland Browns, there and we will sign him to a 'taxi' contract."

I was very grateful to Blanton and told him he would not be sorry, hung up and immediately got Ernie on the phone. I said,

"Ernie, this is a great break for you because Cleveland's your home town, you can live at home, you can be a member of the 'taxi squad' of the Cleveland Browns, and if you're good enough you will eventually worm your way onto the squad."

Ernie was both elated and disappointed—elated at the opportunity to once again play pro football, and disappointed that he didn't have a chance that year to get on the regular team.

So he reports to Cleveland, and he had asked me before he hung up the phone, "How much money should I ask for?"

I said, "Ernie, I have no idea what they pay those people, but I think they pay from week to week. If you want to, why don't you, after you hear Mr. Modell's first offer, tell him that you promised your coach that you'd like to talk with him concerning a contract, and then find a telephone and call me and we'll talk it over before you give him a definite answer."

He said, "That sounds fine."

So the next day he takes off for Cleveland, and the next day he goes to meet Coach Collier and Mr. Modell and after exchanging pleasantries Mr. Modell says, "Ernie, we'd like to have you sign a contract with the Cleveland Browns to be on our 'taxi squad' and we would be willing to pay you $400.00 a week during the season to do that."

Ernie said, "Well, I would very much like to sign with the Cleveland Browns but I promised my coach that I wouldn't do anything until I had an opportunity to talk with him."

So Mr. Modell told him to use the telephone in the clubhouse and give me a call. Ernie goes in and legitimately tries to call me, but at that particular time I'm out of the office, so he doesn't get a chance to talk with me.

He hangs up and goes back out to see Mr. Modell. Mr. Modell says, "Ernie, what did your coach say."

Ernie looked him right in the eye and said, "Mr. Modell, my coach wants me to sign with the Cleveland Browns, but he doesn't think you'll pay me enough money."

Mr. Modell looks at him and says, "All right, we'll pay you $500.00 a week."

Ernie says, "Fine." And he signed the contract with the Cleveland Browns.

Just as I predicted, Ernie was a guy who would hustle around the practice field, and help impersonate the opponent's quarterback even though he was working as a defensive back. He'd study films more than any player they had. The following year he was put on the regular squad, and he has played professional football every year through 1972. Here was a guy who, physically, did not have the qualifications to be a professional player, but he had so much enthusiasm and drive, so much determination that there was no way he was not going to succeed at his goal of being a professional player. I sometimes call him the greatest competitor I ever coached. Without him those first couple of years at Miami could have been very, very rough, but he was a dedicated all-out football player and by far the most valuable player we had during my first two years at Miami in 1963 and 1964.

The usual tenure for a college quarterback is two years, and almost invariably every two years your quarterback changes.

So now Kellermann's gone and we have to play the first guy I ever recruited at Miami—a youngster by the name of Bruce Matte. This was Tom Matte's younger brother. He was a scrawney little kid and knowing Tom at Ohio State, his brother was the first kid I went after. I went after him because he had Matte ability. I mean, he was a highly talented quarterback in high school. He lived in East Cleveland and went to Shaw High School.

Anyway, Matte comes down from Cleveland and he's another writer's dream. If he'd have played at Michigan, he'd have been headlines all the time. A happy-go-lucky kid, personality plus. . .just everything.

So he comes in here and he plays pretty good in freshman ball. But he is the type of player who would fumble the exchange twice in a row and then go back to pass, get trapped and run for a touchdown. And you know what a player like that does to me!

He was a mistake guy and since Kellerman played so well for us, I played Matte at safety in his sophomore year. He was terrible. He'd drive you crazy. He'd make all kinds of mistakes and you'd kick him in the tail and hit him on the head gear. But do you know something? He took it. He responded to this kind of treatment. To look at him, you'd never know it. He didn't seem like that kind of kid.

But he wanted to learn. He didn't have any discipline himself but he was willing to accept it from others.

So I said to myself, "Okay, this is it! If he can take it, I can give it out. I'm going to make a quarterback out of him if it's the last thing I ever do."

So all spring long I tried to get him straightened out. Oh, how I tried. Nobody will ever know how I tried.

I'd stand there and say, "Okay, now stay in the pocket. Don't retreat. Stand there. Don't give ground."

I'd go back while they lined up for the play and the first thing you know here he comes running right back over me, almost knocking me down. The other coaches are looking at me and I'm ready to flip my top, but I know I've got to hold it in. He's going to be quarterback if it kills me.

Well, the kid worked out all summer. . .he really wanted to do it. . .and we go over to play Purdue in our opening game in West Lafayette. Now that may not seem like much except the last time Miami went over to Purdue, Kellerman threw a pass to Bob Jenks for 80 yards to upset the Boilermakers and they were nationally ranked that year. Jack Mollenkoff was coaching the team, so Purdue wasn't going to forget too easily.

We were allowed to carry 38 players on our traveling squad, or something like that, and all the Miami people were there to see our new quarterback. They were all thinking the same thing: Another upset of a Big Ten team.

This was a typical Purdue team. They were big and they ran out about 100 guys before the game and it's 95 degrees and it's band day. In fact, it's so hot the bands don't even perform and when we came in at halftime in a garage behind the locker room, there were hundreds of bandsmen passed out, laying there on the garage floor.

So the game starts and Matte is so nervous he can't even get the ball from center. I'm watching him in the warmup and he can't complete a pass to save himself. I look down at the other end. Who do they have at quarterback? Nobody but Bob Griese.

I can't give you the exact figures but Matte threw something like 24 passes. He completed seven—four of them to Purdue. He failed to get the ball from center twice; he went the wrong way twice; and when the score was really mounting against us, would you believe that he faded back inside our own 10 yard line and as he brings his arm back to throw the ball, it falls right out of his hand. Nobody hit him or anything but the darned thing falls right out of his hand. They recover on our one and go in for another touchdown. I think they beat us, 38-0.

We go back to Oxford and the next day I've got a booster club meeting and they're all down on Matte. When I got into my office, Matte is there waiting for me. He says he doesn't want to play anymore. He's embarrassed. He said he didn't want to disgrace his family. He said he was from a very fine family. He said his dad was a good hockey player in his day and that Tom was a great player at Ohio State and now in pro ball with the Colts.

He said: "I just can't shame them."

You know what? I grabbed him by the collar and put him against the wall. I looked right at him and said: "Listen! There. . .is. . .no. . .way. . .in. . .this. . .world. . . .you. . .are . . .going. . .to. . .quit. You. . .are. . .going. . .to. . .be. . .my . . .quarterback. . .if. . .we. . .both. . .die. . .doing. . .it. Got it!"

The poor kid was shaking. But I think he got it. He stood there nodding. Then I threw him out of the office.

The next week we're playing Xavier and we rolled up a 21-7 lead at halftime. But they've got a guy named Carroll Williams playing quarterback, and this Danny Abramowicz, who goes on to play for the New Orleans Saints. He's their pass catcher and Carroll scrambles for a touchdown with 30 seconds left and they go for the two points and beat us, 29-28. Now we're 0-2 and I don't even want to hear from the boosters club.

The third game is at Western Michigan. Matte plays a fairly decent game and we beat them. It's our first league game, so at least we're 1-0 in the league. I still don't want to see the boosters.

Then we go down to Kent and we're driving through a rain

storm. Now I always have the quarterback sit with me on the bus so we can go over last-minute details. I've got the play book out and I'm telling him this and to watch out for that and do you know what he's doing? He's sitting there looking out the window.

He says to me, "Coach, do you think it's going to stop raining?"

I want to stop the bus and throw him off. Instead, I bite my tongue.

Now he goes out there and has another miserable day. His hands are no bigger than mine and he has difficulty taking the ball from center. He keeps bobbling the exchange or fumbling it and I don't even want to look. He hits maybe five or six passes out of 20 and he has two or three interceptions. It's just awful.

Now we are one win and three losses and maybe that doesn't mean much to you, but down there that was something. They never had a losing season in a quarter of a century and they'd had a string of great coaches and they got great press in Dayton and Cincinnati and particularly in the student paper. So it was very important to them that we weren't winning.

They really got on us. They called us the worst team of the century. They said the coach—that's me—was no good and they said this was the type of team that didn't have any character.

Now I got mad. I thought about Northwestern. I thought about how the seniors quit on Ara and the team didn't win a game for the whole season. That wasn't going to happen here. If we lost we were going to lose fighting. Nobody was going to give up.

I talked to Matte. I talked to the team. You could feel a change in practice that week. I think they'd had enough, too.

They were saying little things like, "Okay, Brucie, let's get 'em!" You could feel them rallying around Matte. All of a sudden he got frisky. He started bouncing around on the practice field.

I looked at him. "Son of a gun," I said. "The guy is an athlete. He wants to win."

"Okay, chief, how about a little dance before I go?"

Bruce Matte, Miami of Ohio Quarterback (Finally!)

So he got fired up and we got fired up and we played Marshall, which hadn't lost a game, and we kicked the daylights out of them. We kept getting better and better. Each week we got stronger. The stronger we got, the more confident we became.

We clobbered Cincinnati in our final game and that locked up the championship and it was the greatest comeback by a football team that I have ever seen. They were a tremendous bunch of kids. They were down but they wouldn't stay down. You should have seen them after the games—punching each other around, wrestling, just going nuts in the dressing room. And you try to tell me that we coach for money!

Matte really became something in his senior year. The pro scouts were coming in to see him from all over.

He got so confident he would come into my office and talk and he'd say, "Okay, chief, how about a little dance before I go." I'd get up. . .you'd die laughing. . .and he'd get up and he'd give me a shuffle step and I'd give him a shuffle step. . .the two of us, standing there dancing.

So if there ever was a guy we made a player out of, it was him. He was a beautiful kid. I don't know where he is now but I'll never forget him.

Following Matte's graduation, we did not have a quarterback on our squad who we could say would be the answer to our problems at that position. During our 20 days of spring practice, we were disappointed with the performances of our quarterback candidates and more than half way through spring practice, as we sat in our staff meeting bemoaning the fact that we felt that we had a good football team but not the talent necessary at that position in order to win, one of my coaches suggested that I take a little-known freshman defensive halfback by the name of Kent Thompson and give him the opportunity to be quarterback of the 1967 Miami team.

As I look back on it, this was an almost impossible situation. Here is a young man who sat in my office the previous winter with his parents. They were farm people from Covington, Ohio. Kent had been an outstanding halfback in this very small Class B school. As I visited with his parents, I told them as directly as I could that their son was a very fine football player, but that at

5'10", and 155 pounds we felt that he was a little bit too small for us to offer him any grant-in-aid assistance to come to Miami.

His dad looked at me and said, "Coach, you're about the tenth college coach who has told us the same thing, so it must be true. But Kent wants to come to Miami, and I am willing to send him here without any financial help if you will guarantee me one thing."

I said, "Well, what is that."

He said, "If you will guarantee me that you won't cut him from the football team. He wants to play so badly and even if he isn't good enough, if he could stay out for football."

I told him, "Under no circumstance will I cut him unless he violates the rules of our team. Otherwise, as long as he is making a contribution in some way I will never cut him from the team."

So Kent Thompson comes to Miami and becomes the best defensive halfback on our freshman team. As a matter of fact, we were looking forward to him playing quite a bit of football for us as a sophomore in our defensive secondary.

Now in spring practice, we cannot conceive that anyone could take a youngster who wasn't good enough for grant-in-aid, who was too small to even play at Miami, who had never played quarterback before, and halfway through spring practice convert him into a quarterback with a possible opportunity to be the regular quarterback at Miami in 1967.

The following day, I took Kent out with our starting center and showed him how to take the ball from center. He was a good athlete. He had big hands, he was quick, he had good running ability. He had never passed before, but techniques such as the center-quarterback exchange, footwork and ball handling—things of that nature—came rather easily to Kent. And so I put him in that first day and had him run a few plays with our varsity and, believe it or not, he looked fairly good. The following day we were to have a third-and-eight scrimmage. The third down, long yardage situation in football, as you know, is the most critical. We were trying to work as much as could to be able to control the third down play, and you must have outstanding performances from your quarterback in order to get first downs in those situations.

While I started our other quarterback for about 20 plays—and I believe we got only three first downs—our offensive team was very dejected. They were a pretty good ball club, but they didn't have the quarterback who could hit the pass or scramble for the first down. Our defensive team was higher than a kite because they were really taking it to the offense and this was our first offense against our first defense. It was the toughest situation that we could get them in.

Things were going so badly that I didn't think there was any way it could get worse, so I called Kent over, and I said, "I know you don't know a lot about our football right now, but you just listen to what I tell you, and do the best job you can. Let me see what you can do in there."

So he said, "Okay, coach, I'm ready to go."

The first play I called was a pass play with a hook to our wide receiver. Kent took the ball from center and came back, set up and drilled it in for a first down.

Everybody was elated, patting Kent on the back and showing a lot more enthusiasm. The defensive team, under coach Jim Young, did not like the idea of this youngster coming out there making their defense look bad, so on the next play you know what they are going to do. They put on the blitz, and when we had a pass play called and Kent went back to pass our offensive line picked up the blitz beautifully—except for one man, the backside end, big Ron Butcher. He came storming in on Kent, and since he was coming in on the blind side he put his headgear right in between Kent's shoulder blades and hit him as hard as I have seen a quarterback hit from the blind side.

Kent's helmet flew off, the ball flew up in the air and the defensive team recovered and got up shouting and patting each other on the back. Kent got up off the ground and he looked over at me and I said, "Kent, those situations are going to happen to you every once in a while and when they do, for God's sake, don't drop the football!"

So Kent goes back in there again and on the next play the defensive team blitzes again, and this time we picked up the backside end and blocked him. But we missed Errol Kahoun, the defensive left tackle, 6'4", 250 pounds—the biggest man on

Ernie Kellermann

Kent Thompson

Don Moorhead

Tom Slade

the Miami team. As Kent was standing back ready to pass, he could see Errol Kahoun coming right straight at him. So sensing the situation and remembering what I had told him, he ducked his head and put the ball under his arm, and he and Kahoun hit head to head.

The force of the blow knocked his helmet down over Kent's nose, peeling the skin off the front of his nose, and blood trickled down his cheeks. But he did not fumble the football.

When he got up I called him aside and I said, "Kent, I want to apologize to you. I had no right to put you in there under these circumstances, especially allowing the defense to blitz. I think we better go with our quarterbacks until I have an opportunity to work with you a little more."

He looked at me with blood streaming down his cheeks and he said, "Coach, I know what they're doing now. Don't take me out. I think I can get the job done."

I said, "Okay, we'll give her another go."

On the next six plays, Kent Thompson passed for three first downs and ran for three when they tried to blitz. Six consecutive first downs. Our offensive team was whooping it up. We had found our quarterback.

Kent Thompson, during the next two years, demonstrated all the qualities that you like to have in a quarterback. He was a very courageous player. He was a fine leader, a dedicated worker. He had all the character in the world. He did not fluster easily. He was a confident kid, and as he learned the position he became tougher and tougher to beat.

I'll never forget that first year after we had lost a couple of games with Kent at quarterback. One night, as I arrived home about eleven o'clock following a game which we had lost, it was pouring down rain. Kent Thompson's dormitory was about three miles from my house. He walked all the way through that rain out to my house. I opened the door when he knocked, and he was standing there soaking wet.

He said, "Coach, I think I'm letting you down and I just wanted to come out and talk with you."

I called him into the house, gave him something to eat, and I said, "Kent, there is no way you are ever going to let me down. Any youngster who has so much concern about doing a good

"Okay. I'm your coach and this is what we're going to do."

Bo Begins Miami of Ohio Coaching Career

MIAMI ATHLETIC HALL OF FAME

Five men have been selected for induction into Miami University's Athletic Hall of Fame. They include Bob Brown, Ernie Kellermann, Marv Pierce, Bo Schembechler and Charles Shugert,

The addition of these five men will bring the Miami Athletic Hall of Fame to 23 members. Charter members include Walter Alston, Earl Blaik, Paul Brown, Jay Colville, Wilbur Ewbank, Ara Parseghian, John Pont and George Rider. Selected two years ago were Carmen Cozza, Wayne Embry, Jim Gordon, Virgil Perry, Chester Pittser and Tom Sharkey. Inducted last year were John Brickels, Paul Dietzel, Bill Mulliken and Mel Olix.

WHAT MIAMI HAS MEANT TO ME
Bo Schembechler

Miami University has given me two of the greatest opportunities in my life time. First, it gave me the opportunity for a college education and second it gave me the opportunity of my first coaching position. Consequently, I have been fortunate enough to have spent nearly a quarter of my life time in the friendly surroundings of beautiful Miami.

As a senior in high school Coach Sid Gilman encouraged me to enroll at Miami, when at that time I knew very little about the school. I decided to enroll immediately after my first visit to the campus. My four years at Miami were tremendous.

Both academically and athletically my association with the coaches and players were very close; and many of those men are my dearest friends today. I also met many other faculty and students outside of football that have meant a great deal to me and have also developed into lasting friendships from those associations.

My greatest thrill in coaching was being asked to return to my alma mater as the Head Football Coach. I am sure many people entered into the decision

to hire me, but I would like to particularly thank at this time John Brickels who was then Athletic Director.

During my six years as Miami's coach I had an opportunity to coach many fine Miami men. There always seemed to be the same spirit and enthusiasm in those teams as on the ones that I enjoyed playing on in Miami many years earlier.

Miami will always leave its mark on those who have been associated with her.

Miami of Ohio Hall of Fame—1972

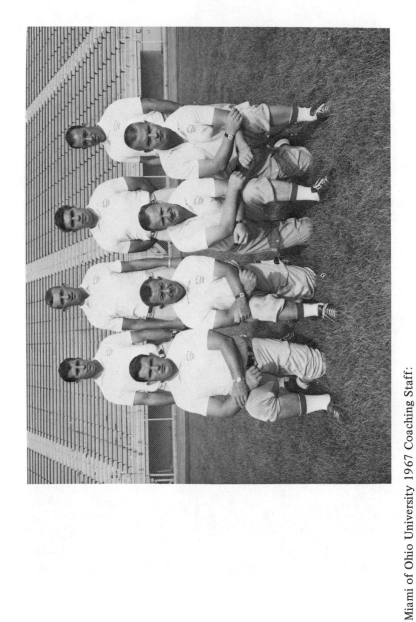

Miami of Ohio University 1967 Coaching Staff:
Top (Left to Right)—Dick Hunter, Larry Smith, Gary Moeller, Chuck Stobart—Bottom (Left to Right)—Joe Galat, Jerry Hanlon, Head Coach Bo Schembechler, Jim Young

Bo Schembechler—Miami of Ohio

job for me will never let me down. I did not feel our loss today was your responsibility, and you have always given me a great performance."

The fact that he had walked all the way out there because he was concerned about how I felt made me feel that I would never have to worry about my quarterback as long as Kent Thompson was at the position.

Upon arriving at Michigan in January of 1969, I knew that Dennis Brown, the fine little quarterback from the year before, was to graduate and I was hopeful that I would be fortunate enough to have a quarterback as good as Ernie Kellermann when I first went into Miami to run the Michigan team in 1969. Everyone told me about the "heir apparent" to Brown's quarterback position, a youngster from South Haven, Michigan by the name of Don Moorhead. He was the backup quarterback the previous year, a big youngster, almost 6'3" tall and 195 pounds. I was very much impressed with him the first time I met him. He had a pleasing personality, a tremendous desire to be the Michigan quarterback, excellent physical potential. Yet to be determined would be how he would react running the team. In discussions with the various players all of them indicated great confidence that Moorhead would be an outstanding quarterback.

You so often hear about football players who are first out onto the field and the last to leave. But I, in two years, cannot recall a situation when I walked on the practice field early and Don Moorhead was not out there waiting on us. He was an eager football player. He was an excellent passer and he learned to run our option plays equally well. He was a strong runner, with good moves and good speed.

From the very beginning of spring practice until the end of his senior year, Don Moorhead was our quarterback at Michigan. He was the type of youngster who always exuded great confidence. I can recall in 1969 before the Ohio State game saying in our quarterback meetings I was sure that Moorhead was going to play his greatest game. He and all the rest of us felt that if we played well, we would definitely win. In two years at Michigan Moorhead broke five career records. He was in on more plays and gained more yardage in total offense than any player in Michigan history. He threw more passes, completed more passes, and gained more yardage passing than any quarterback Michigan has ever had.

As luck would have it, upon taking my second head coaching job, a great quarterback was waiting for me. Don was a most determined competitor. After we had lost to Michigan State in 1969 and went up to play that critical game in Minneapolis against Minnesota with a record of three wins and two losses, in the first half we trailed 9-7. At halftime, Don had sustained a very painful hip pointer, the type of injury that was not serious but very, very difficult to play with. I suggested to him then that he not play the second half, but he was adamant in his demand that he be allowed to play. During the second half of that game, he led us to four touchdowns and a 35-9 victory over Minnesota. From then on, it was clear sailing into the Rose Bowl.

During his two years at Michigan where he ran and passed so frequently, only on one occasion—when he had run the football to the one yard line against Arizona in the opening game of the 1970 season and he was shaken up and I took him out of the game for one play—is the only time in his two years at Michigan that I can ever recall that we had to play without Don Moorhead.

After Moorhead moved on to play professionally in Canadian football, we knew that in 1971 we probably had the most talented football team we ever had, except that we were faced with the prospect of going with a sophomore quarterback. It was obvious that the passing game was not going to be a strong weapon in the 1971 arsenal. So early in the season, we chose a youngster by the name of Tom Slade, a pre-med student from Saginaw, Michigan who had a fine football mind. He was an excellent ball handler, could run the option plays well, and did an excellent job of leading our power sweep and blocking for Bill Taylor.

We almost completely avoided the passing game, and with Slade at quarterback we went through eleven consecutive games and into the Rose Bowl. Only in that ball game—where that fine Stanford defense made it difficult for us to move and we lost by one point—did a Tom Slade-quarterbacked team lose.

Tom Slade had done a magnificent job for us in 1971 as a sophomore.

In 1972, he was to lose his position to a sophomore by the name of Dennis Franklin, a youngster who came to Michigan with wonderful potential and immediately put it to use in his effort to become the No. 1 quarterback at Michigan.

Imagine the situation that young Tom Slade was in. He had led Michigan through an undefeated season to the Rose Bowl, losing by only 1 point in the only game he had ever quarterbacked in a losing effort. Then he was losing his position to another sophomore. No matter how you look at it, it was a very difficult situation. I suppose I have even gained more respect for Tom Slade since he was beaten out at his position than I had when he was the regular quarterback for us.

Just prior to the opening game against Northwestern in 1972, I was giving a written examination to our quarterbacks on which I asked them questions concerning our automatics for the game, formations, and plays, special situations. The second-to-last question I asked them was: "What can they do to beat Northwestern?"

Slade's answer was this: "Show great enthusiasm. Be a leader and encourage Denny and give him every show of confidence and encouragement before, during and after the game. Be ready for any situation. The point after touchdown, the field goal, injury to quarterbacks. Be aware of what is going on on the field in case I do get to play. Help Mike Lantry by trying to relax him and keep him as cool as possible. Catch the ball and place it perfectly on the tee. Cover field goals. Be alert and be sharp."

That's the answer that Tom Slade gave when he knew, going into the Northwestern game, that perhaps his only assignment that day would be to hold the football for the extra points and field goals.

The last question on that exam was: "What does poise mean for the quarterback?"

This is the way Tom Slade answered it: "Poise for the quarterback means 'Be cool.' No hotdog antics. No expressions of extremes. Keep his head up at all times. To me personally it means being sharp, diplomatic. You call the officials 'Sir.' Say

'Yes' not 'Yeah,' etc. And it means being basically expression-less. The quarterback can't flail his arms and stomp his feet at a bad call. He must take the good with bad. He must stave off any injuries as minor and be an example to his teammates. He must lead, yet he must maintain control at all times without being overbearing and dictatorial with his teammates. He must make them want to follow him.''

Those were the answers Tom Slade gave after he had lost his position as the Michigan quarterback.

In 1972 Dennis Franklin led us to ten consecutive victories before a 3-point loss to Ohio State in Columbus. Although it may be heresy to talk about quarterbacks who are presently on your team and have not yet completed their careers, it is fitting to note that Dennis Franklin falls into the mold of all the out-standing quarterbacks that I have had in the past.

Denny came to Michigan from Massillon, Ohio where his team was undefeated and won the state championship and had an outstanding success. He is a very goal-seeking young man. He wants to be the best at his position. He has all the necessary attributes to be a truly outstanding quarterback. He has wonderful ability, both as a runner and passer, tremendous poise and confidence, great courage, willingness to work, an unselfish attitude about football—all of the things that you would like to see in your quarterback. Whatever happens to this young man in the next two years will be interesting to watch, for he very well could be the best quarterback I have ever had.

When you analyze a quarterback, one thing becomes per-fectly clear—that in every case he is usually a hell of a lot more than just another football player. His qualities as a person exceed his football talent.

Chapter 17

Just Call Me Stick-In-The-Mud

I guess there are some people in Ann Arbor who think I'm a stick-in-the-mud. Or maybe even anti-social. The truth is, I'm just not much for socializing.

It's not that I don't enjoy people. I do. You can't be in this business and not have a feeling for those around you. But I'm just not much for parties. I don't go to cocktail parties, for instance. When I first came here, people were inviting me all the time. Now they don't. They know I don't go. I guess I could do better by my wife, Millie, if I got around more. But I am what I am and, well, after work I'm just not one to run downtown and have a few drinks and jazz around. When I'm through at the office, I just like to light out for home.

What I enjoy doing the most is just sitting down and relaxing with the kids. I just enjoy being home. I know I am going to have a nice meal cooked for me and I have a nice home and Millie just does a tremendous job with those kids.

This is my second marriage. The first ended in a divorce. You just learn to appreciate what you have. Take Millie. She's an independent gal and she has strength herself but she is a woman and like all women she has her weaknesses. But basically, I think she understands that I enjoy what I'm doing. This is her second marriage, too—her first husband died—and having been without a husband for such a long period of time, she is able to understand when I am gone more than some other wife might.

Millie has great character. Do you realize she was 40 years old when we had Shemy. Now that had to be a tough deal on her, what with having to put up with me and having the other

The Tough Coach with Son Shemy

"See you after the Ohio State game, honey." Bo and Millie
at home

three boys around the house, but she handled it all.

I like to read. . .Time, Newsweek, the sports pages. . .I love reading sports pages. . .but I don't play golf or bowl or anything like that. Golf takes too long and I'm just not interested in those other things. I hate to admit it but I've never seen a ball game in Tiger Stadium. I've never been inside Tiger Stadium. I have never seen a football game there; I have never seen the Red Wings, only on television, and I've never been to a Detroit Pistons basketball game.

I never go to the movies either but when it was Geoff's birthday—he'd just turned 15—I went home and said: "All right, men. It's on me tonight. Look it up and I'm taking the three of you to the movies." Chip is 17 and Matt is 13 and they all go inside and look up the movie schedule.

"We're all set, dad," they come back and tell me.

I ask them, "What are we going to see?"

They tell me, "Deliverance."

I'm pretty naive about movies. I don't know anything about this film and so I ask them what it's all about.

They tell me it's about some guys on a canoe trip and they get ambushed and it takes place in the woods. The ad shows the guys carrying the canoe along the water and it looked pretty good to me.

I said to them, "How come it's marked 'R'?"

They say, "Aw, it's because they've got shooting and stuff like that when they get into the woods. It's okay, dad."

So we drive out to the theater and it's packed. The movie comes on and all of a sudden here are the guys driving to the waterfront and one of them says, "Well, are we going to take the trip on the 'bleeping' river." I just about want to fall out of my seat.

I look at the kids and the kids look at me. Nobody says anything. And that's how it goes all through the movie. . .one bad word after another.

The kids know I'm mad. They just keep looking straight ahead. When we walk out to the car, nobody says a word. Matt, the youngest one says, "Hey, dad, that wasn't so bad after all."

I say, "Shut up!" and we drive home in silence.

When we get home, Millie asks how the picture was and the boys say okay. But they go right to bed. Nobody else says a word and we've never talked about it again.

That's how exciting a life I lead.

Millie Schembechler:

I met Bo through mutual friends. I lived in St. Louis at the time and I met him through his trainer's wife—his trainer at Miami. She is Merle Pollins and her husband, Marvin, is now the trainer of the Cincinnati Bengals. She and Marvin had been going to camp together since they were youngsters and my three boys and I went to the same camp with them three years in a row. For a couple of summers Merle decided she would like to play Cupid and she had a couple of guys she thought I would like to meet and Bo was one of them. It took a great effort and a lot of time on Merle's part to bring us together.

I met Bo on the last weekend in May of 1968, but before that Merle had the boys and myself come down to their home in Oxford, which was about four doors away from where Bo lived at the time. She invited us down for a weekend and she had a party and invited Bo. Bo didn't show up, naturally. He is not too great on parties, so that was a definite disappointment.

Merle didn't give up. The next summer she called at about eleven o'clock one night. I said, "Good heavens, what are you calling me at this hour for?" She said she was with Cheryl Smith, who was the wife of Larry Smith, who was one of the coaches at Miami. They were sharing a duplex at the time and they were down at their apartment—the two girls—and Bo was with them. They had laughingly asked Bo to come by and put out the garbage cans since their men were out of town— and, surprisingly, Bo did. Well, they had a couple of beers and Merle got out all the old camping pictures of all of us— the boys and me—and I guess he stayed there long enough and had enough beers so that Merle got on the phone at eleven o'clock and called me.

She said, "I have somebody who wants to speak to you,"

Millie: *"I have been most happy to let him run the show."*

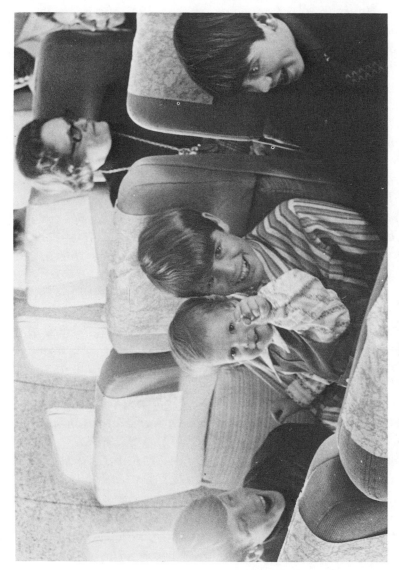

Bo's Future Backfield—(Left to Right)—Sons Matt, Shemy, Chip and Geoff with "Grandma" Betty Schembechler on Rose Bowl plane

and she put Bo on the phone.

At the time, I couldn't pronounce his name, much less spell it, and so I just let him talk. He was very cordial and nice and he said he just happened to have an occasion where he would be in St. Louis in another week and he thought perhaps we could have dinner together. I told him to give me a call and that was the whole conversation.

When he got to town, he came out to see us and he made a big hit right away with the kids. The first thing he did, of course, was get out there and play a little ball with them. He threw the ball around with them and it was pretty hot and so they came inside and started playing a card game—poker. He had a pocket full of change and he let them win it all, so right away you knew he was very popular with the boys.

Frankly, I was most impressed with him. I liked the way he took to the boys and I liked the way he looked—he was athletic and healthy looking— and he was very nice and sweet. So we went out to dinner and we talked until four or five in the morning. Knowing Bo now and how awkward he is around women, it was surprising that he was so relaxed with me. As a matter of fact, he extended his stay and we went out again.

We didn't talk football—only when the boys would ask him something. We talked about our philosophies of life; how we felt about living; how I felt having the responsibility of three boys all alone and what a frightening situation it was for me. My husband had died in December, 1964, so we had been alone for four years. I was working as a nurse at a school and prior to that, I had worked at St. John's Hospital.

When Bo stayed over, we went to the St. Louis Arch and to the zoo. We had the boys with us all that day and I liked that. I had always thought that if the situation was not good and right for the boys, I would never consider remarrying.

I wanted nothing more than to find somebody who would be right for all of us because the boys were getting to the age where they needed the male influence more than ever.

So I took Bo to the airport on Sunday evening and the boys stayed at home. When I came back—and this was such a twist because the boys had always resented anyone I had ever gone out with. . .when I got back to the house, Geoff said to me,

"Matt cried when you left." Matt glared at his brother. "You almost did, too," he said. Already they loved Bo.

We got married so quickly it is almost a disgrace to talk about it. He called every night for the next two or three weeks and we were talking about the possibility of getting married. Well, it happened on August 3, about three months after I first met him. It was a funny thing, you'd think we would have had a great deal of fears and apprehensions—which I'd always had before—but this time it seemed so right that we really didn't ask many questions of each other.

I realize what a great effort it has been on Bo's part to suddenly become the father of three teenage boys, and then to have another boy shortly after you're married. I honestly cannot recall a single awkward moment about this whole situation. I have been most happy to let him run the show. . . because after having the full responsibility of a house, a yard, the boys and my job. . .it was such a relief to have a man come to my side and help me out.

It is interesting the way Bo and the boys get along. I'll find them sitting in the corner of a room somewhere. They'll be talking and I am really not welcome. He will come home at night and start in with Shemy. He'll wrestle him all over the floor. Then he'll talk to the boys, alone or all at once—whatever is needed. Sometimes it'll be a few words, sometimes a long conversation. But he always talks to them.

Bo loves to read. He devours the sports pages. If he is reading or watching television, he is so consumed by what's happening that it's hard for us to get to him. This is one of the little things which annoys me and the boys. His concentration is fantastic.

Bo is helpless around the house. I mean, fixing things. That's my job. I do the painting, the fixing and the gardening. We made that agreement when we got married. He said, "You know, I won't be very much help around the house."

We made one other agreement.

I do the cooking.

He does the eating.

The Ghost Speaks:

241

I've followed one rule through most of my newspaper career: Never socialize with an athlete, a coach or a manager.

I figured it was too dangerous.

How could I become friends with someone I had to write about? That, I felt, would be a breach of responsibility.

I felt my responsibility was to my readers, the people who buy my newspaper, not to the people I write about.

So, all these years I have remained aloof from the athletes and coaches and managers.

This has been a mistake on my part.

I don't think it is wise to be an extremist in any circumstance. I see that now. I have gone into Bo Schembechler's house and had dinner with his family. I have sat at the kitchen table and talked with them. And it's been beautiful. They have learned some things about me, and I have learned some things about them.

If nothing else, writing this book has changed my ideas about dealing with people in sports. I see now that it's unwise, and also unfair, to remain so distant. I see now that you can get close to a person and keep your sense of responsibility at the same time.

All you have to do is keep the ground rules clear—that you are, primarily, a newspaperman and that your responsibility is to your readers.

People have said to me: "How can you ever write objectively about Bo again after writing a book with him? How can you ever criticize him?"

Just watch.

Chapter *18*

Pasadena Revisited: What Heart Attack?

I'm always asked: "How'd you feel going back to the Rose Bowl the second time?" I guess what they mean is, how'd you feel about going back to where you had your heart attack?

To tell you the truth, I didn't think too much about it. I guess I should have but I didn't. I mean, I didn't relive any of those moments, except up at the monastery.

Mostly I was bugged because we couldn't get a place to practice. Of course we lost again. Stanford beat us, 13-12. But to say I was thinking of my illness all the time—it just didn't happen.

Our second trip to the Rose Bowl. . .this was after the '71 season. . .was tougher than the first. We were supposed to practice at a junior college near Pasadena and the Friday before we went out there, the groundskeeper turned on the electrical watering system and left it on. He was supposed to set it so it shut off in a couple of hours but it kept running and running, all weekend it ran—Friday, Saturday and Sunday. So when the rains came, the place already was soaked and it became one big mud puddle. And the rains continued for days.

I spent all Christmas Day traveling around Los Angeles looking for a place to practice. Nothing. Everything was wet. We started making phone calls and by noon the only place where they had a dry field was up in Bakersfield, across the other side of the mountains. I was pretty tired, so I got a car and a driver and we went across those mountains. It was Bakersfield Junior College. Here it is Christmas Day and I'm making motel arrangements at the Holiday Inn and I'm look-

Schembechler with 1972 Rose Bowl Queen Margo Lynn Johnson and Billy Taylor

ing at the field and I'm thinking of all the things we have to do to get the team here. The turf was wet but it wasn't as bad as we had in Los Angeles.

So I got back to our hotel in Pasadena and everyone is half-way through the evening meal. I haven't even seen my family yet. So I just went in and grabbed something to eat and went up to my room. I had to start telling everyone we were going to Bakersfield in the morning.

We had some pretty good workouts up there but what fouled things up for us, we had to come back to town for the Big Ten party. Can you imagine breaking up your practice program to go to a banquet? I guess I'll never get with all the hoopla that goes with the Rose Bowl game.

I'm getting apprehensive about the whole thing because I know we are not ready to play a ball game. We didn't have the right practices set up—I thought we could do it on a one-a-day basis—and we never had a really good field to work on and the whole thing became a mess.

But the game is coming up and so it's back to the monastery and you know, the priests gave the same cocktail party, at the same place and the same time. You can imagine what that made *me* think of. In fact, I pointed out the spot to the other coaches where I had that terrible pain. That gave me a strange feeling, I'll tell you.

But you're talking about a guy who probably weighed 180 pounds now—a guy who was in shape. I felt confident about myself. No way was I going to let the memory of my heart at-tack have any effect on our plans to get ready for the game. I just wouldn't let it.

I thought about going over to St. Luke's, to say hello to the people there, but I never got around to it. Dr. Weinstein, the one who took care of me, came out to practice with his son one day. I let him in and we talked and I gave him a couple of tickets for the game. He said that I looked pretty grim but he didn't ask me if I had any problems. He didn't even ask how I felt. I think he knew it was over, so why bring it all up again.

We went out there with the idea we could get by with one practice a day. From a psychological standpoint, we thought it would be good for the players. But we got into a situation where some of the sessions wound up inside gymnasiums. I mean, we had no choice—but do you know what it's like to try to work out on a wooden floor? I wanted one good practice a day—that's all—but I could never get it until we went to Bakersfield. We got one or two good workouts under our belt, then we had to go back for the Big Ten party.

I suppose you could say Stanford was having the same problems. But I wasn't thinking about Stanford.

I slept well the night before the game. In fact, everything was normal. I spoke to the players as I always do and I spoke to the coaches. None of that stuff bothered me. Looking back now I realize I made a great tactical mistake by having my players wear too long a football cleat.

I was psyched out by the weather. It was so bad for so long and the fields were so chopped up, I thought they needed a long cleat for traction. I felt we'd be doing a lot of slipping and sliding out there.

Well, I guessed wrong. I think the longer cleat tired their legs, I really do. We would have been a lot better off with a shorter, lighter cleat. The field was solid enough for a shorter cleat.

Stanford wore the right kind of cleats. In fact, most of them wore their artificial turf shoes.

The game itself was disappointing. We didn't execute very well and they played some outstanding defensive football. Our defense was superb in the first half. We shut them off pretty cold. We didn't move the ball, though. We didn't run it and what it really boiled down to is that we couldn't throw the ball. Our ineffective passing really killed us. They gave us the full pass and we couldn't take advantage of it. If we threw at all, I usually ended up catching the ball on the sidelines. Stuff like that.

I'm not being critical of any particular player. I'm just saying that in this game we didn't do a very good job of executing our offense. I know we didn't block. We didn't block at all.

The thing is, we were never behind. We weren't playing well but we were never behind. What was it at halftime—7-0 or 7-3? Something like that. It was very close. We were either tied or leading but we were never behind. In other words, it looked to me like this was going to be a game that we'd pull out. I thought to myself, "We're going to win it without playing well." I knew we were being out-statisticed but I thought sure we were going to win.

Well, on their last drive we made a great tactical mistake that cost us the game. We gave them the opportunity in a hurry-up sequence to throw the ball against a standpat defense. In other words, they knew that by us not going into a huddle, we weren't changing our defensive and secondary coverages. We weren't giving them any problem other than to read our basic defense. Since that time we've developed a system where we can give any defense without a huddle, but we didn't have it then and they took advantage of it. If we'd have made just one adjustment—which would have been to bring our end off to the wide side of the field to help handle the flooding—we would have shut them off. But we never did.

So, I learned something—right there I learned something. That's the way this game is. You'd always better be learning. Our defense over the last eight years is a result of trial and error. There isn't too much room for error. We've faced almost everything there is to face and it's hard now for anyone to catch us in a situation we can't adjust to.

When Stanford lined up for their winning field goal, I had a terrible feeling. I knew they were going to make it. You can just sense things like that. I felt bad since we had gone 11 and 0 and now this had happened to us. And then there was all this business about the "free spirit" of Stanford against the "establishment" of Michigan—that sort of junk that was being printed in the Los Angeles papers. Their band against our band. The Free Spirits against The Establishment.

We're not an Establishment team or any other kind of team. We're just a football team and a darned good one. What is an Establishment team—one that wins? If that's so, I guess maybe we're guilty.

We just did a bad job out there. They took advantage of the weaknesses in our offense. They also caught us in a weakness in our defense. Give Stanford some credit. I think our players tried hard enough, though it wasn't one of their great performances of that season.

I've been asked if I think I'm jinxed in the Rose Bowl. Or by playing out on the West Coast. I don't feel that way at all.

Do you know what we did when we went out to play UCLA in our second game of the 1972 season? We went and stayed in the same hotel! I put them in the same rooms and when we worked out the night before the game, we worked out in the Rose Bowl with the lights on. I did everything the same. We slept in the same room, ate in the same rooms—everything was exactly the same. I told them the night we were in the Rose Bowl, "Look around, guys. Take a good look. . .because you'll be coming back here." I told them, "We're going to win in California and nobody is going to stop us."

Then we went into the coliseum and kicked the daylights out of them. I'll tell you, we were good that night—awfully good. The score was 26-9 and there was that much difference in the two teams.

Nobody can tell me the Big Ten isn't at a big disadvantage out there. I don't care how you add it up, it is true. Back in the old days we were so powerful we could play mediocre football and win. Today that isn't true. The Pac Eight has good football teams and you have to be ready to play them.

One disadvantage is that you stay out there too long. After you've gone to Disneyland and Marineland and a couple of other places, what is there to do? Southern California is just Southern California. You can't tell me it doesn't hurt you to get into a bus and drive a half hour to the practice field and then get back in the bus and drive another half hour back to your hotel. And the rain—the rain was a joke when we went out there to play Stanford. And being away at Christmas—now you can't tell me that is too helpful.

If you go back with the players who have been there before, you've lost a lot of the excitement. If it's new to them, then they're enthusiastic. But what is a guy going to think who's been there before?

It is just not like getting ready for a regular season game. You've got distractions everywhere and I'm just not a guy who likes to have his concentration broken.

Now if I were in Southern California and could practice at home, I'd be a lot better off. Who knows, I might even be a Rose Bowl winner.

Joe Falls
Sports Editor

Why Didn't U-M Work on Passing?

Jan. 3, 1972

For 11 Saturdays in the autumn of 1971, Bo Schembechler was asked: "Why don't you pass more often?"

And for 11 straight Saturdays, he replied: "Why should I?"

It was difficult to argue with the man. Not only difficult, but impossible. He was doing the thing he was supposed to do.

But now, after his shattering setback in the Rose Bowl, he is going to hear it again ..... and again ..... and again. He will have to live with it through these winter months and into the springtime, when he begins getting ready for 1972.

He will probably hear it through all of 1972. They will forget those 11 straight victories. They will only ask about No. 12, the one that got away, the Rose Bowl Game.

In a way this is a great tribute to Schembechler. It shows the degree of excellence he has created at Michigan. There was a time around Ann Arbor when even the most partisan of Michigan fans were resigned to two or three defeats a year . . . even more.

But now they lose one and people are whispering. They're unhappy. They're distraught. Some of them are slightly shattered. How could it happen?

They're all spoiled and Bo Schembechler is the man who spoiled them.

The last thing Bo wants, or needs, is my pity. He is a strong enough man to take it all himself but I couldn't have been more impressed with him than the way he stood in that dark storeroom under the Rose Bowl on New Year's night and faced all of he writers and gave it to them straight.

He offered no excuses. No alibis. He said simply that his team didn't deserve to win because it didn't do the things a football team has to do to win. It didn't block properly. It didn't move the ball consistently. It didn't get those key first downs.

The Wolverines didn't do a lot of things, really...

It took some kind of courage for Schembechler to stand there and talk about these failures.

Completed Only 3 of 11

It is difficult to explain this man if you don't know him but defeat to him is like a hammer blow. Almost a mortal blow. I have seen it all but destroy him, turn him into an angry and irrational man.

I try to understand his dedication. A lot of men are dedicated to what they do in life. But I have never met one quite like Bo —one who is so completely consumed by what he does.

So failure comes exceptionally hard to him . . . harder than any of us can ever understand. That's why I had to admire him as he stood there and talked to us Saturday night and spoke honestly and openly, for deep down you knew he was literally dying.

This is going to sound like the same old song, but the thing that puzzled me about the whole game is how Michigan WAS so utterly inept in trying to throw the ball. I couldn't understand how the Wolverines couldn't even come close to pulling off a decent pass play — not even one.

They tried to throw the ball 11 times. They completed three passes. Two of these were made possible only by diving catches on the part of Glenn Doughty. They didn't make a single first down through the air.

I can't believe that a team of this talent can't mount some sort of passing attack. Even a feeble one. Just enough to keep the other team off balance.

Bo had insisted his team could pass when it needed to. Well, the Wolverines needed to in Pasadena and couldn't do it.

So you have to ask — why?

Bo says he passed when he had Don Moorhead at quarterback. That's true. Young Tom Slade is no Don Moorhead.

But does that mean that Michigan has to all but abort the pass?

What gets me is that I think Bo is a good enough coach that he should have been able to think of some way to get the ball into the air. Hit the backs. Throw a short screen. Try a swing pass. Anything to keep the defense honest.

Was Bo's Pride to Blame?

Was he being stubborn, again trying to prove that his was the right way? Was he trying to prove his conviction that the only way his Michigan team could go was on the ground?

I hope not ..... because it would be a sad thing if he was beaten by his own pride...

I saw Michigan in only three games this season. The last three. They were the toughest three. I saw them squeeze by Purdue and Ohio State, when Bo's will prevailed in the end, and I saw the disaster in Pasadena.

Everybody has a reason why Michigan lost on Saturday. Mine is this: I wonder if Bo, in his insistence to run the ball so much, to keep running the same plays over and over, didn't inadvertently aid the opposition?

After all Stanford had a chance to study Michigan's game films and watch the Wolverines work the same plays again and again.

You may not believe this, but some of the writers were even calling Bo's plays in the press box in Pasadena — Ed Shuttlesworth on the slam with fourth and one, Billy Taylor on the power sweep to the right in a similar situation.

These were the plays that had worked all season — worked for 11 straight victories. Maybe Bo had a right to believe they would work again. But the point is, this time they didn't. Stanford . . . and also Purdue and Ohio State . . . were ready for them.

There just wasn't enough variation in the Michigan attack.

Remember this: In his three years at Michigan, Bo has lost his last game each season. Even he has to ask himself why, if he's honest with himself.

University of Michigan Wolverines—1972 Big Ten Co-Champions

No "Missing Man" This Time

Bo and Chuck Stobart on Sidelines at 1972 Rose Bowl Game

PHOTOGRAPHY

Bowling Green University - Pages 202, 203
Miami of Ohio University - Pages 68, 184, 219, 223, 225, 226, 227, 228
The University of Michigan - Pages 3, 21, 38, 46, 60, 63, 90, 104, 105, 116, 118, 122, 132, 140, 145, 152, 157, 170, 191, 223, 238, 239, 244, 250
Northwestern University - Page 206
Ohio State University - Page 84
Presbyterian College - Page 199
Stuart Abbey - Pages 123, 151
The Ann Arbor News - Pages 34, 67, 97, 153, 234
Disneyland Photo Service - Page 32
Jack Glazier, Credits Page Drawing
Malcolm Emmons - Page 83
Merv Lew Photo - Pages 24, 33, 175, 251
1969 Rose Bowl Committee - Page 23
1972 Rose Bowl Committee - Page 241
Scene Magazine - Page 93